GAYS AND THE FUTURE OF ANGLICANISM

RESPONSES TO THE WINDSOR REPORT

EDITED BY

ANDREW LINZEY & RICHARD KIRKER

Marilyn McCord Adams, Thomas E. Breidenthal,
Anthony P. M. Coxon, L. William Countryman, Sean Gill,
Elaine Graham, Rowan A. Greer, Charles Hefling, Carter Heyward,
Lisa Isherwood, Gareth Jones, Philip Kennedy, Christopher Lewis,
George Pattison, Martyn Percy, Carolyn J. Sharp, Martin Stringer,
Vincent Strudwick, Adrian Thatcher, Keith Ward, Kevin Ward

Copyright © 2005 O Books
O Books is an imprint of John Hunt Publishing Ltd., The Bothy,
Deershot Lodge, Park Lane, Ropley, Hants, SO24 0BE, UK
office@johnhunt–publishing.com
www.O–books.net

Distribution in:
UK
Orca Book Services
orders@orcabookservices.co.uk
Tel: 01202 665432 Fax: 01202 666219 Int. code (44)

USA and Canada
NBN
custserv@nbnbooks.com
Tel: 1 800 462 6420 Fax: 1 800 338 4550

Australia
Brumby Books
sales@brumbybooks.com
Tel: 61 3 9761 5535 Fax: 61 3 9761 7095

New Zealand
Peaceful Living
books@peaceful–living.co.nz
Tel: 64 7 57 18105 Fax: 64 7 57 18513

Singapore
STP
davidbuckland@tlp.com.sg
Tel: 65 6276 Fax: 65 6276 7119

South Africa
Alternative Books
altbook@global.co.za
Tel: 27 011 792 7730 Fax: 27 011 972 7787

Text: © individual contributors.

Design: BookDesign™, London, UK

ISBN 1-905047-38-X

A CIP catalogue record for this book is available from the
British Library.

Printed in the USA by Maple–Vail Manufacturing Group

Gays and the Future of Anglicanism

Responses to the Windsor Report

EDITED BY

Andrew Linzey &
Richard Kirker

BOOKS

WINCHESTER UK
NEW YORK USA

CONTENTS

PART IV: JUSTICE FOR GAYS

THE CONTRIBUTORS

Marilyn McCord Adams is Regius Professor of Divinity at the University of Oxford and Canon of Christ Church, Oxford. Formerly, she was Horace Tracy Pitkin Professor of Historical Theology at Yale University and Professor of Philosophy at UCLA. Her publications range over medieval philosophy and theology, and philosophical theology, and include major books: *William Ockham* (2 vols, University of Notre Dame Press, 1987) and *Horrendous Evils and the Goodness of God* (Cornell University Press, 1999), as well as many articles.

Thomas Breidenthal has been Dean of Religious Life and of the Chapel at Princeton University since January 2002. Previously, he was the John Henry Hobart Professor of Christian Ethics at the General Theological Seminary in New York City. An Episcopal priest, he received a DPhil in Theology from Oxford University. His professional work has been focused on interfaith dialogue, political theology, and the role of faith in shaping personal relationships. Publications include: *Christian Households: The Sanctification of Nearness* (Cowley Publications, 1997; reprinted Wipf and Stock, 2004). He lives in Princeton, New Jersey, with his wife, Margaret, and their two children.

L. William Countryman is the Sherman E. Johnson Professor in Biblical Studies at the Church Divinity School of the Pacific in Berkeley, California. He is also a member of the Core Doctoral Faculty of the Graduate Theological Union and serves on its Interdisciplinary Committee. He has written on a variety of topics in biblical studies, Anglican studies, and spirituality. He is perhaps best known for *Dirt,*

Greed, and Sex (Fortress, 1988) on New Testament sexual ethics, *The Mystical Way in the Fourth Gospel* (Fortress, 1987), and *Living on the Border of the Holy* (Morehouse, 1999) on priesthood. Recent books include: *The Poetic Imagination* (Darton, Longman and Todd, 1999) on poetry in Anglican spirituality, *Interpreting the Truth* (Trinity Press International, 2003) on biblical studies and the church, and a book on gay–lesbian Christian spirituality, written with M. R. Ritley, *Gifted by Otherness* (Morehouse, 2001). His most recent book is *Love Human and Divine* (Morehouse, 2005), a brief plea for the importance of eros to Christian spirituality.

Anthony P. M. Coxon is currently Honorary Professorial Fellow at the University of Edinburgh and Emeritus Professor of Sociological Research Methods, University of Wales, and prior to that was Professor in the Departments of Sociology and of Health and Human Sciences at the University of Essex. He originally trained for ordination at Mirfield, and his doctorate was in the recruitment, selection and socialization of Anglican ordinands, published with Dr Robert Towler as *The Fate of the Anglican Ministry* (Macmillan, 1979). He has researched and published extensively in the fields of research methods, sociology of religion and sexual behavior, identity and lifestyles and was co–founder and principal investigator of Project SIGMA, Britain's national longitudinal study of gay men under the impact of Aids. He has authored or co–authored 10 books on these topics. He also contributed entries on "homophobia", "sexuality" and "same–sex relations" to *Dictionary of Ethics, Theology and Society* (edited by Andrew Linzey and P. A. B. Clarke, Routledge, 1995). He is currently Bishop's Adviser on Mission and Ministry in the Diocese of Argyll and the Isles.

Sean Gill is Senior Lecturer in Theology and Religious Studies at the University of Bristol; he was previously Lecturer in Theology and Religious Studies from 1976–1996, and Head of Department from 1997–2000. His research and teaching interests are in the areas of modern Anglican history, and religion, gender and sexuality. His publications include: *Women and the Church of England from the Eighteenth Century to the Present,* (SPCK, 1994), *Campaigning for Justice, Truth and Love: A History and Reader of the Lesbian and Gay Christian Movement* (Cassell, 1998), (co–editor) *Religion in Europe: Contemporary Perspectives* (Kok Pharos, 1994), and *Masculinity and Spirituality in Victorian Culture* (Macmillan, 2000).

Elaine Graham is the Samuel Ferguson Professor of Social and Pastoral Theology at the University of Manchester. Publications include: (co–edited with Margaret Halsey) *Life–Cycles: Women and Pastoral Care* (SPCK, 1993), *Making the Difference: Gender, Personhood and Theology* (Mowbray, 1995), *Transforming Practice* (Mowbray, 1996, 2nd Edition, Wipf and Stock 2002), *Representations of the Post/human* (Manchester University Press, 2002) and (co–edited with Heather Walton and Frances Ward) *Theological Reflections* (SCM Press, 2005).

Rowan A. Greer is Professor of Anglican Studies Emeritus at Yale Divinity School. His previous appointments include Associate Professor of New Testament at Yale, and Chaplain of the Theological College of the Scottish Episcopal Church, Edinburgh. He is author of eight books including, *Origen: An Exhortation to Martyrdom and Commentaries* (Limited Editions Club, Oxford: At the Clarendon Press, 1977), (with James L. Kugel) *Early biblical interpretation* (Library of Early Christianity, Westminster Press, 1986), *Broken Lights and Mended Lives: Theology and Common Life in the Early Church* (Penn State Press, 1986), *The Fear of Freedom: A Study of Miracles in the Roman Imperial Church* (Penn State Press, 1989), and *Christian Hope and Christian Life: Raids on the Inarticulate* (Crossroad, 2001).

Charles Hefling is a professor in the Theology Department at Boston College, Chestnut Hill, Massachusetts; Editor–in–Chief of the *Anglican Theological Review;* and the Examining Chaplain to the Bishop of

Massachusetts. He is the author of *Why Doctrines?* (Boston: Boston College, 2000), the translator of *The Incarnate Word* by Bernard Lonergan, and has edited *Our Selves, Our Souls and Bodies: Sexuality and the Household of God* (Boston: Cowley, 1996) and Oxford University Press's forthcoming *Guide to the Book of Common Prayer.*

Carter Heyward is the Howard Chandler Robbins Professor of Theology at Episcopal Divinity School in Cambridge, Massachusetts. Previous publications include: *Flying Changes, Horses as Spiritual Teachers* (Pilgrim Press, Spring 2005), *God in the Balance: Christian Spirituality in Times of Terror* (Pilgrim Press, 2002), *Saving Jesus From Those Who Are Right: Rethinking What It Means to Be Christian* (Fortress, 1999), *Staying Power* (Pilgrim Press, 1995), *Touching Our Strength: The Erotic as Power and the Love of God* (Harper Collins, 1989), *Speaking of Christ: A Lesbian Feminist Voice* (Pilgrim Press, 1989), *Our Passion for Justice: Images of Power, Sexuality, and Liberation* (Pilgrim Press, 1984); *The Redemption of God: A Theology of Mutual Relation* (University Press of America, 1982), and *A Priest Forever: Formation of a Woman and a Priest* (Harper and Row, 1976). She resides in the mountains of North Carolina in an intentional community, where she work with horses and people who love them, is a liturgical coordinator for a small Episcopal, justice and peace seeking mission, and writes whenever she can.

Lisa Isherwood is Professor of Feminist Liberation Theologies at the College of St Mark and St John, Plymouth. She is an Executive Editor of the international journal *Feminist Theology* and Co–Director of the Britain and Ireland School of Feminist Theology. Her publications include: *The Power of Erotic Celibacy* (Continuum, 2005), (editor) *The Good News of the Body* (SAP, 2000), *Introducing Feminist Christologies* (Continuum, 2001), *Liberating Christ* (Pilgrim Press, 1999), and (co–edited with Marcella Althaus–Reid) *The Sexual Theologian: Essays on Sex, God and Politics* (Continuum, 2005). She is editor of three international series: *Religion and Violence* with Rosemary Radford

Ruether (Equinox), *Gender, Theology and Spirituality* (Equinox), and *Queering Theology* with Marcella Althaus–Reid (Continuum).

Gareth Jones studied Theology at Cambridge University, completing his PhD on Bultmann in 1988. He then spent three years at Keble College, Oxford, as Bampton Fellow, before moving to Birmingham University as Lecturer in Systematic Theology in 1991. After spending eighteen months as theological consultant to the House of Bishops of the Church of England, he was appointed to the Chair of Christian Theology at Canterbury Christ Church University College in 1999. He is the author of *Bultmann* (Cambridge University Press, 1991), *Critical Theology* (Cambridge University Press, 1995), *Christian Theology* (Cambridge University Press, 1999), and Editor of the *Blackwell Companion to Modern Theology* (Oxford University Press, 2003).

Philip Kennedy studied music at the University of Melbourne before joining the Dominican Order in 1977. His graduate studies in Theology were undertaken in Switzerland and the Netherlands, after which he lectured on Theology in Australia, United States of America, and England. He has been based in Oxford since 1994. From 2000–2004, he was Lecturer in the History of Modern Christian Thought in the University of Oxford, and is now the Senior Tutor of Mansfield College, Oxford. He is the author of *Schillebeeckx* (Geoffrey Chapman, 1993), *Deus Humanissimus: The Knowability of God in the Theology of Edward Schillebeeckx* (University of Fribourg Press, 1993), and forthcoming, *A Modern Introduction to Theology: New Questions for Old Beliefs* (I. B. Tauris, 2005).

Richard Kirker is Director of the Lesbian and Gay Christian Movement, a post held since 1979. LGCM, a UK–based but internationally active ecumenical charity, with a predominantly Anglican/Episcopal membership, campaigns against homophobia and for an inclusive church. He is ordained a deacon in the Church of

England, has written dozens of articles, makes regular media appearances, edits *Lesbian and Gay Christians,* and has been involved in establishing links with a wide variety of Church organizations and ecumenical bodies globally.

Christopher Lewis is Dean of Christ Church, Oxford. He was previously Vice–Principal of Ripon College, Cuddesdon from 1976–1982, Residentiary Canon of Canterbury Cathedral from 1987–1994, Director of Ministerial Training for the Canterbury Diocese from 1989–1994, and Dean of St Albans from 1994–2003. His publications include: (edited with Dan Cohn–Sherbok) *Beyond Death* (Macmillan, 1995), and (edited with Stephen Platten) *Flagships of the Spirit* (Darton, Longman and Todd, 1998).

Andrew Linzey is a member of the Faculty of Theology in the University of Oxford, and Senior Research Fellow of Blackfriars Hall, Oxford. He is also Honorary Professor of Theology in the University of Birmingham, and Special Professor at Saint Xavier University, Chicago. He has written or edited 20 books including: *Animal Theology* (SCM Press and University of Illinois Press, 1994), (with P. A. B. Clarke) *Research on Embryos: Politics Theology and Law* (LCAP, 1988), (edited with Dorothy Yamamoto), *Animals on the Agenda: Questions about Animals for Theology and Ethics* (SCM Press and University of Illinois Press, 1999); *Animal Rights: A Historical Anthology* (University of Columbia Press, 2005), and *Dictionary of Ethics, Theology and Society* (Routledge, 1995) both edited with P. A. B. Clarke.

George Pattison is Lady Margaret Professor of Divinity in the University of Oxford. Previously, he spent fourteen years in parish ministry, was Dean of Chapel at King's College, Cambridge from 1991–2001, and Associate Professor in Practical Theology at the University of Århus (2002–2003). His publications include: *Kierkegaard and the Crisis of Faith* (SPCK, 2002), *The End of Theology* *and the Task of Thinking about God* (SCM Press, 1998), and *Thinking about God in an Age of Technology* (Oxford University Press, 2005).

Martyn Percy is Principal of Ripon College Cuddesdon, Oxford. He is also Adjunct Professor in Theology and Ministry, Hartford Seminary, Connecticut, USA (since 2002), and Honorary Professor of Theological Education at King's College London. He is also Canon Theologian of Sheffield Cathedral. After training at Durham, he served as curate at St Andrew's, Bedford, from 1990–94, and was then Chaplain and Director of Theology and Religious Studies, Christ's College, Cambridge from 1994–1997. In 1997, he was appointed Founding Director, Lincoln Theological Institute for the Study of Religion and Society. His most recent book is *Salt of the Earth: Religious Resilience in a Secular Age* (Continuum, 2002). His main research interests are Christianity and contemporary culture, modern ecclesiology and practical theology. He is a regular contributor to *The Guardian, The Independent,* Radio 4, and the World Service.

Carolyn J. Sharp is Assistant Professor of Old Testament at Yale Divinity School. She is the author of *Prophecy and Ideology in Jeremiah* (T & T Clark, 2003). Her current book project, *Irony and Meaning in the Hebrew Bible: The Power of the Unspoken in Sacred Texts,* explores hermeneutical and theological issues involved in interpreting irony in scripture.

Martin Stringer studied Social Anthropology at Manchester University, completing his PhD on the congregation's understanding of worship in 1987. He then spent five years as a church based community worker working for the Diocese of Manchester, before moving to Birmingham University as Lecturer in the Anthropology and Sociology of Religion in 1992. He was elected Head of the Department of Theology and Religion at Birmingham University in 2002. He is the author of *On the Perception of Worship* (Birmingham

University Press, 1999) and *A Sociological History of Christian Worship* (Cambridge University Press, 2005).

Vincent Strudwick is Chamberlain of Kellogg College and Associate Chaplain of Corpus Christi College, Oxford. He is an Emeritus Canon of Christ Church, Emeritus Fellow of Kellogg College, and an Emeritus (but still teaching) member of the Oxford University Faculty of Theology. He was previously Director of Theology Programs in the Department for Continuing Education, University of Oxford. Following ordination in the Church of England in 1959, he was Tutor in Church History and Sub–Warden of Kelham Theological College before moving to the Chichester Diocese in 1971. There he worked as Diocesan Adult Education Adviser while also Tutor in Church History at Chichester Theological College. Following four years as the Ecumenical Education Officer for Milton Keynes New City, he became Director of Education and Training in the Diocese of Oxford from 1981–1988, when he was appointed Principal of Oxford Ordination Course, which in 1990 became the St Albans and Oxford Ministry Course. During this period, he researched and taught historical theology, specializing in the formation of the Church of England and of the Anglican Communion. His publications include: *Christopher Wordsworth, Bishop of Lincoln 1869–85* (Honeywood Press, 1987), *Is the Anglican Church Catholic?* (Darton, Longman and Todd, 1994), "English Fears of Social Disintegration, and Modes of Control 1533 –1611" in *The Bible in the Renaissance* edited by Richard Griffiths (Ashgate, 2001), "Bishops and the Formation of Anglicanism" in *The Call for Women Bishops*, edited by Harriet Harris and Jane Shaw (SPCK, 2004), and "Herbert Hamilton Kelly" in the *New Dictionary of National Biography* (Oxford University Press, 2004).

Adrian Thatcher taught Theology at the College of St Mark and St John, Plymouth, from 1977 until his retirement in August 2004. He became Professor of Applied Theology there in 1995. He is now part–time Professorial Research Fellow at the University of Exeter. His most recent publications include: *Marriage after Modernity* (Sheffield Academic Press, 1999), (editor) *Celebrating Christian Marriage* (T&T Clark/Continuum, 2001), *Living Together and Christian Ethics* (Cambridge University Press, 2002), and *The Daily Telegraph Guide to Christian Marriage* (Continuum, 2003). Formerly a Baptist minister, he became an Anglican in 1988.

Keith Ward has taught Philosophy at the Universities of Glasgow, St Andrews, London and Cambridge. He has taught Theology at London, Cambridge and Oxford. He was F. D. Maurice Professor of Moral and Social Theology, and then Professor of the History and Philosophy of Religion at London University, and Regius Professor of Divinity at Oxford University. He has been a priest of the Church of England since 1972. He is a Fellow of the British Academy. His most recent books are: *God: A Guide for the Perplexed* (Oneworld Press, 2002), *Christianity: A Short Introduction* (Oneworld Press, 2000), and *What the Bible Really Teaches* (SPCK and Crossroad, 2004).

Kevin Ward is Senior Lecturer in the Department of Theology and Religious Studies at Leeds University, where he teaches African religious studies. An Anglican priest ordained in the Church of Uganda, he worked in East Africa from 1969–1990 as a schoolteacher and theological educator. He is a trustee of the Church Mission Society, and member of the General Synod of the Church of England. He has written extensively on issues of church and society in East Africa, on the East African revival movement, and on issues of sexuality within African Christianity. He is currently writing a history of the worldwide Anglican Communion.

INTRODUCTION

"MISTAKES OF THE CREATOR"
Andrew Linzey

I

"All inmates with pink triangles will remain standing at attention". We stood on the desolate square ... our throats dry from fear ... Then the guardhouse door of the command tower opened and an SS officer and some of his lackeys strode toward us. Our *Kapo* barked: "Three hundred criminal deviants present as ordered." ... We learned that we were to be segregated in a penal command and the next morning would be transferred as a unit to the cement works ... We shuddered because these bone mills were more dreaded than any other work detail ... "You don't have to look so dumb, you butt fuckers," said the officer. "There you'll learn to do honest work with your hands and afterwards you will sleep a healthy sleep. You are a biological mistake of the Creator. That's why you must be bent straight ..."[1]

---

1 Reminiscences of L. D. von Classen–Neudegg, cited in Richard Plant, *The Pink Triangle: The Nazi War Against Homosexuals* (Edinburgh: Mainstream Publishing, 1987), p. 174. Plant's book is a cool and lucid account, and I am indebted to it. See, also, the first full–length account by a gay inmate, Heinz Heger, *The Men with the Pink Triangle* [1972] (Boston: Alyson, 1980), and especially the groundbreaking research by Rüdiger Lautman and Hanns Wienold, *Das Sexuelle Abwehrstem gegen sexuelle Abweichung, insbesondere Homosexualität* (Bremen: privately published, 1978). Lautman led a team at Bremen University that examined the dossiers of 1,572 homosexual prisoners.

The above is part of a testimony from an inmate at Camp Sachsenhausen in June 1942. The inmate was, of course, gay. And conditions for gays in the death camps were often the severest of all. While gays suffered in the camps along with antifascists, Jews and Gypsies, virulent homophobia extended even to fellow inmates. Some were sexually exploited by SS guards who used the younger inmates, usually Poles or Russians, as their "dolly boys" (*Piepel*).[2] For such acts, the gay inmates were held accountable, and often tainted by the crimes of homosexual guards – even though they themselves were the victims.

In addition to frequent sexual abuse, and being shunned by non–gay inmates, the number of homosexuals used for experiments was disproportionately large.[3] Because gays were regarded as degenerates or "contragenics", they were seen as fair game for scientific vivisection, in a quest to locate the physiological source of their "abnormality". And if we ask: why it is that information about the treatment of gays is not more widely known, then, the answer is even more grotesque. Although it is reasonable to suppose that only a small proportion of camp inmates were gay, their actual numbers and first–hand knowledge of their conditions is very limited for this reason: in comparison with other inmates, very few actually survived.[4]

Even worse (if such is possible), the very small number that *did* survive the death camps were still not released by the liberating armies since, under German law, homosexuals were still classed as criminals.

---

2 Plant, *Pink Triangle*, p. 166.

3 Plant, *Pink Triangle*, p. 175, and pp. 176f. for details of the Buchenwald experiments explicitly on homosexual prisoners.

4 No exact figures are known for the number of homosexuals interned, but Plant estimates that "the number of males convicted of homosexuality from 1933 to 1944 at between 50,000 and 63,000, of which 4,000 were juveniles" (p. 149), but given that there were estimated to be 1.2 million homosexuals in Germany in 1928, the figures seem on the low side. Himmler himself estimated the number at 2 million (p. 148), and his policy was explicitly to exterminate every one. The treatment of homosexuals has been a neglected topic in holocaust studies and historians have almost entirely ignored the issue.

Some American and British jurists, "on learning that an inmate had been jailed and then put into a camp for homosexual activities, ruled that, judicially, a camp did not constitute a prison", therefore, if "someone had been sentenced to eight years in prison, had spent five of these in jail and three in a camp, he still had to finish three years in jail after liberation".[5] Even three or four years in a Nazi concentration camp was thought insufficient penalty for homosexual activity.

But it is not the conditions, or the survival rates of victims, that I want to focus on, but the reported words of the SS officer who saw their crippling work as a means of theological reformation: "You are a biological mistake of the Creator. That's why you must be bent straight ...". Was it not enough that those who wore the pink triangle had to suffer what other inmates suffered, sometimes to a worse degree, without also enduring the ultimate theological insult of being classed as "mistakes" of their Creator?

The sense that lesbians and gays are not "quite right", "handicapped", "deformed", or "perverted" does not come from nowhere. It has been fuelled by centuries of Christian theology. In that, of course, gays are not unique. I remember, years ago, being confronted by a professor of Judaism with the details of the holocaust. Squirming inside, I feebly protested that Christianity couldn't really be all to blame, only to face the full thunder of his question (which has remained with me since): "Where else, then, did it come from?"[6] Since for at least ten centuries before the holocaust, Christianity held unique sway over European culture, where else indeed? But the same question, except with added force, must also be pressed in relation to homophobia. During the Third Reich, there were some Christians who protested against the treatment of the Jews, but I have been unable to discover

---

5 Plant, *Pink Triangle*, p. 181.
6 See, his book, Dan Cohn-Sherbok, *The Crucified Jew: Twenty-Five Centuries of Christian Anti-Semitism* (London: HarperCollins, 1992).

even *one* Christian group who protested against the holocaust of homosexuals.[7]

Now, I know that some readers will say that I am emotionally over–loading the argument before I have even begun, but theology operates some unusual canons of sympathy when it comes to moral issues. Why, for example, should it be right for theologians to go to sometimes extraordinary lengths to "contextualize" their necessary "reappraisal" of Judaism in the light of the holocaust – a position that now extends even to the highest apologetic regions of the major churches – while, at the same time, utterly failing to do so in the case of gays – for whose treatment Christian thinking was arguably more responsible than anything else? If today theologians declared, in all seriousness, that Jewish practices were "perverted", "deformed" or "handicapped", their utterances would receive universal condemnation – and rightly so. But, nowadays, bishops can typify homosexual behavior as "objectively disordered" or "intrinsically evil", without even attracting the mildest of censure. It is as though Christians have at last woken up to the fact that their thinking about Jews helped lead them to the death camps, but cannot quite grasp that Christian thinking also helped lead gays to the same destination.

"Ah, but," comes the reply, "we have no objection to homosexual *orientation*, it is homosexual *behavior* that we regard as immoral". Well, in Nazi Germany even Christian terminology concerning "intention" and "acts" was formally utilized: in 1936 Nazi courts ruled that "illicit sexual acts" do not have to be acts; "intent is what counts".[8] Like eager moral theologians, the Nazis saw that even a

---

7 Christian culpability is most clearly demonstrated by the silence of the churches as anti–homosexual, and anti–semitic, prejudice mounted during the years *prior* to Hitler's rise to power. By the time explicit legislation was enacted against Jews and homosexuals in 1935, hatred was the norm. For an account of the lethargy of the churches, see Klaus Scholder, *The Churches and the Third Reich*, Vol. 1, *Preliminary History and the Time of Illusions, 1918–1934* [1977] translated by John Bowden (London SCM Press, 1986), for example: "In the decisive days around 1 April [1933] no bishop, no church administration, no synod objected publicly to the persecution of Jews in Germany" (p. 268). Needless to say, the position was even worse for gays.
8 Plant, *Pink Triangle*, p. 214. The ruling was on 10 December, 1936. Plant notes that throughout 1936 alone approximately 90,000 Germans were arrested.

Some people say that they are not "homophobic", using the word in its etymological sense. Perhaps they are right – they don't *fear* gay people. Gay people do, however, turn their stomachs. That's the point. It isn't just being frightened. It's *loathing*, disgust, an *aversion*. Persons so inclined want to get away from gay people, not (or not simply) because gay people might harm them (maybe that's "fear"), but because gay people might *pollute* them. But homophobia in the relevant sense isn't just a feeling – though certainly feeling comes into it. Homophobia is an "existential" state of mind and heart, constituted, and reinforced by two thousand years of Christian propaganda. As the song in "South Pacific" has it: "You've got to be taught before it's too late, before you are six or seven or eight, to hate all the people your relatives hate".

I want to emphasize that in what follows I am not pointing the accusing finger at any individual, or claiming in any sense to be "holier than thou", but rather trying to register our *common* problem as Christians – namely, our unconscious (sometimes even conscious) fear of gays. This suggestion should not surprise us. After all, so much of what we do and think is made up of a range of attitudes, impressions and experiences mediated to us through our family, our society and – in the case of Christians – the churches to which we belong. We acquire senses of right and wrong, natural and unnatural, long before we are able to digest and appropriate them for ourselves. And in the Christian community the sense that homosexuality is "not right" has such a long and deep history that it should not surprise us that attitudes to gays are often deeply ingrained, even "habits" of thought. Feelings are tutored. *All* feelings are tutored.

Let me give a brief example. In the 80s, I attended a small weekend conference of Christians who supported the ordination of women. It was an unusually good conference and many people spoke frankly about the issues that concerned them. When we broke up into small groups, the group of which I was a member spent time talking generally about sexuality, and the subject of homosexuality arose. "I don't know what it is", said one member of the group, "but I always feel uncomfortable around homosexuals". "But you don't feel uncomfortable around me, do you?" responded the person sitting next to him. What followed was what I. T. Ramsey used to call a "moment of disclosure" – the individual concerned had to confront his own fear, and when faced with reality – to think again. Whether the cognitive "insight" or disclosure was sufficient to both confront *and* overcome his irrationality, I shall never know. But it was certainly a start.

In many ways, I believe that the Anglican Communion is facing the kind of disclosure moment that that person – I shall call him John – experienced at that conference years ago. It is having to confront its own fears and test them in the light of its experience of real people.

III

How would the church know that it was homophobic if it was? Windsor says the usual things:

> ... any demonising of homosexual persons, or their ill–treatment, is totally against Christian charity and basic principles of pastoral care. We urge provinces to be pro–active in support of the call of Lambeth Resolution 64 (1988) for them to "reassess, in the light of ... study and because of our concern for human rights, its care for and attitude toward persons of homosexual orientation" (57, para 146).

But Archbishop Rowan Williams, in his speech to General Synod in 2005, offered us a rare acknowledgement that all might not be well: "If the acceptance of the recommendations of the Windsor Report or something similar to them were to be simply a mask, a stalking horse, for prejudice or bigotry, for collusion in violence, then I think the report would have failed, and worse than failed it would have made us less than the body of Christ."[12] Although the Archbishop doesn't apparently believe that the Windsor recommendations are influenced by homophobic sentiments, he accepts that it is a *possibility* that its recommendations could become a "mask" for them. But I think the situation is a great deal more serious than Archbishop Rowan supposes, and that there is already evidence that the debate so far has uncovered tangible signs of homophobia.

Consider, first, *the intemperance, even vehemence, of anti–gay language*. Now, I don't want to apologize for the rough and tumble of moral debate. People have the right to state what they believe to be right and wrong, and to criticize those actions they believe are sinful. Nevertheless, there are some kinds of arguments that disturb more than their arguers might suppose. Here is the first paragraph of a press release from "the Resistance Movement" sent to gay organizations:

> Denouncing homosexual behavior as, "a perversion of one of the most intimate and beautiful acts between consenting adults." and calling it, "satanic," and, "a neurological disorder," John Conner, author of *The Resistance Manifesto* offers no apologies. "I'm not homophobic. I'm a pervert–a–phobic. I'm afraid of perverts. I'm afraid of perverts destroying decency in society and in the media. I'm afraid of perverts being able to get married and ruining the meaning of marriage. I can't believe that this kind of behavior is not only accepted, but celebrated in society today. MTV, has long celebrated homosexuality and other satanic behavior. And in recent years, the major networks have also introduced gay characters and gay storylines. We're calling for a return to decency. A replenishment of morals in the media." Connor insists, adding, "these queers make me want to puke."

---

12 Archbishop Rowan Williams, Speech on the Windsor Report, General Synod of the Church of England, 17 February, 2005.

In case this is thought to be an extreme example, I choose another from an Anglican Primate:

> With this tragic topic on the agenda of the Anglican Church worldwide, the Church has regrettably come to a crossroads … The majority of us still believe that communion is important, and it is cherished by us all. However, this is not at the expense of vital communion with God, and certainly not at the cost of shepherding more than 17 million Nigerian Anglicans into harm's way by leading them into the wilderness of morally empty theologizing. Homosexuality or lesbianism or bestiality is to us a form of slavery, and redemption from it is readily available through repentance and faith in the saving grace of our Lord, Jesus Christ.[13]

Note the underlying argument here: homosexuality isn't just wrong, it "is *at the expense of* vital communion with God"; it leads to "the wilderness of *morally empty* theologizing"; homosexuality and lesbianism is placed in the same category as "bestiality", and is depicted as "a form of slavery". In the same article, it is made clear that there can be no tolerance of what is called "the permissive and *satanic* spirit" that leads to "an *acquired* aberration" (my emphases). Note especially the emphasis upon the "satanic" in both statements. I do not believe that I have selectively quoted, and the words are actually those written (rather than reported) in a newspaper article penned by its author. Remember, these words are from an Anglican Primate, a member of the 38–member body that constitutes one of the supposed "Instruments of Communion". Whatever is at work here, it is more than simple disagreement about the rightness or wrongness of certain behaviors.

---

13 Archbishop Peter Akinola, Primate of Nigeria, "Why I Object to Homosexuality", *Church Times,* 4 August, 2005.

Consider, second, *the absence of dialogue with those who differ.* The Primates' communiqué in February 2005 states: "In reaffirming the 1998 Lambeth Conference Resolution 1.10 [which, *inter alia*, opposed the ordination of gays] as the present position of the Anglican Communion, we pledge ourselves afresh to that resolution in its entirety, and request the Anglican Consultative Council in June 2005 to take positive steps to initiate the listening and study process which has been the subject of resolutions not only at the Lambeth Conference in 1998, but in earlier Conferences as well."[14] At their face value, these seem admirable intentions. But, in fact, way back in 1978, the Lambeth Conference called for a "deep and dispassionate study" of homosexuality, which should include a consideration "both [of] the teaching of Scripture and the results of scientific and medical research".[15] It never happened. In fact, only the Episcopal Church of the United States (ECUSA) and the Anglican Church of Canada have begun to initiate any such study or "listening" process. What the Primates resolved in 2005 was to pass on the issue to the Anglican Consultative Council to "take positive steps to *initiate* the listening and study process" which should actually have started way back in 1978. We know from attendees at the Primates' meeting that, far from actually listening and studying, 14 or so Primates refused even to share holy communion with their fellows. Moreover, one Primate, subsequent to agreeing to the communiqué, attacked press reports that he was willing to "listen" to homosexuals. I quote the news report virtually in full:

---

14 Anglican Communion Primates' Meeting Communiqué, 24 February, 2005, Anglican Communion News Service, para 17. It is astonishing that such notice has been taken of the Primates' response to Windsor since the Primates' meeting has no juridical, executive or even advisory authority within Anglicanism.

15 The 1978 Lambeth resolution was remarkably measured noting that "an adequate understanding of, and response to, homosexuality will not be found until society as a whole, and Christians in particular, can approach the subject compassionately without prejudice", and it therefore called for further study. *The Report of the Lambeth Conference 1978* (London: CIO Publishing, 1978), Section 1, E, p. 64. Compare this with resolution 1.10 of the 1998 Lambeth, which condemned homosexuality. It appears as if the bishops' view was strengthened in the *absence* of further study called for in 1978.

The Archbishop of the COU [Church of Uganda], Henry Luke Orombi, ruled out any debate with homosexuals, saying they either repent and adopt the biblical teaching of sex or go their way. "I do not think there is a debate. When God gives his word, you either take it or leave it. We either agree with God or go our own way," Orombi told journalists he called to brief on the Anglican leaders' meeting which resolved to suspend the American and Canadian Churches from the Anglican Communion because of consecrating gay Church leaders. Orombi said, "The Bible defines marriage as between one man and one woman. The Episcopal Church of America hasn't followed the biblical teachings on sexuality and that's why we're against them."[16]

Even allowing for press distortion, it seems a fair reading that the "listening and study process" advocated by Lambeth and the Primates is not being endorsed here. Despite official and apparently authoritative pronouncements, the Anglican Communion as a whole, has not been, and is still not, involved in any "listening and study process".

Consider, third, *the denial of human rights to homosexuals.* Windsor, it should be remembered, opposed "any demonising of homosexual persons, or their ill–treatment", and recalled the Lambeth 1988 declaration of pastoral care for gays "because of our concern for human rights". I will not dwell here on the many places in the world where Anglican churches fail to oppose draconian measures against homosexuals (including, prison sentences and capital punishment), rather I shall focus on the situation in the United Kingdom. I simply ask: How can the statements from Lambeth, Windsor and the Primates be reconciled with the successful attempts by church leaders in Britain (actively supported by the Archbishop to Canterbury) to amend human

---

16 "No Debate on Gays, says Orombi", *The New Vision*, March 4, 2005, and the previous report, "Orombi Okays Gay Debate in Church", *New Vision*, 1 March, 2005.

rights legislation to enable faith–groups to sack employees specifically and exclusively on the grounds of their sexual orientation? The remit includes clergy and educators – though the range could well be extended further. I have yet to hear any convincing justification for this position. This is the moment to recall those lofty words of the Primates' communiqué: "The victimization or diminishment of human beings whose affections happen to be ordered towards people of the same sex is anathema to us".[17] Really? People wiser than I might be able to explain how it is possible with integrity (that is, without self–contradiction) to publicly oppose any "diminishment" of people with a homosexual orientation while also actively working to enable their sacking on grounds of their sexual orientation. The frequently made claim that the Anglican Communion upholds the rights of homosexuals "as persons" flies in the face of not inconsiderable evidence.

Consider, fourth, *the disproportionate attention that the subject receives*. For many, the issue of gays has become a litmus test as to whether the Communion upholds "biblical morality", maintains the "supremacy of scripture", even whether a church is "orthodox". These are extraordinary notions, and can only be rationally justified if sex, and especially gay sex, is the most important moral issue facing Anglicans today, or at least one of the most important. But, in fact, even highly "orthodox" theologians have never given sex this kind of prominence. Consider, for example, these words from that icon of conservative Anglicanism, C. S. Lewis:

> … though I have had to speak at some length about sex, I want to make it as clear as I possibly can that the centre of Christian morality is not here. If anyone thinks that Christians regard unchastity as the supreme vice, he is quite wrong. The sins of the flesh are bad, but they are the least bad of all sins.

---

17 Anglican Primates' Communiqué, para 6.

Lewis goes on to say how the worst pleasures are in fact "spiritual": putting "other people in the wrong, of bossing and patronizing and spoiling sort, and back–biting; the pleasures of power and hatred … that is why a cold, self–righteous prig who goes regularly to church may be far nearer hell than a prostitute. But, of course, it is better to be neither".[18]

By this standard, pursuing the debate in the acrimonious spirit that has so far characterized Anglican intercourse on this subject is a greater sin than engaging in homosexual intercourse itself. Within Christendom, there never has been a consensus that sex is the main, or most significant sin, let alone the criterion for membership of the Anglican Communion. Even if one regards homosexual practice as immoral, the attention, time, energy (not to mention, money) devoted to this issue by anti–gay campaigners is indicative of a deeply disproportionate understanding of Christian morality.

Consider, fifth, *the inconsistency in the way church statements are selected and advanced.* Those who are anti–gay use the 1998 Lambeth Conference statement as a talisman of Christian orthodoxy, or as Windsor actually puts it "the standard of Anglican teaching". In fact, the claim is bogus because Lambeth has only an advisory role at best. But if one really believed that Lambeth was able to declare official, incontrovertible teaching one would surely want to take *all* Lambeth resolutions with great seriousness. Is that what we actually find? By no means. As I have indicated in my own chapter, the strongest of all Lambeth resolutions have been about war, and the stark "incompatibility" between armed violence and the teaching of Jesus. And yet, in reality, individual Christians, clergy, and even individual Anglican provinces take a wide variety of views about warfare, and some clergy are actually employed as military chaplains. Why of all the Lambeth resolutions about moral issues (some of them highly

---

18 C. S. Lewis, *Mere Christianity* [1952] (London: Fontana Books, 1962), p. 91. Originally given as broadcast talks on "Christian Behavior" in 1943.

contentious) from birth control through to temperance, armed conflict to sexuality, should gay sex be singled out as the cornerstone of contemporary Anglican orthodoxy? Such inconsistency in applying apparently "authoritative" teaching indicates a process of selection, at best.

Consider, sixth, *the disparity between what the church says and what the church does.* We have seen that there is a disparity between what the church says about listening to homosexuals and their human rights, and what it actually does. Gay people would be right to be skeptical about Anglicanism on these grounds alone. But there are other grounds too. The chief one is the way in which it actually operates its "no–gay" policy. One example may illustrate my point. After Windsor was published, I remember discussing its contents with a friend of mine, who happened to be one of those in charge of theological education for ordinands in the Church of England. I explained my objections to Windsor and why I thought it bode ill for the church. He sought to dispel my concerns by insisting that gay candidates continue to be selected for ordination and were, in fact, ordained by sympathetic bishops. He concluded by saying that: "In judging a church one really must look at what a church does as well as what it says". The words have remained with me ever since.

Well, what does the Church of England "do"? Against its own stated, public policy, it selects, ordains and employs hundreds, if not thousands of gay people on the understanding that they are "discreet". The tacit agreement is that so long as they remain quiet, and do not call attention to themselves, they will not be disciplined or sacked. There is a word for this situation and that word is "hypocrisy". There is no nice way of putting it, because it is not a nice thing. There are, it is true, literally a few (I mean, very few) gay priests who are "out" and have not been sacked (as yet), but they of course live under the constant threat of it. For the rest, they content themselves with the belief that they have responded to God's call (as they see it) and struggle on, as best they may, with a church that largely tolerates them for its own purposes. In case it is thought that my comments relate to just a small group of otherwise marginal priests, I should add that not a small number of senior posts in the Church of England are held by what are termed "closeted gays". As has been humorously pointed out, some are so far in the closet that they are almost in Narnia. Only a most unusual kind of phobia could make an institution want to operate such a hypocritical, and (humanly speaking) such a diminishing system.

These, then, are my grounds for believing that the Anglican Communion is homophobic. It is not often that we use the "h" word and it should be used sparingly, but the evidence seems to me to be overwhelming. It is the only explanation that fits all the various facts, as we know them. Now, some will argue that it is a very low argument to seek to call into question another person's position on the basis of some perceived psychological disposition. In general, I agree, but simply ask: even when one believes it to be true – *and* can supply rational grounds for supposing it to be true?

But if further evidence is needed, there is the very fact that the Anglican Communion had to set up a blue–ribbon panel and issue a weighty Report, all because the third largest church in the world is – or thinks it is – about to break up, *not* over an article of faith, but over the issue of same–sex relationships. The strangeness of this situation should not go unremarked. As reported, Jesus said nothing about gay sex. There are no Anglican creedal statements on sex, let alone same–sex. The great ecumenical statements of faith of Nicaea and Chaldedon make no reference to sexual behavior. Even the comprehensive Thirty Nine Articles do not touch on homosexuality. Likewise, the *Book of Common Prayer*. The elevation of *one* view of sexual behavior to the status of incontrovertible teaching, so incontrovertible that it is allowed to become the *criterion* of being in communion is without parallel, historical precedent, theological and moral justification – in fact, so preposterous that unless it had actually happened it would be scarcely credible.

IV

And does it matter if the Anglican Communion is homophobic? Viewed from one perspective, especially yes. And that is provided by the teaching and ministry of Jesus. "Truly, I say to you, as you did it to one of the least of these my brethren, you did it to me". Such is the reply of Jesus as recorded by Matthew (25:30), to "the righteous" who expect eternal life. The parable as a whole, and Jesus' interpretation of it, is a remarkable challenge to the narrowness of moral concern exemplified by the ruling religious elite of the time. Matthew's account is sometimes challenged by those who claim that parts of the gospels present a caricature of Jewish groups – such as the Pharisees – or even misrepresent their teaching. But even allowing for this possibility, there can be no dispute about the position advocated by Jesus at this point. He is at pains to extend the fullness of moral obligation even to those in his own society who possessed reduced or diminished moral standing:

> I was hungry and you gave me food, I was thirsty and you gave me drink, I was a stranger and you welcomed me, I was naked and you clothed me, I was sick and you visited me, I was in prison and you came to me (Matthew 25:35–39).

Jesus does not just commend charitable works in a way that indicates how all circumstances being equal (since of course they never are for those who are really disadvantaged) we should help those who are worse off. Rather, he makes care for the outcast a *test* of religiosity, and therefore of true righteousness. Indeed, nothing less than his whole personal authority before God is at stake in the way the question is posed and answered: "… for *I* was hungry and you gave *me* no food, *I* was thirsty and you gave *me* no drink" (25:42; my emphases).

This absolute identification of the moral claims of Jesus and, by implication, of God himself, with those of suffering, disadvantaged humanity would be striking enough simply as one parabolic episode in Matthew. But what we find here is one single and consistent strand throughout all the gospels. In Mark (9:35–45), Jesus commends the way of sacrificial loving that is to become the hallmark of his disciples. In John (13:1–20), Jesus washes the dirty feet of his apostles and sets before them an example, which they are to manifest to the world, and in Luke, the very beginning of Jesus' ministry begins with his bold identification with the words of Isaiah:

> The Spirit of the Lord is upon me, because he has anointed me to preach good news to the poor. He has sent me to proclaim release to the captives and the recovery of sight to the blind, to set at liberty those who are oppressed, to proclaim the acceptable year of the Lord. (4:18–20, cf. Isaiah 61:1–2).

If we are to take this teaching seriously, we are led to the disturbing thought – not only that the vulnerable and the outcast ought to command our moral concern – but also that Jesus himself gives *priority* to those who are deemed "least of all". In the light of this, theology that legitimates suffering, or renders us more insensitive to it, cannot be *Christian* theology, no matter how religious it may be.

In our context, it is a terrible thing to discuss theological issues merely as issues, and fail to see the human dimension – the suffering and misery of those affected most directly. It is utterly wrong to discuss gays as if they were just some pawns in an ecclesial game of chess, or some "cost" that has to be factored into some scheme of maintaining church unity. Our common belief in Jesus ought to save us from these instrumentalist conceptions of fellow human beings. Most importantly, it ought to save us from fear itself. "Have no fear, I am with you". Jesus frequently appears in the gospels and repeats these words. They represent then, as now, the abiding challenge of living by faith.

V

Assembled here is a range of essays that address various aspects of Windsor. It is no exaggeration to say that they come from some of the most accomplished theologians in the Anglican Communion. Although all are critical, there has been no attempt to impose a line: all contributors have addressed the issues they felt to be the most important, and in their own way. All are the work of individuals who take responsibility for their own views – as I alone am responsible for the views expressed here, and in my later chapter.

Taken together, these essays constitute such a comprehensive and detailed critique of Windsor that it is difficult to see how that document can honestly be regarded as a way forward for the Anglican Communion at the present time. It is curious, to say the least, that theologians have been so little consulted in the (actually rather hastened) "response period" to Windsor. But now that they have spoken – or rather that 23 of them have done so – it is to be hoped that their arguments will at least receive as much attention as the voices from the other side. It is often said that one of the strengths of the Anglican Communion consists in its long tradition of theological learning and its preparedness to follow where reason leads. It is difficult to think that there has ever been a time when rational debate is more needed than it is now. My own phobia – and I freely state it – is that on this issue something so deeply visceral is involved that rational argument can hardly prevail against it. In these troubling times, I pay tribute to my fellow contributors for having the courage to raise the standard, and for their impressive, erudite, even inspiring work. And I wish the reader much intellectual stimulation.

Andrew Linzey
Blackfriars Hall
University of Oxford
andrewlinzey@aol.com
April 2005

I would like to thank Charles Hefling and Priscilla Cohn for their helpful criticisms of an earlier draft of this paper. Needless to say, I am alone responsible for the views expressed.

PART I

ISSUES OF AUTHORITY

I

POLITICS, POLITY AND THE BIBLE AS HOSTAGE

L. William Countryman

Windsor is primarily a practical document that will succeed or fail primarily on the level of current politics. Will it, or will it not, help to make time for ongoing conversation among Anglicans of different perspectives – enough time to prevent the passions of the moment from tearing the Communion apart? Nonetheless, it does make theological claims, and we have to consider it in those terms, too. Indeed, if we neglect to do so, we may find ourselves moving in directions incompatible with our faith and our tradition simply because we are frightened by the problems of the moment, or seduced by an apparently reasonable solution to them. In this essay, I take up two issues to examine, the first an issue of polity, the second the role of scripture in the present conflicts. They are more closely related than might a first appear.

Windsor proposes a revision of the polity of the Anglican Communion that would place new constraints on the autonomy of the separate provinces. It argues that this is simply an effort to rebalance the relation of parts to whole, a reemphasis on the interdependence that forms the rightful context of autonomy. For those provinces that, until recently, formed part of the British Empire, this may seem like something of a return to earlier circumstances, albeit with broader global participation. From the quite different historical perspective of the Episcopal Church in the United States (ECUSA), it looks different – less a recovery of a lost wholeness and more a shifting of power to bishops and, more specifically, the Primates.

Anglicans have been united in their acceptance and practice of episcopacy, but have not held to a single understanding of its nature nor, at least since the late eighteenth century, to a single way of integrating it into the structure of the church as a whole. The Chicago–Lambeth Quadrilateral acknowledges this diversity in its carefully chosen language about the episcopate. It names, as one of four bases for Christian reunion, "The Historic Episcopate, locally adapted in the methods of its administration to the varying needs of the nations and peoples called of God into the Unity of His Church." By referring to the "Historic Episcopate," the Quadrilateral avoids making any particular theory of the meaning of this institution a requirement of unity. By speaking of local adaptation, the document acknowledges that not even Anglicans all have the same kind of organization, or assign to their bishops exactly the same authority.

The situation of the Episcopal Church in the United States is one of the "local adaptations" to which the Quadrilateral refers. The circumstances leading to the independent existence of the American church were unusual among Anglicans. There was no orderly devolution of local autonomy from the imperial power or the missionary organization. The church grew up in the Thirteen Colonies with little oversight, and largely under lay initiative and leadership. There were no bishops among us before the Revolution, partly because of lethargy on the part of the Church of England and partly because of American resistance. Most American colonists, even those loyal to the Church of England, wanted no part in the hierarchical "lord bishop" they saw as normal to that church.

After the Revolution, American Anglicans were in disarray. Many had been Loyalists and some of these fled the new country. Many others had been Patriots and were faced with the question of how to give shape to their community of worship under changed circumstances.

The result was a polity that maintained the office of bishops, while balancing their authority with that of other clergy and of lay people, acting in local parishes and in diocesan and national conventions. The idea of a bishop who can dictate to the diocese is not absolutely unknown in ECUSA, but it exists, where it does, by local custom, not by canonical right.

The American church is thus markedly different from some of the Anglican provinces that might be called "Commonwealth churches" by virtue of their devolution from the British Empire. We did not originate in a top–down fashion. Nor are we presently organized in such fashion. Such an arrangement is at home neither in our history, nor in our culture. An effort to turn the American church into a top–down, episcopally controlled structure is not only unlikely to succeed, but it would violate the fundamental Chicago–Lambeth criterion of an episcopate adapted to local needs.

Some Anglicans, to be sure, understand bishops as successors to the apostles and conduits through whom the grace of God and the Gospel flow to those below them in the church. But this is just one view among many, and it has probably never been the majority position. It is difficult to demonstrate the historical grounding of such a view in the first Christian century; and it is very difficult to render it intelligible in terms of contemporary Anglican or ecumenical understandings of ecclesiology. The *laos* is the church, not the clergy. While we value the classic polity of the three orders for its capacity to link churches to one another today and to the past, Anglicans do not generally understand the historical episcopate as the church's unique link to God or to Christ.

Why, then, is there pressure for a stronger episcopate at the present time? Windsor emphasizes the bishop as a teacher of scripture (58–60). Its effect is to put more power in the hands of local bishops. But the *de facto* beneficiaries of such increased power are a much smaller group, the Primates (58). This is an even more problematic proposal from the perspective of American Episcopalians. We treat our Presiding Bishop as a Primate for reasons of courtesy, but for practically no other purpose. Originally, the holder of this office was simply the senior bishop, who presided over meetings of the House of Bishops. Even now, our Presiding Bishop cannot speak for the whole American church in the way that the Archbishop of Canterbury can for the Church of England. Nor can the House of Bishops. Only the entire General Convention can do this.

Nothing is more astonishing in our present conflicts than the sudden prominence of a group that did not even exist a few decades ago and has no real grounding in our ecclesiology: the Primates' meeting (65). We have never distinguished an order of Metropolitans or Primates as if they were anything other than bishops, albeit bishops with somewhat broadened responsibilities. Windsor, however, elevates them to one "Instrument of Unity" among four. And the Primates themselves have now gone on to turn themselves into the principal such instrument by presuming to give directions to another of the instruments, the Anglican Consultative Council (ACC).

From an American perspective, if either of these two "Instruments of Unity" might seem to embody some particular authority for Anglicans, it would have to be the ACC. A group like the meeting of Primates, which does not include the voice of the larger *laos*, presumes a model of church in which the people are connected with God only through their highest liturgical officer. It is, in fact, a papal model, even if the Report proposes, in effect, a council of popes as distinct from a single one. One could debate the relative merits of one pope or many, of course, but my own preference – and I daresay the classic Anglican preference – is for none at all.

Why this sudden rush to quasi–papal authority? Why the sudden desire on the part of some Anglicans for the Communion to have an authoritative voice to which all must yield obedience? It is difficult to believe that this goal is being sought for its own sake. The primary movers are not, for the most part, anglo–catholics who adhere to the theory of bishops as successors to the apostles and conduits of grace, but evangelicals, who in principle ought to be skeptical of such an amplification of priestly authority. Indeed, some of them are evangelicals of the extreme Sydney variety, whose real preference in polity seems to be presbyterian.

The absoluteness of papal authority was surely one of the principal targets of attack for the English Reformers. For them, it was not simply the Church of Rome that had to be rejected, but the whole notion of an omnicompetent vicar of Christ. They never suggested that Canterbury was a new Rome or that the Archbishop took the place of the Pope. The Church of England was not even claimed to be beyond error. In framing the Articles of Religion, the Reformers practiced a certain restraint about defining orthodox opinion on every topic of the day. They did not share the need of some of their modern successors to define everything; and, accordingly, they did not require a mechanism for doing so. While they acknowledged the idea that a general council of Christians might settle controverted issues (Article xxi), they had a pretty strong suspicion that no such gathering would be convened.

Yet, the Report treats the meeting of Primates almost as a theological given, reflecting New Testament ideas of apostolic leadership (65) – precisely the position that the Chicago–Lambeth Quadrilateral avoided endorsing with regard to the episcopate at large. Polity here is not being treated – as it deserves to be treated – under the heading of ecclesiology, but as a political device. The determining influence is not the proper constitution of the church or even of the Anglican Communion, but the rough–and–tumble of contemporary ecclesiastical politics and a perceived means of gaining closure by giving one party the upper hand. The *de facto* effect is to establish a group that happens to be dominated by proponents of contemporary right–wing evangelical theology (with a smaller band of right–wing anglo–catholics in tow) as the guarantors of an eternal and unchanging orthodoxy for Anglicans. In other words, what Windsor really proposes is a palace coup, however far that idea was from the minds of most of the members of the committee.

Anglicans, classically, have seen a certain humility and reserve in theological matters as one of the great graces poured out by the Spirit on our tradition. We believe that no one theological expression of Christianity has ever achieved perfection and that none ever can. We must ask ourselves whether we are prepared to hand over so much power to the Primates. For what the Report comes down to – particularly now that the Primates have revealed their willingness to give directions to the other "Instruments of Unity" – is that no further development of thought or practice will be permitted within the Anglican Communion that is not first approved by them. This, in turn, implies that the authority of church synods, the autonomy of provinces, and the role of the local bishop can be freely overruled.

This is a problematic model for a global Communion that has historically been suspicious of theological absolutism. One basic fact of any genuinely global community is that it will have to exist simultaneously in a great many different cultural and historical contexts. Questions that have great power to create conflict in one place may be meaningless in another. It would be easy, for example, for North Atlantic Anglicans to dismiss the question of how Anglicans in East Asia should or should not honor ancestors. We might dismiss the question as intrinsically insignificant (something that could not possibly justify theological reflection even among Anglicans of East Asia) or as something of no real importance to us (invoking "tolerance" as a dismissal) or as a threat to Christian orthodoxy (and therefore to be suppressed, if necessary, by pressure from outside).

None of these "solutions," however, is appropriate in a truly global Christian community. Christians of the North Atlantic community have no business dictating the details of theological reflection to Christians in today's mature Asian churches. Even in a missionary period, there are limits as to how far an emissary of Christ from one culture can determine the best way to incorporate Christian faith in another. And in a mature global Christian context, our proper response to one another is respect – a respect made manifest by both questioning and encouragement. It is important to think what the various solutions to this particular question will offer to all Christians, not just those of East Asia. A global decision can only follow a period of thoughtful and reflective experience by the faithful within each culture. Sometimes this will mean that our sisters and brothers in other parts of the world do things that surprise any one of us.

For this reason, the classic Anglican pattern of "bonds of affection" is actually a superior model, and more responsive to the needs of a global communion today, than is the proposed collegial papacy of Windsor. It allows for theological conversation. It allows for new ideas to be contemplated and tested over time. The North American churches have relied on exactly these bonds as they try to follow the leading of the Spirit in their own cultural context. What is threatening to destroy the bonds of affection today is that some other parties are trying to replace them with an alternative, more centralized structure that they fully expect to control.

Despite the Report's efforts at revising history (126), if the proposed structure had been in place twenty or thirty years ago, we would not now have any women as bishops in the Anglican Communion. Indeed, we would be unlikely to have any in the foreseeable future. If it had been in place in the eighteenth century, we probably wouldn't have the lay participation in church governance that we have now. Change does not, historically, happen by first persuading central authorities to agree to it. A central authority is invested in continuity, not in change (unless, to be sure, the change enhances the central authority's power). A John XXIII is an occasional miracle of grace, not the norm of papal or quasi-papal power. Change that can open the church up to new experience of grace normally comes from below, from the willingness of Christians on the ground to live out their experience of God's goodness in ways that may seem startling at first to others. It does not follow, of course, that every such innovation will be of enduring value. But the ones that will must show themselves by having the chance to be tested by the faithful in the life of the church.

The Report's proposal to focus authority in the Anglican Communion in the "Instruments of Unity" ultimately comes down to reposing it in the council of Primates. The Archbishop of Canterbury will be reluctant to resist them, as we have already seen. And neither the Lambeth Conference, nor the ACC, meets frequently enough to be an effective counterbalance. And, if there were any doubt before as to the willingness of the Primates to use their weight against another "Instrument of Unity," we need doubt no longer. The Report offers no real argument on behalf of this sort of change in structure except to say that we need it at the moment. No, what we need, in this respect, is more careful ecclesiological thinking.

The treatment of scripture in Windsor – and, indeed, the use of scripture generally in our present troubles – is intimately related to the interplay of polity and politics that I have sketched above. Here, however, the Report does much better in providing a theological account of the role of scripture in Anglican faith (53–62). This is basically sound and could form an excellent foundation for further dialogue among Anglicans. The problem is whether the context for this dialogue exists, either as it is implied in the Report, or as it is becoming known to us in the playing out of the current conflicts.

First, however, the positive elements. The Report recognizes that the attachment of the Anglican Reformers to the holy scriptures was somewhat different from that of their reforming contemporaries: along with repeated reference to the Fathers, "it was part of their appeal to ancient undivided Christian faith and life" (53). They did not take the Bible out of context as an isolated legal document, a kind of perfected Sinai Covenant, as Puritans often tended to do. Rather it was the central element in their appeal to a Christianity that preceded both the excesses of the Middle Ages and the divisions of their own time. They sought to return to the unity of that era in its own terms, as a network of churches bound together by their basic faith and worship, a bond that found one of its images in the episcopal college. Even if they did not use the phrase themselves, "bonds of affection" describes such a unity well – as opposed, on the one hand, to the exercise of one–sided power by the papacy or, on the other, to the Puritan commitment to an absolute uniformity of faith and practice claimed to be found in scripture itself and given detailed expression in confessions.

The Report rightly adds that the authority of scripture always points beyond itself to the authority of God (54). It can never substitute for the latter. To treat scripture as if it were the very voice of God in the present moment is to commit the favorite sin of the religious: idolatry. Idolatry takes some good gift of God and treats it as if God were so fully involved in it that one can no longer tell the two apart. This is what we are doing whenever we assume that the Bible, by itself, can provide us with complete and unproblematic access to the authority of God here and now – the idea that a single text or a short catena of texts can resolve complex problems like the ones Anglicans are now debating.

If scripture is truly to represent the authority of God to us, it cannot, in any case, simply proclaim law, for that is not the goal of scripture any more than it is the goal of the incarnation. This is not to say that law is of no value to us, but law conveys God's good purpose only if it comes to us as an implication of the larger proclamation of good news. The authority of scripture is made known when, through it, the Spirit breaks in upon us to declare the good news of God's grace and to transform lives (55).

The Spirit, of course, is never under our control. We cannot summon such an inbreaking, we can only remain open to it. This is one reason why common prayer remains the central place for our encounter with scripture (53). It is also a reason why, as the Report emphasizes, scripture always stands in need of interpretation (59). Our pious temptation is to let the existing interpretations substitute for the word of scripture itself, just as we are also tempted to allow scripture to stand for God. The presumably "obvious" meaning of the text sometimes turns out, on closer examination, not to be wellfounded in the words themselves. Better knowledge of those words' ancient cultural, religious, linguistic, or historical context may even suggest that they originally meant something quite different, or that they are embedded in cultural presuppositions that are no longer intelligible, or even morally acceptable in our own time.

If we propose to let the text have something like its own voice and not be merely an echo of our own, we have to cultivate a spirituality of reading that leaves the text free to contradict conventional interpretation and produce conversion in us. This spirituality entails our pursuit of learning in order to read the text well; it also entails humility and an openness to the movement of the Spirit. Neither learning nor openness is sufficient by itself. Accordingly, the reading and interpretation of scripture calls for a variety of voices, which may well produce a variety of results. The Report very properly rejects the Enlightenment notion that there has to be a single meaning of the text and that this can only be discerned by representatives of the academy – presumably the male, white, western academy (60).

Unfortunately, the Report does not go far enough in this regard. The end of Enlightenment presuppositions must signal more than the simple introduction of one imperialism in place of another – the imperialism of Primates in place of professors (58). What the post–Enlightenment situation creates is an opportunity for more voices, not fewer, to enter into conversation in seeking what God wishes to communicate to us through scripture in the Spirit. For any of these voices to begin by excluding others makes no sense; indeed, it invalidates the whole conversation. The test to which we must all hold one another is not, "Does this agree with the present interpretation of the church?" – that would be to silence scripture before it has spoken. The only possible questions are, "Where do you find what you are saying in the text? And how do you see this as part of God's saving grace?"

In the Report's basic treatment of the authority and interpretation of the Bible, there is nothing for any party within Anglicanism to fear. Indeed, if we could embrace this set of principles, we might be able to resume some healthy and mutually respectful conversation. It may turn out that we really do all believe the things that Windsor says here about Anglicans and the Bible. And, if we do, we may find that we can learn how to talk about the issues on which we disagree while maintaining a sense that we are talking together in God's presence, and in the hope that the Spirit will nurture our community of worship, and use it as a means for the salvation of all humanity. I can imagine no more desirable result.

Two things, however, stand quite obviously in the path of this hope. One emerges in Windsor itself, but looms even larger in recent practice. The other is an issue that the Report seems uncomfortably aware of, but refuses actually to name. And it may turn out to be the factor that will tear the Anglican Communion not just in two, but also into ever–multiplying fragments.

The first is the new role suggested for the Primates, which I have already discussed in terms of ecclesiology, but which also figures in the Report's treatment of scripture. The Report speaks glowingly of bishops as teachers of scripture (58), which it sees as an essential component of their authority. "The accredited leaders of the Church . . . must be people through whose prayerful teaching ministry the authority of God vested in scripture is brought to bear . . ." This is a dangerously ambiguous statement. If it simply expressed the *desideratum* that Anglicans should elect people steeped in scripture to the episcopate, it would be quite all right, though it would probably have little effect. Bishops are elected for a wide range of reasons, including the perceived threats and opportunities of the present moment, reverence for the new bishop's predecessor, rejection of the same, complex political maneuvers, the candidate's actual gifts and graces, the candidate's perceived gifts or graces, a certain level of learning (evaluated either positively or negatively), the treacherous influences of unfaith and hatred within the church, the gracious influences of the Holy Spirit, and so forth. It is all very well to desire that all bishops should be prepared to reflect and communicate the authority of the scripture, having assimilated it in a life of prayer, humility, study, and openness to the

Spirit. But it is impossible to ascribe such a thing to them merely because they have been duly "accredited."

In any case, the bishop as a single voice will never be able to take the place of the larger, more complex conversation about scripture going on in the church as a whole. The Primate is, if anything, even less capable of such a task, given the greater size and complexity of the Christian community over which he or she presides and the more extensive demands of the task. While we look with great admiration and gratitude on the occasional archbishop who maintains a very active life of prayer and study and speaks to the rest of us out of that, it would be foolish to pretend that this is something we can routinely expect from Primates. Not every archbishop is a William Temple.

The Report, in any case, sneaks this supposed biblical ministry of the Primates in as a kind of appendage to that of the bishops (58), almost as if it were equally obvious, when it is not at all. The Anglican Reformers did retain existing primatial organizations within the Tudor dominions (England and Ireland), but they never ascribed to them any ecclesiological necessity. They specifically relegated, not just Rome, but all the most ancient patriarchates to the human realm of error, actual or potential (Article xix). They could scarcely have thought Anglican Primates of the twenty–first century any more likely to be preserved from error. Windsor, however, gives the Primates a central role in mediating scriptural authority to the Communion as a whole. The only apparent reason is that, being few in number, they might offer a hope of producing some kind of mutually consistent interpretation that the bishops cannot offer. After all, there are bishops on all sides of our current conflicts. And all of them understand themselves to be speaking out of the message of scripture.

Some Primates have happily adopted their new job description, freely proclaiming that the Bible is on their side of our disputes. They have little trepidation about speaking authoritatively. If the professors of scripture do not all agree with them, it is a fairly easy matter to sweep them aside (58). If other faithful people do not all read the scriptures in the same way, they have not been given the "accreditation" that the Primates enjoy. On the topic of biblical authority and interpretation, the Report is already being read by a number of Primates as license for them to clothe themselves in scriptural authority as the chief teachers of the Bible and therefore, to all intents and purposes, the voice of God. If the virtues of the Report's discussion of scripture are to make any headway, they will have to be liberated from this political development.

But this may prove impossible for a reason that Windsor avoids mentioning. The larger background of our current crisis lies in the way some Anglicans have long used scripture to authorize their particular partisan versions of our shared tradition. This was true already with Puritanism. Richard Hooker argued long ago that it first adopted its position and then "proved" it out of scripture. Everything the Puritans believed, whatever its origin, was presented as just the "plain sense" of scripture. The great challenge for classic Anglicanism was whether it could save scripture from being treated as a strangely organized lawbook that only a Puritan could interpret. Its great achievement was to preserve the scriptures as something more like what they had been in earliest Christianity – a book of mysteries, in which, and through which, God might meet you at any moment, and without warning. And the God who meets you there will meet you with the good news of grace.

Yes, there will also be moral demands, spiritual demands, the awareness of judgment, even the occasional "example of life and instruction of manners." But all these will reach us as manifestations of the central reality of good news – a good news that surprises us with forgiveness and love, inspires forgiveness and love in return, and winds up transforming us into citizens of the age to come. Much Christianity, however, has never gotten beyond the rules. There is no lack of this in Anglicanism. Some of us are imprisoned by the rules of tradition, some by the rules of what is currently fashionable in theology, some by the rules of particular ways of reading the Bible.

The last has become the particular province of right–wing evangelicals in our tradition. They have a complete account of what the

Bible means. They regard this account in somewhat the same light as the conservative Roman Catholic regards *ex cathedra* pronouncements by the Roman pontiff. To question even details of this evangelical account of scripture is grounds for one's expulsion from the ranks of the elect. There is no room for conversation, no possibility that their interpretation might be less perfect than scripture itself. For every claim they wish to make, the rubric – often unexamined – is "The Bible says." Those who disagree are questioning not them, but the Bible itself.

The long period of dialogue in ECUSA leading up to the ratification of Gene Robinson's election was marked by a "godlike" refusal of the evangelical right to participate. It was a refusal that took various forms. To a great extent, they simply did not attend parish and diocesan events intended to encourage dialogue. When they did attend, they simply repeated their existing position without any particular effort to show how it might connect with other perspectives. Most damaging of all, they refused to listen to the other people present and merely dismissed everyone and everything with which they disagreed. After the "dialogue," they went right on identifying their position with that of the Bible as if nothing else were possible, as if no one else had ever read scripture or argued for a different reading of the texts.

This behavior can only be described as abusive toward the community as a whole, and its effects are still unrolling before us in the threat of schisms by which they propose to replicate in organizational ways a long–standing refusal to treat their fellow–Anglicans as faithful Christians. Windsor rightly notes that "A mention of scripture today can sometimes seem actually divisive, so aware are we of the bewildering range of available interpretative strategies and results" (62). A more critical factor in producing this result is the insistence of one party that only its voice deserves to be heard. The Report hopes that "our shared reading of scriptures across boundaries of culture, region, and tradition" can guide "us together into an appropriately rich and diverse unity by leading us forward from entrenched positions into fresh appreciation of the riches of the gospel as articulated in the scriptures." If that is to

2

ECCLESIAL AUTHORITY AND MORALITY

Keith Ward

Does the Christian church have a special authority in matters of morality? The Roman Catholic Church has a clear view on this issue. The magisterium of the church, ordinarily rooted in the normal teaching of diocesan bishops, but ultimately based on the teaching of the pope, provides authoritative teaching on moral issues. When defined or ratified by the pope, this teaching is binding on all believing Catholics. It is forbidden for teachers of Catholic theology publicly to question such teaching. For Christ promised that the Spirit would guide the church into all truth, and the pope is the channel through which this guidance is given. So if the pope says that homosexual practice is sinful, then it is.

Anglicans do not accept this position. If they did they would be members of the Roman Catholic Church. Nor do Anglicans hold that, though the pope is not authoritative in his moral teaching, the Archbishop of Canterbury is. Indeed, it looks as though Anglicans are committed to denying that there is any magisterium in matters of morality. The twenty–first of the Thirty Nine Articles of the Church of England states that, "general councils may err, and sometimes have erred, even in things pertaining unto God". Anglicans are committed to saying this, since the Church of England is officially defined (for instance, in the Royal Accession Service) as a protestant church, one that rejects many defined doctrines of the Catholic Church, such as transubstantiation and "the Romish doctrine of Purgatory".

In Anglicanism there is a long tradition of patristic scholarship, and some theologians have held that at least the first six or seven councils of the undivided church are authoritative. It seems irrational, however, to hold that God guided the church for the first few hundred years, but then gave up. So while Anglicans give the early councils of the church great significance, they are not bound by the decisions of councils, if those decisions do not seem in accordance with scripture and reason.

The Thirty Nine Articles do give the scriptures of Old and New Testament a great authority, and it is a normal Anglican position that nothing can be held binding on faith if it cannot be "proved" by scripture. There are, however, notorious difficulties with this position. Virtually all patristic theologians agree that the doctrines of the incarnation and trinity, as they came to be formulated in the early councils, are not to be found in that form in the Bible. John's Gospel seems unequivocally to say that the Father is greater than the Son (John 14:28), which was denied by the early church. And the full divinity of the Holy Spirit was not defined until the Council of Constantinople, in 381 AD. If you deny authority of interpretation to the church, it is obvious that there are many ways of interpreting scripture, as the great number of protestant churches shows, all of them claiming to be "Bible–based", yet all disagreeing on biblical interpretation with each other.

The Fourth Commandment: the Bible and moral teaching

A good example of diversity in interpreting the moral rules of the Bible is provided by treatment of what most protestants call the fourth commandment (Exodus 20:8–11). Are Christians to keep the Sabbath rules or not? Are we to keep all of them or some of them? John Calvin, in the *Institutes* taught that we should not keep any of them. This was in accordance with Paul's teaching that there should be no special times and seasons, and with Calvin's own view that the whole of the ritual "law" (the Torah) had been superseded by Christ's sacrifice on the cross.

What most Anglicans seem to do is to ignore most Sabbath regulations in the Old Testament, change the holy day to Sunday, and keep a small selection of the ancient rules (like not working), though even then not very rigorously. What justifies selecting not working, while rejecting rules about not traveling and not lighting fires? Nothing in the New Testament does so. The only appeal can be to church tradition – that is, the decisions of a group of bishops of the early church. But since that is agreed not to be binding, we Anglicans are in fact choosing to follow some ancient traditions, presumably because we find them helpful, but dropping others, presumably because we find them too inconvenient or simply irrelevant. We are picking and choosing, and our ultimate reason is not what is in the Bible, but what we find relevant and helpful, in our situation. It would be equally plausible just to drop all the Sabbath regulations – since we have dropped some of them anyway – or to adopt all of them – since that would obey our Lord's command to keep every minute detail of the law (Matthew 5:18–19).

In case we think this is a trivial matter, we should remember that this is one of the ten commandments, written up on many Church of England walls on either side of the altar. My own view would be in agreement with Calvin – that this commandment has to be interpreted symbolically, so that it enjoins us always to be mindful of God, but allows us to work on the Sabbath. But I have to admit that if someone wants to take it literally, and keep all the Sabbath laws, I can understand that. And if someone wishes to keep only some of the laws (the ones explicitly mentioned in the fourth commandment, for example), that is their decision. It seems to me an arbitrary decision, since it seems obvious that the commandment implies that its hearers should keep all the Sabbath laws, not just the one about not working. It also contradicts Paul's rule not to keep special days. But I can understand the decision, and, as an Anglican, I am even prepared to go along with it. It is, after all, not a grave moral issue in my eyes, and it will not hurt me to follow the tradition of my own church. What I cannot say is that "this is what the Bible says".

If, and only if, you take the fourth commandment completely out of context, it can be made to say that you should not work on the Sabbath. But if you put it into its total biblical context, you get a more complex story.

First, in its original Jewish context, it says that on Saturdays you should not work, leave home, gather wood or light a fire. You should double the daily sacrificial offering (Exodus 16 and 20, Deuteronomy 5, Numbers 15 and 28, Exodus 35).

Second, if you appeal to the recorded teaching of Jesus, you should certainly keep these rules literally (Matthew 5:19). But you should look for their deeper spiritual meaning (perhaps, remember God at all times, but set apart some special time, especially perhaps on one day of the week), and make sure you keep that too.

Third, if you appeal to the letters of Paul, it seems that all ritual rules that set apart Jews from Gentiles are superseded, and that no special days and festivals are to be kept.

Fourth, in Acts 20:7, it is mentioned that Christians met "on the first day of the week" to break bread. That day is called "the Lord's day" in Revelation 1:10. In 1 Corinthians 16:2, Paul asks that Christians set aside offerings on that day. So Sunday was beginning to be the regular weekly day for Christian meetings. No reference is made to Jewish Sabbath rules, however.

That is all the biblical evidence there is. What shall we make of it? I think the original Sabbath rules have been dropped, despite the teaching of Jesus about keeping the law. This is a major problem, to which not enough attention is usually given. How can Christians disobey the teaching of Jesus? Probably the best explanation is given in Acts 15, sometimes called the first council of the church, where the issue of whether Christians should keep the law was raised. It is obvious from this account that Jesus had not unambiguously told the apostles that the law need not be kept. On the contrary, all of them who had known

Jesus personally, especially James the brother of Jesus and Peter, had insisted in keeping the law rigorously. It was Paul, who had never met Jesus, who insisted that Jewish laws should not be imposed on Gentiles.

There was perhaps some ambiguity about the teaching of Jesus – Mark thought that Jesus had, at least by implication, declared "all foods clean" (Mark 7:19), whereas Matthew denied that Jesus ever taught the law could be abandoned (all incidents like eating corn or healing on the Sabbath were in fact allowed by liberal interpretations of the law, widely accepted by contemporary rabbis). But there is no doubt all the apostles wanted the law kept at the first council, which implies that was what they thought Jesus had approved. However, they recognized that they were now in a new situation. Jesus had spoken only to Jews, before his death. Now perhaps his death had brought the law to an end, burst the bounds of Judaism, and opened the way to a religion of grace, not laws. So they compromised, saying that circumcision was not compulsory, but eating only kosher food remained a rule. As we know, the rule about kosher food was soon abandoned too. At that point, the Jewish law was definitively superseded.

But the salient point is that there was no clear unambiguous teaching from Jesus that settled this issue – the first major debate about how Christians should live in the history of the Christian church. The apostles just had to make a decision. The decision they made was that the literal teaching of Jesus, given in a specific context to a specific group of people, did not remain binding in a different context, and to different people. Rather, they appealed to more general considerations of "what seemed good to the Holy Spirit". They took a decision, they changed the rules, they did not follow what was recorded by at least one Gospel tradition as the literal teaching of Jesus, and they appealed to the Holy Spirit, not to a written text or previous authority, as their guide.

Of course, the remembered or recorded teaching of Jesus was important. It could not simply be dismissed. But its literal application was seen to apply in a limited context – namely, to Jews before the death and resurrection of Jesus. The decisive consideration was that the universal grace of God had transformed the law whose purpose was to set apart the Jews from everyone else. The moral appeal, in other words, was not to a literal interpretation of the words of Jesus. It was to what a gospel of universal grace and unbounded love seemed to require in a new situation, where there were no binding precedents to follow.

Just to complete the story about the Sabbath, it was not until the fourth–century Council of Elvira that it was made a rule not to work on Sundays. And it was only in the English and Scottish Reformations that the prohibition of games and sports on Sundays became part of the Puritan agenda. The way we view Sundays is the result of this long set of legal decisions and traditions. If we want "the biblical view" we have to say that it allows for a range of decisions to be made, that might well differ from one another. The decision that is nearest the biblical is, to my mind, that Sundays are not special at all, except as days to celebrate the Lord's supper. But I am prepared to allow that the Anglican compromise is a possible (though unlikely) interpretation of the biblical material. Even then, it is not just "what the Bible says". It is the result of decisions made after thinking about the Bible. As a decision, it might have gone differently. It is changeable for good reason, and it is adopted because it is thought to be spiritually helpful, in our ever–changing situation. I am prepared to accept this odd compromise. But I am not prepared to say that it is the only, let alone the best, interpretation of the Bible. And any appeal to the ten commandments must be made in the light of thorough theological reflection on the Pauline Gospel of grace, on the way in which Jesus' teaching was modified by the early church, and on the sort of authority that the decisions of church meetings have for us. For Anglicans at least, treatment of the fourth commandment is not based simply on the Bible or on some authoritative church decision. It is revisable in the light of differing situations and of what is found spiritually helpful. In default of further argument, what goes for that biblical command must go for the others too.

Homosexual practice

My concern is with the exercise of church authority in matters of morality. I have appealed to the Sabbath regulations as an example of how complex and difficult appeal to the Bible is on this issue. I have emphasised the Church of England's position that any church meeting or council is liable to error, even in matters concerning God. I have shown, by reference to this one commandment, how even the interpretation of the ten commandments, central to Christian morality, is affected by church decisions and extra–biblical factors. And I have shown how a main precedent for Christian decision–making (the Council of Jerusalem) is, not an appeal to a literal and direct application of written words, even from scripture or from Jesus, but an appeal to what the Holy Spirit is believed to suggest in changing situations.

The inescapable conclusion is that the interpretation of the Bible is difficult and always liable to dispute by the most competent and pious scholars. The decisions of church councils, while they should no doubt be heard with due consideration, are liable to error. I have always loved the Church of England because it has shown some knowledge of the pluralism and diversity of biblical interpretation, and the fallibility of its committees and leaders. Accordingly, it has claimed no moral magisterium, whereby one small group of people can tell the world what is right and wrong without fear of error. Instead, it offers the Bible, a complex and difficult text that can be interpreted in a variety of ways. And it offers the advice of carefully chosen expert committees – advice that contributes to open debate, and is made in the light of a basic commitment to the moral demand and universal love of God. But no specific interpretation of the Bible, and no adherence to the teachings of its committees and bishops, has been demanded. It is a church in which the Bible is treasured as a source of inspiration, and prayerful scholarship offering guidance in moral issues is taken seriously. But it is not a church in which definitive and binding answers are given to perplexing moral questions I think it would not be unfair to add to this that most church decisions have, for most of history, been taken by groups of rather conservative, unmarried elderly men. That is a reason for not expecting them to show innovative, creative and radical solutions to the ethical problems facing them. So the great moral reforms of recent centuries – a stress on the equality of human beings, on human rights, on the emancipation of slaves, on women's rights, and on the wellbeing of animals – have not generally been led by the church. On the contrary, the church has been seen as the enemy of liberal democratic thought, of human rights, and of freedom of thought and expression. It is wise to be aware of the conservative bias of the church when debating highly controversial issues like that of same–sex partnerships.

There can be little doubt that most Christian churches have opposed the ratification of same–sex partnerships throughout their history. The Bible too has little to say in favor of them. So it is not surprising that the natural conservative attitude is to oppose them. But is such opposition rationally defensible? I will examine Bible teaching on same–sex partnerships in precise parallel with the way in which I have examined teaching on keeping the Sabbath (the latter is arguably more important, since it is one of the ten commandments, whereas the former is not).

First, homosexual practice, in some form, is condemned in the law. The penalty for intercourse between man and man is death (Leviticus 18:20). No reason is offered, though it is characteristic of the law to condemn any "mixing of kinds", like mixing linen and wool, ploughing with oxen and asses, or wearing clothes belonging to the other sex. Homosexual intercourse was possibly seen as one of these dangerous confusing of kinds. If so, it would be best regarded as a primitive taboo, which should have been long ago left behind.

Further, we know that many of the laws are primitive and unacceptable to us – worshipping another God is punishable by stoning to death, all the Amalekites are to be exterminated, and adultery is punishable by death. No one would today advocate genocide, stoning to death, or physical punishment for apostasy. The most orthodox Jew would mitigate these laws, and there are rabbinic legal decisions that do so.

So the fact that homosexual practice is condemned in the law does not settle the issue of whether this is part of the law that should be mitigated. Most of us would mitigate it by not insisting on the death penalty. But is it a primitive taboo or a universal moral command? That we cannot so far tell.

Second, if the teaching of Jesus is considered, there is nothing specifically on this issue. Sexual sins are mentioned, but they largely seem to be matters of demeaning the humanity of another, or of breaking human relationships of loyalty and affection. The New Testament sin of *porneia* is probably the sin of using sex without maintaining respect for the personhood of another. That would at least preserve a belief that Jesus' moral teaching is about inner attitudes of the heart, about respecting the personhood of others, and about "doing to others as you would have them do to you" (Matthew 7:12). It does seem a plausible interpretation of Jesus' teaching that it is concerned not so much with a set of rules (though he does not deny the rules), as with the attitudes such rules might be meant to express.

Third, the one thing that does seem clear in the New Testament is Paul's teaching that Christ is "the end of the law", that "the letter kills but the Spirit gives life", and that the whole law is summed up in love of neighbor. If Paul teaches that the whole law has been set aside by Christ, then appeal to the law to back up a moral view has been rendered impossible. To appeal to the moral beliefs of Paul, who taught that we should not be bound by any written words, would hardly make sense. But Paul, like Jesus, does give us a criterion by which to decide what is right or wrong. That criterion is love of neighbor, concern for their wellbeing. Such neighbor–love is to be modeled on the example of Jesus, which asks for self–giving, humble, unreserved and unlimited concern for the good of others.

My conclusion is that the question of the acceptability of

homosexual practice cannot be decided by appeal to the law, which is superseded, or to the explicit teaching of Jesus, which is unspecific. It is to be decided by the New Testament criterion of whether homosexual practice shows true love of neighbor, whether it respects human personhood, and whether it expresses the compassionate and self–giving love that was seen in Jesus.

My decision would be that, when safeguarded by a stress on the need for loyalty and total commitment in relationships, and by an insistence that sexual practice should express and be subordinated to mutual personal love, a sexual relation between two people of the same sex who are by nature attracted to one another is acceptable and natural. Further, it is worthy of being blessed by the church, which exists to support loving relationships and especially to support those who tend to be socially ostracised or to be objects of unthinking social prejudice.

It is very important to note that this is a principled, bible–based decision. But it is a decision. I do not think that the Bible is easy to interpret, and I am aware that other interpretations exist, even though I am pretty sure they are inadequate. I know that my decision has not been shared by the majority of Christian moralists throughout history. I therefore need to justify it by pointing to new knowledge of human gender and sexuality, and by showing that such new knowledge extends and deepens understanding of what it means to be concerned for human good and the wellbeing of other persons. I believe this has been done, but I rather expect a diversity of opinions on this topic among Christians.

Moral diversity in the church

Diversity extends much more deeply than to matters of biblical interpretation. Most of the biblical scholars of whom I am aware view the Bible as a very complex and nuanced document, from which few clear and indisputable doctrines and moral beliefs can be drawn. If Christians are seriously concerned for truth, they have to admit that there is room for serious dispute about how far many biblical records are legendary or symbolic. They have to admit that many committed Christian scholars hold that there is much legendary material in the gospels. I myself am of a naturally conservative disposition. I would like to see as many of the gospel records as possible as accurate reports of events as they happened. But I have to admit that many of the best biblical scholars find much embroidered and legendary material in the gospels, and I have to take this into account. It is dishonest to claim that we know for certain that the Bible is accurate in detail when we know that many people of devotion and scholarly expertise have good reasons for doubting such accuracy. I can still maintain the view that I conscientiously hold. But I cannot honestly claim that mine is the only acceptable view. Truth compels me to say that a diversity of beliefs about the literal truth of the gospel records exists in the academy and in the church. I have argued that, even taking the Bible as strictly accurate, there is room for diversity of interpretation, and that acceptance of same–sex partnerships is compatible with commitment to a fully biblical morality. But, in view of the findings of biblical scholarship in the last 150 years, we must also accept diversity in assessment of the extent to which various biblical records are literally accurate, or metaphorical or legendary.

A further layer of diversity, enshrined at the very heart of the Anglican Communion, is diversity in the formulation of Christian doctrines. At the Reformation, doctrines of the sacrifice of the mass, transubstantiation, purgatory, the sacraments and the nature of the atonement were challenged and reformulated. It is agreed that such doctrines were originally formulated by various church councils, and that they were rejected or reformulated by various protestant church bodies. The Church of England has for many years now contained members, priests and bishops who take completely opposite views on such issues, as whether the mass is a sacrifice, whether purgatory exists, and whether veneration of the saints is permissible. Catholic and evangelical "parties" have lived in the same church, and accepted bishops belonging to the other party, for some time. An important part of Anglican tradition has also been an open or liberal "party", that seeks to be informed by the best critical biblical scholarship, and to look for creative reformulations of Christian beliefs in the light of new knowledge, particularly from the natural and social sciences.

The church is able to embrace these diverse approaches precisely because it accepts no magisterial teaching authority. These issues are treated as matters of personal decision and allegiance. So the personal beliefs of bishops are not considered binding on others. Has the bishop, then, no teaching authority?

A distinction needs to be made between two sorts of teaching. One form of teaching simply tells you what is true, and demands that you believe it. A different sort of teaching seeks to extend and deepen understanding, and to put people in a position to make an informed decision. It is part of the teaching role of a bishop in the Anglican tradition to ensure that the range of diversity in the church, and the reasons for it, is made clear, so that a sympathetic understanding of the views of others is possible, and conversation between proponents of diverse views is encouraged. That is a real and important teaching role. It is not a magisterial authority that tells you what you must believe. It is a vehicle of encouragement to extend knowledge and understanding and to frame responsible beliefs of your own. If people wish for guidance, it can make that guidance as informed and charitable as possible, while not pretending that differing views do not exist, by simply ignoring them.

Anglican teaching authority, in other words, is an authority of guidance and advice, not a magisterial capacity to define what is definitively true. The church holds together because it accepts the Bible as its scriptural text, without defining how it should be interpreted. It accepts baptism and the eucharist as normative rites, without insisting on one set of detailed doctrines to explain them. And it accepts Jesus as the true image and liberating act of God, without presuming that there is just one correct way of understanding how this is so.

I have argued that the church should support same–sex relationships of long–term commitment and fidelity, and that such a policy is based on a legitimate interpretation of scripture in a society in which new insights about gender and sexuality have been gained. I have also acknowledged there is a diversity of views. There is nothing new in this situation. There are catholic, evangelical and open churches in the Anglican Communion. They may keep a certain distance from one another, but they live in the same Communion. For the Anglican Communion is not a group of people who all agree. It is, and always has been, a fellowship of diversity, in which people of very different views are inspired by one Lord, Jesus Christ, and seek to worship the God who is disclosed in Jesus, as they see him in many different ways. Such an acceptance of diversity requires an acceptance that one's own beliefs are not obviously and certainly correct. It requires tolerance and a willingness to learn from others.

At the present time, it requires that there should be inclusive churches, whose vision of human relationships as related in Christ includes those living in same–sex partnerships. There is no reason why bishops in committed same–sex relationships, appointed by proper procedures, should not have pastoral oversight of such churches. There is no reason why they should not be accepted as full bishops of the Anglican Communion, even though some churches would apparently not accept their oversight.

If there is to be any hope of Christian unity in the world, Christians will have to learn to embrace diversity of interpretations, doctrines and ways of life, while always seeking to relate those diverse patterns to the disclosure of the divine nature in the biblical records of the person of Jesus, and in the creative power of the Holy Spirit. The attraction of the Anglican Communion for many of us is that this is what it seeks to do. If it fails to do this, it will impede the process of Christian unity for many years. It will betray the Anglican vision of comprehensiveness, diversity, and a rejection of magisterial authority. That, in my view, would be a great loss for the church and for the world.

3

BEYOND PROOFTEXTING

Carolyn J. Sharp

Oh that I knew how all thy lights combine,
And the configurations of their glory!
Seeing not only how each verse doth shine,
But all the constellations of the story.
This verse marks that, and both do make a motion
Unto a third, that ten leaves off doth lie:
Then as dispersèd herbs do watch a potion,
These three make up some Christian's destiny:
Such are thy secrets, which my life makes good,
And comments on thee: for in ev'ry thing
Thy words do find me out, and parallels bring,
and in another make me understood.

George Herbert, from *The H. Scriptures*

What does it mean to hold scripture at the center of our common life as Anglican followers of Jesus Christ? We may say with confidence that scripture reveals to us the glorious Creator whose sacrificial, Spirit–breathed love incarnates our every hope of redemption and fruitfulness. We learn from scripture that God has searched us and known us (Psalm 139:1); scripture "finds us out," as George Herbert intuited. Such acclamations as these would be fully in line with the diverse hermeneutical positions of many Anglican readers of scripture throughout the history of Anglicanism. But they would not, yet, articulate more than a basic awareness of how God's lively and powerful Word invites us into discipleship, challenges us, troubles us, changes us. A great deal is at stake every time a believer picks up the Bible with hope or trepidation or holy curiosity. Particularly in times of intense theological debate over core matters of ecclesial identity, Christian readers of scripture are called to examine attentively the ways in which reading practices shape our identities as individual believers and communities of faith. Contemporary believers who understand the value of creative and faithful thinking about scripture need, in the idiom of St Paul, not milk, but solid food with regard to biblical hermeneutics.

The aim of the present essay is to respond to the overt and implicit claims about scripture and hermeneutical practices made in the Windsor Report. Specifically, I will pursue a query about ways in which we may understand the relationships among propositional, narratological, and poetic biblical texts, arguing that the notion of community is inscribed in scripture texts as a continually shifting, dynamic engagement among multiple claims concerning insiders and outsiders. I hope to show that scripture's intertextual allusions, multivocality, and self–conscious reflections on its own dynamic reinterpretation in new contexts may provide a useful and responsive hermeneutical model for contemporary readers engaged in ecclesial debates.

I

Windsor rightly locates scripture at the center of the beliefs and practices of devout Anglicans. Its emphasis on the ongoing and lively activity of the Holy Spirit through scripture is noteworthy, for in this, the Report explicitly moves beyond any simplistic notion of scripture as a repository of static authoritative pronouncements to be mined for proof texts at the convenience of disputants. Such a model of prooftexting, which has unfortunately been used by not a few Anglicans of various perspectives in our current debates, constitutes a deplorable commodification of scripture and, in many instances, amounts to a use of scripture in anger as a weapon to disenfranchise believers who read differently. That God's life–giving and transformative Word might be wielded by one believer in order to shame or silence another is one of the bitterest ironies in the history of the Christian Church's reception of the Logos. The Report is right to caution against such destructive hermeneutics (55, 61).

Windsor begins to get at something crucial in its proleptic hope for the "appropriately rich and diverse unity" into which scripture–reading, rightly performed, should lead us "across boundaries of culture, region and tradition" (62). Of utmost importance is the Report's call for Anglicans everywhere to give sustained attention to biblical interpretation – to "re–evaluate the ways in which we have read, heard, studied and digested scripture" and, where so directed by the Spirit, to "read and learn together from scripture in new ways" (61). That it refrains from offering even the rough outline of a way forward on this, apart from a general call to "mature study" and "wise and prayerful discussion," may perhaps be expected given its mandate to focus on issues of ecclesiology and polity; but it is regrettable. The present essay aims to address itself to that lack. Two preliminary observations are in order.

First, it is unfortunate that Windsor virtually ignores the place of the witness of the Old Testament, except for a fleeting nod to the inbreaking of God's rule having been "long promised and awaited in Israel" (55) and a mention of the importance of ongoing discussion about the "respective authority of the Old and New Testaments" (56). Given that disputants in our current debates refer with predictable frequency to Leviticus, it is essential that Anglicans examine closely our hermeneutical positions regarding the following, among other issues: the roles of tradition and innovation in the inner–biblical preservation of multiple understandings of covenant and holiness; theologically and hermeneutically viable ways in which Christians may construct and deconstruct the authority of 2,500–year–old Semitic law in our establishment of contemporary liturgical and social practices; and, the diverse ways in which ancient Hebrew storytelling, cultic legislation, psalmody, prophecy, and sapiential writings invite contemporary believers and communities of faith into faithful relationship with God and loving relationship with one another, or may exclude from such relationship. The Report hurries past these and other crucial hermeneutical issues on its way to Romans, Ephesians, and 2 Corinthians, leaving the lamentable and subtly polemical impression that our consideration of scripture may begin and end appropriately with the writings of the apostle Paul.

Second, Windsor tries to get at the influential role that cultures and ideologies play in our readings of scripture, but more might have been hoped for on that score. It rightly notes the importance of sophisticated historical–contextual work for understanding the significance of scripture texts. Further, it offers a salutary reminder that the "assumptions and entrenched views" of both the Enlightenment and anti–critical conservatism should be tested and explored in dialogue rather than taken for granted by their respective constituencies. Yet while noting that Biblical scholarship "cannot pretend to a detached 'neutrality'" (60), the Report seems to assume a neutral or universally accepted center to the church's life and tradition that could theoretically stand uncontested as we wrestle over more peripheral hermeneutical variables. Windsor acknowledges the important role of enculturation in our reading practices (67), a fine point that implicitly (if perhaps unwittingly) directs the attention of the Anglican Communion not only to indigenous readings of all sorts but to feminist, womanist, liberationist, queer, and postcolonial approaches to biblical interpretation as well.[1] But the Report may be criticized for suggesting elsewhere a subtly monolithic view of the church itself that seems intent on ignoring the very diversity that lies at the heart of our current ecclesial debates.

Representation of the church as an unproblematized unity, whether in some romanticized past or in the present day, is neither accurate nor appropriate. Women, individuals who are openly gay or lesbian, and the poor have been systematically excluded from ecclesial and conciliar decision–making throughout the history of the church, rare exceptions to the contrary notwithstanding. There is no neutral notion of "church" to which all may cleave as we debate the finer points of polity. There is no neutral received tradition of major stature in Christian history that has not itself been, to one degree or another, the product of exclusion of those whose participation in the sacramental life of the church is now being debated. Given this, it is surprising that the Report speaks without qualification of such notions as the "ancient canonical principle that what touches all should be decided by all" (51), "ancient undivided Christian faith and life" (53), "loyalty to the community of the Church across time and space" (60), "the consensus fidelium" (68), and so on. More helpful would have been a candid acknowledgement of the inescapable biases of the ecclesiological traditions and decision–making operations of the church since its very inception within the thoroughly patriarchal matrix of ancient Jewish cultic praxis and Greco–Roman culture. Acknowledgment of bias in the church's own structures and authoritative traditions should be an

---

1 The biblical interpretation generated by feminist, womanist, and liberationist readers is too vast to be cited in any detail here. Queer theory and postcolonial studies being newer on the hermeneutical horizon and possibly less familiar to non–specialists, it may be helpful to cite the following volumes of interest: Robert E. Goss and Mona West (eds), *Take Back the Word: A Queer Reading of the Bible* (Cleveland: Pilgrim, 2000); Fernando F. Segovia, *Decolonizing Biblical Studies: A View from the Margins* (Maryknoll: Orbis, 2000); and R. S. Sugirtharajah, *Postcolonial Criticism and Biblical Interpretation* (Oxford: Oxford University Press, 2002).

essential part of any discussion of cultural conditioning and ideological assumptions, however one may then weigh the implications of that bias in particular instances. By articulating no awareness of that problem, the Report has missed a crucial opportunity for leadership regarding one of the central problems affecting the adjudication of our current ecclesial disputes.

Windsor presents scripture as the first of three "bonds of communion" that hold together the diverse bodies and beliefs that constitute the Anglican Communion (the other designated bonds being the episcopate and discernment). This decision to name scripture as a primary means to "draw us together and hold us in fellowship" (52) presses a noteworthy claim about the reading practices of Anglicans in communion, namely, that our common reading of scripture might fairly be expected to be a "means of unity, not division" (62). While the cherishing of God's Holy Word has unquestionably drawn together believers otherwise quite multifarious in liturgical praxis and social perspective, it by no means goes without saying that a deep attentiveness to scripture will leave readers in a more unified state of communion than before. Where new understandings of scripture challenge the limitations and biases of very human readers in fragile ecclesial communities, the result is likely to be anxiety, struggle, avoidance, overcompensatory assertions of certitude, and the polemical clash of divergent witnesses. Encounters with scripture are transformative, but they are not always easy, and certainly do not always result in a deeper unity. In the seeking, we may draw nearer to one another, to be sure. But in the finding, we may be given powerful grounds for contesting each other's views, whether that may mean proclaiming new visions of justice, reclaiming fidelity to tradition, or taking some other kind of position that disrupts, energizes, and reconfigures the reading communities gathered around God's Word. While this may not be comfortable, it is likely salutary. As Rowan Williams has observed, "When Christian speech is healthy, it does not allow itself an over–familiarity with, a taking for granted of its images – its Scriptures, its art, its liturgy; it is prepared to draw back to allow them to be 'strange', questioning and questionable."[2] Windsor's preemptive emphasis on the unifying force of scripture, then, seems somewhat suspect. It seems to be too eager to avoid the struggle, questioning, and risk that are an integral part of transformation in community.

Also worthy of critique are statements in the Report that draw a needlessly polarized distinction between scholars and the church:

> Where a fresh wave of scholarship generates ideas which are perceived as a threat to something the Church has always held dear, it is up to the scholars concerned, on the one hand, to explain how what is now proposed not only accords with but actually enhances the central core of the Church's faith. And it is up to the Church, on the other hand, not to reject new proposals out of hand, but to listen carefully, to test everything, and to be prepared to change its mind if and when a convincing case is made. (60)

May we assume that what is discovered by scholars will necessarily enhance the core of the church's faith? Of course, so long as the church is always fully committed to understanding and proclaiming what is true. But it is not necessarily the case that what is true will enhance "the central core of the Church's faith" in transparent or unproblematic ways. Windsor seems to rely at several points on a simplistic view of church tradition as the unimpeachable arbiter in an antagonistic confrontation with scholarship. This supposed neutrality

---

2 Rowan Williams, *Resurrection: Interpreting the Easter Gospel* (2nd edition; Cleveland: Pilgrim, 2002), p. 66. Also relevant here is Williams's observation that a truly catholic understanding of ministry and mission "strives to show, to embody, the way in which the incalculable variety of human concerns can be 'at home' in and with the confession of faith in Jesus. It does not seek to impose a uniform Christian culture or a preconceived Christian solution: it aims only to keep open and expanding the frontiers of the community of gift" (p. 57).

of the church, again, is specious: the voices of countless people on the margins of institutional power have characteristically been silenced or

ignored during the crafting of church polity and doctrine. Further, the hostility of the Report to the so–called "threat" posed by biblical scholarship is palpable and does not advance the discussion.

Windsor rightly insists, "We can no longer be content to drop random texts into arguments, imagining that the point is thereby proved" (61). Which developments within biblical scholarship, then, might aid ecclesial communities in coming to a fuller and deeper understanding of the scriptures that heal and trouble us, that confirm God's love, that unseat our idols, that call us into renewed prophetic witness and evangelistic mission? The following discussion will consider the rhetorical performativity of different kinds of texts, biblical multivocality, and intertextuality as potential avenues into fuller conversations about scripture.

II

Developments in biblical hermeneutics have been prolific and far–reaching in recent decades. But it would seem that important gains made in biblical interpretation have gained little purchase within churchly discussions of scripture. One senses that major paradigm shifts in our understandings of the rhetorical functions of texts, reader agency, and the situated and highly contextual nature of meaning–making have only begun to be noticed and addressed in some ecclesial quarters. Windsor's emphasis on the central role of Christian leaders as teachers of scripture (58) may be heard, then, not only as an affirmation of clerical didactic authority but as an urgent call to renewed engagement with the best of biblical scholarship.

Scripture texts perform their truths and meanings – in engagement with readers and reading communities – through diverse kinds of dictions. Of the most interest here, scripture enacts its rhetorics particularly through propositional, narratological, and poetic means of expression that inscribe and construct meaning in different ways. This has profound significance not only for descriptions of biblical literature, but also for the ways in which we understand biblical texts to invite readers into engagement with revelatory truths. That is, it matters whether we are reading proposition, story, or poetry when we attempt to discern the truths of scripture for our own beliefs and identity in community. Proposition, story, and poetry can be seen to construct, affirm, interrogate, and contest each other within the Bible. Ideological critics have long recognized that scriptural truths are imaged, performed, and reinscribed in a kaleidoscopic panoply of insiders, outsiders, and conflicting views. There was no one single view of true Israelite or Christian community historically represented within scripture texts, nor could there have been, given the many competing claims for identity and authority that we see in both Old Testament and New Testament texts.[3]

It follows, then, that meaning in scripture has always been enacted and apprehended by means of dialogic processes among numerous intertexts (biblical and extra–biblical), processes of response and rereading, and negotiation of a variety of faithful claims and counterclaims. These dialogic processes are not extraneous to scriptural signifying, but are intrinsically constitutive of scripture's characteristic responsiveness both to changing historical circumstances during the composition and editing of scripture, and to the demands and invitations of varying genres and forms encountered and enculturated in new contexts. Communities of readers that try to claim a static and unchanging message for any given scripture text, without considering the multiple pressures and constraints offered by larger literary contexts,

---

3 See here the important work of Walter Brueggemann on scripture's essential character as a dialogue of testimonies and countertestimonies: *Texts Under Negotiation: The Bible and Postmodern Imagination* (Minneapolis: Fortress, 1993) and *Theology of the Old Testament: Testimony, Dispute, Advocacy* (Minneapolis: Fortress, 1997). While Brueggemann's work has its weaknesses – among them its reliance on an overly aestheticized notion of biblical rhetoric – it is imaginative and well worth consideration by those interested in exploring the multivalence and dialogical nature of scriptural signifying.

by numerous intertexts constructed by biblical authors, and by contemporary reception of the Bible, fundamentally misunderstand the nature of scripture as a living, dialogical, and contextually responsive divine Word.

I turn now to one particular group of Old Testament texts to illustrate the above hermeneutical points in concrete terms: legal material in Deuteronomy 23. The diction of legal prescriptions and prohibitions presents itself as uncompromising and clear, and has been commodified as such in contemporary ecclesial debates. But here, the interpreter would do well to attend to the ways in which legal discourse offers opportunities for deconstruction and contextually subtle reconstruction. In passing, we may note that there are several distinct law codes preserved in the Hebrew Bible (traditions usually referred to as the "Covenant Code", the "Holiness Code", and the "Priestly School"), and these distinct legal corpora by no means always agree with each other on particulars of cultic observance or on conceptual matters lying behind individual laws. Further, the extraordinarily rich midrashic literature on *halakha* in Jewish tradition gives ample testimony to the diverse ways in which law may be understood, questioned, and reheard for new cultural contexts. So when one appeals to legal diction in the Bible as objective and transparently applicable in any context – in a word, when one engages in prooftexting – one is choosing to beg a number of important questions concerning literary context and reception history, not to mention complex questions of cross–cultural applicability. The inadequacy of such an approach should be clear.

A hermeneutical path beyond prooftexting may be charted by means of an examination of the ways in which propositional legal diction is frequently contextualized, complicated, and contested through biblical narratives themselves. Now to our text, an ostensibly uncompromising group of *halakhic* assertions:

> *No one whose testicles are crushed or whose penis is cut off shall be admitted to the assembly of the Lord. Those born of an illicit union shall not be admitted to the assembly of the Lord. Even to the tenth*

generation, none of their descendants shall be admitted to the assembly of the Lord. No Ammonite or Moabite shall be admitted to the assembly of the Lord. Even to the tenth generation, none of their descendants shall be admitted to the assembly of the Lord, because they did not meet you with food and water on your journey out of Egypt, and because they hired against you Balaam son of Beor, from Pethor of Mesopotamia, to curse you (Deuteronomy 23:1–4).

Some basic observations may be helpful at the outset of our exposition. The first categorical restriction, on males whose genitals have been mutilated or excised, likely refers to (voluntary) eunuchs, although other causes of genital mutilation may also be in mind here. The reference to illicit unions bespeaks incestuous relationships as well as other proscribed means of sexual engagement. The references to "even to the tenth generation" are probably meant to signal exclusion of the relevant groups in perpetuity; they should not be read literally as meaning up to exactly ten generations and no more.

Now, how does biblical storytelling complicate these exclusionary laws in Deuteronomy 23:1–4? We have some notable stories of proscribed relationships in scripture. The indiscretion of Ham with his drunken father Noah we may pass over in silence, the evidence remaining inconclusive regarding the precise nature of Ham's transgression. But attentive readers of scripture will remember two stories of incest narrated with scrupulous attention to narratological detail: the intercourse of Lot with each of his daughters that generates the Ammonites and the Moabites (Genesis 19), and the act of incestuous intercourse between Tamar and her father–in–law Judah in Genesis 38, which results in her giving birth to a son in the genealogical line that eventually yields King David.

Was Genesis 19 composed in order to mock the shameful origin of two of Israel's traditional enemies, the Ammonites and the Moabites? Perhaps in part, but the narrative of Genesis 19 is far more complex than that, and contemporary readers will necessarily privilege various aspects of the story to suit their own discernment of meaning and their own veiled, or explicit, ideological commitments within their reading communities. Lot, nephew of Abraham, hosts two angels unawares, and these divine beings are threatened with sexual violence by the men of Sodom. Lot upholds the ancient Near Eastern standard of hospitality with an obsessive focus on the wellbeing of his guests, urging earnestly that the men of Sodom leave the guests unharmed, "for they have come under the shelter of my roof" (Genesis 19:8), and instead sate their coercive intentions on the bodies of Lot's own two daughters. The ironizing of Lot's host mentality in the narrative is quite clear. No host concerned for the welfare of those in his house would go so far as to offer up his own daughters to the violent will of an unruly mob in order to make a point about hospitality, earnest assertions by scholars of the importance of hospitality in the ancient Near East notwithstanding. Lot bows excessively and unimaginatively to tradition here, leaving the trust in his own family shattered. The angels continue on their mission to destroy Sodom, and Lot's family suffers still more, his future sons–in–law and his own wife perishing in the divine conflagration. Lot, traumatized, is manipulated by his daughters into impregnating them. The daughters' actions are repugnant according to incest taboos in ancient Near Eastern cultures, and of course, in the view of the narrative, they are misguided in their concern that all men on earth have been destroyed. Yet, these daughters, acting to preserve life, are blessed with offspring. We are left with a picture of the genesis of two of Israel's most intractable enemies, Moab and Ammon, by means of the sexual exploitation of an unaware, unimaginative, and cruel nephew of Abraham himself, the one through whom "all the families of the earth shall be blessed" (Genesis 12:3). The connection to Abraham has proven, even this early, to be a mixed blessing for Israel itself, yielding ironic vulnerabilities as well as strengths.

The other prominent incestuous relationship narrated with significant implications for Israel is the single act of intercourse between Tamar and Judah. Genesis 38 artfully manipulates themes of veiling and revealing through ironic reversals to underline the point that the (probably) Canaanite woman who poses as a prostitute to entrap her father–in–law is "more righteous" than Judah himself. One scholar has argued that we see throughout the Joseph cycle (Genesis 37–50) the growth of Judah as a moral character, from one who dodges responsibility in the selling of their younger brother into slavery to one who can admit his wrongdoing in the matter of impregnating his daughter–in–law and who can affirm the value of tradition.[4] Others, however, see the character of Judah rendered as risible, his obtuseness regarding the identity of the "prostitute" and subsequent hyperbolic overreaction to the guilt of Tamar making him a buffoon in the eyes of the implied audience. Sharp–edged ironies abound in this story. Judah is lacking in discernment and honor, and the genealogical result of his incestuous liaison is a scion, Perez, in the lineage of King David. What would Deuteronomy say? If Perez should be barred from the worshipping community because of his clearly incestuous origin, then David must be barred. This is a complication indeed for our exclusionary proposition in Deuteronomy 23:2.

Consider now a third narrative that problematizes Deuteronomy 23: the Book of Ruth. Ruth the Moabite works her way into the Israelite community at Bethlehem and, through highly unusual sexually aggressive machinations, manages to become an ancestor of King David as well. Putting this narrative in dialogue with the Deuteronomic proscription fatally undermines the uncompromising diction of the legal material. Israelite law pronounces in stentorian tones that Moabites must be excluded from the congregation of Israel – doubly, of course, by virtue of their incestuous origin and by virtue of

---

4 See Anthony J. Lambe, "Judah's Development: The Pattern of Departure – Transition – Return," *Journal for the Study of the Old Testament* 62 (1994): 37–48.

their Moabite ethnicity. So there seems to be no chance for any hermeneutical nuance, any subtle rereading of this prohibition for a new context. And yet, Moabites are already irrevocably and powerfully present in the Israelite assembly through Lot as nephew of Abraham himself and through Ruth as matriarch of Israel's most glorified king, David.

The "Other" has quietly, fruitfully infiltrated the worshipping community even as the sentence of perpetual exclusion is being pronounced. Straightforward prohibitions in the law of ancient Israel have been thoroughly ironized and contested by no fewer than three foundational narratives in the storytelling of those same ancient Israelites. Propositional and narratological truth–claims collide in a frisson of undecidability.[5]

Intelligent and faithful readers are invited into dialogue with each other through the silences, nuances, and complexities of this single intertextual conversation in scripture. And there are many other such conversations: fierce internecine disputes within the Book of Jeremiah itself, not to mention theological debates raging among Isaiah, Jeremiah, and Ezekiel; divergent politicized uses of the theme of the nations streaming to Zion in Isaiah 2 and Micah 4; radically different reflections on the old refrain that God is slow to anger in Jonah 4, Joel 2, and Nahum 1; and on and on. With regard to the intertexts gathered around Deuteronomy 23: for some readers, the divinely ordained stability of law may exercise a welcome exegetical control over the messiness and ambiguities of story, over the fractures and failings of embodied living. But for others, the dramatic stories of incest and Moabite ethnicity that narrate the paradigm of Israel's leadership speak a more compelling word about the urgency of social, ethnic, and moral

---

5 For some readers (including patristic exegetes), Ruth may represent the paradigmatic righteous Gentile convert. For others, she may be a self–actualized heroine, a manipulated object of patriarchy, or an assimilated ethnic "Other" robbed of her heritage. For feminist, womanist, and postcolonial readings of Ruth, see Athalya Brenner (ed), *Ruth and Esther: A Feminist Companion to the Bible (Second Series)* (Sheffield: Sheffield Academic Press, 1999).

inclusion; the legal prohibition, in reluctant dialogue with the storytelling, may come to seem overanxious and ineffectual, a hyperbolic attempt to police communal boundaries that never did work in the tumultuous social history of Israel's life. The point is not, of course, that one or another reading is correct. The point is that attentiveness to these intertextual conversations offers us an invaluable opportunity to continue to read together as these texts interrogate, construct, and challenge each other.

Bring, now, the dense and elusive signifiers of Hebrew poetry into view. What texts may be said to have bearing on whether David might be admitted into the congregation of Israel? The Psalms are important here, particularly those psalms whose superscriptions refer to events in the life of David. David is not only a descendant of incest (twice over) with Moabite blood in his veins. He is the king of Israel, and as the paradigmatic Psalmist, he is the voice of Israel at prayer to its God. But traces of irony may be seen even in the Psalter. David asserts that the Lord "hates the lover of violence" (Psalm 11:5). Can this be the same David whose bloody mercenary raids for the Philistines paint him as one of the most opportunistic and brutal chieftains ever portrayed in ancient literature? David acclaims as worthy to enter the worshipping congregation those who "do not take a bribe against the innocent" (Psalm 15:5), and he praises God as the "father of orphans and protector of widows" (Psalm 68:5). Are there not freighted silences here, hushed ellipses concerning David's shameful extortion of Nabal and subsequent taking of Nabal's widow (1 Samuel 25); concerning his coercive treatment of Saul's son Mephibosheth, made an orphan precisely because of David's military assistance to the Philistines who eventually killed his father, and by David's own subsequent ruthless campaign against the house of Saul (1 Samuel 27–2; Samuel 3); and concerning David's betrayal of Uriah and subsequent taking of Uriah's widow Bathsheba (2 Samuel 11)? Even readers of scripture accustomed to valorizing David as a model for faith must acknowledge the evidence plainly writ in the Books of Samuel: David may have been many things, but he certainly was a ruthless and immoral leader.[6] Yet, not only is David allowed into the worshipping congregation; he all but leads it, coming to embody the very voice of the congregation of Israel in its laments and praises.

> *Those born of an illicit union shall not be admitted to the assembly of the Lord. Even to the tenth generation, none of their descendants shall be admitted to the assembly of the Lord. No Ammonite or Moabite shall be admitted to the assembly of the Lord. Even to the tenth generation, none of their descendants shall be admitted to the assembly of the Lord.*

Indeed? These clear and direct legal pronouncements of scripture have been radically destabilized, ironized, and renarrated, as we have seen, multiple times within scripture. Members of the Windsor Commission surely have read Genesis, Deuteronomy, and Ruth; yet they can ask pointedly, as if they were completely innocent of all of the texts just cited above, how it might be possible to read scripture as permitting the leadership of gay and lesbian persons in the church (135). Here we may well affirm the Report's confession – for such it must be taken to be – that "it is by reading scripture too little, not by reading it too much, that we have allowed ourselves to drift apart" (67). Would this be the moment to bring into the conversation the compelling scriptural evidence that David himself, the leader and the very voice of Israel at worship, was deeply homoerotically engaged with Jonathan, son of Saul? It is not feasible, the contortions of conservative exegetes notwithstanding, to dismiss the biblical representations of David's and Jonathan's passionate love as simple platonic friendship.

---

6 See Baruch Halpern, *David's Secret Demons: Messiah, Murderer, Traitor, King* (Grand Rapids: Eerdmans, 2001) for detailed argumentation that David is portrayed as a ruthless schemer and usurper by significant blocks of tradition in the Deuteronomistic history.

The intensity of the closeness of David and Jonathan is unprecedented in biblical literature, and as such, it is transparently marked as "Other".[7] However that particular exegetical issue be adjudicated, the opportunities we have for moving beyond atomistic prooftexting are rich indeed.

By way of denouement, we may note a final point of contrast between our central passage from Deuteronomy 23 and a powerful voice for inclusion within scripture: the prophet Isaiah. Isaiah 56 invites eunuchs fully into the worshipping community despite the Deuteronomic prohibition on those with mutilated genitals. Eunuchs are offered extravagant promises of blessing that surpass even those whose status in the community was already assured due to their heteronormativity (Isaiah 56:4,7). Isaiah's rewriting of the prohibition against eunuchs illustrates the dynamic way in which authors of scripture recontextualize earlier traditions in response to visionary insights for new contexts. This pattern of revoicing earlier traditions continues into the New Testament: a eunuch hears the Word and is joyfully baptized into the believing community of Israel (Acts 8);

---

7 Immediately after David has introduced himself to Saul, "the soul of Jonathan was bound to the soul of David, and Jonathan loved him as his own soul" (1 Samuel 18:1): love at first sight, nothing less. When Jonathan and David part, they kiss each other and weep for a long time: this close contact and protracted weeping show unmistakably the intensity of the emotional connection between them. The lament song of David underscores this intensity in an explicitly sexualized analogy: "my brother Jonathan, greatly beloved were you to me; your love to me was wonderful, passing the love of women" (2 Samuel 1:26). Perhaps most telling in the mustering of evidence for a homosexual relationship between David and Jonathan is the diction an outraged Saul uses to shame Jonathan concerning his loyalty to David: "You son of a perverse, rebellious woman! Do I not know that you have chosen the son of Jesse to your own shame, and to the shame of your mother's nakedness?" (1 Samuel 20:30). The terms in which Saul disgraces Jonathan are unmistakably sexualized, obscene terms. The "nakedness" word is the same used of the uncovering of Noah by Ham in Genesis 9; it is used in Ezekiel 16 and 23 in the prophet's extended sexualized rants against Jerusalem figured as a nymphomaniacal whore; and it is used in Leviticus 18, in a section of law dealing with prohibited sexual relationships including incest and male homosexuality. Given the silence of the biblical text regarding overt sexual activity between the two men, David's and Jonathan's homoeroticism will never be "proven" to the satisfaction of exegetes who worry fetishistically about whether the officially proscribed male–male penetration happened. Yet, at the very least, the intensive marking of this relationship in sexualized terms in the Books of Samuel suggests that the burden of proof should lie with those who want to argue for platonic friendship.

circumcision itself, the erstwhile nonnegotiable mark of God's covenant with Israel, is metaphorized and understood anew; the evangelist Matthew chooses to name Tamar and Ruth in the lineage of the Messiah with no indication that their history of incest and Moabite identity should exclude Jesus' participation in the worshipping community (Matthew 1).

III

This reflection on texts from Deuteronomy, Genesis, Ruth, Isaiah, and Matthew has argued that one may indeed read scripture faithfully and well to support the church's radical inclusion of those whom one or another scripture text has identified as engaging in "abominable" acts, or who were at one time seen as permanently unsuited for inclusion in the worshipping community. There will be readers for whom the exegetical arguments traced above beg a prior question: how can a biblical text be called "holy" at all if it calls for the permanent rejection of any of those made in God's image? Some readers will doubtless prefer simply to reject misogynistic, homophobic, racist, xenophobic, and other exclusionary scripture texts as no longer authoritative in any way. But other readers may choose to bring difficult texts into intertextual conversations that may yet yield fruit for interpreting communities. As George Herbert reminds us, scripture texts continually gesture toward other texts and toward the heart of the believer.[8] These gestures inspire and trouble us, inviting us into a dialogic process of hearing and contesting and honoring the truth of God's lively Word as best we can discern it with the help of the Holy Spirit. Many avenues of response are possible.

---

8 Consider a relevant irony of Herbert's strophe from *The H. Scriptures* cited at the beginning of this essay: there is a disputed term within its central analogy for scriptural intertextuality. The verb in the line, "as dispersèd herbs do watch a potion," has resisted all attempts to find transparent sense. No emendation may finally be considered authoritative either, and Herbert's poetic vision stubbornly remains, resistant and elusive and breathtakingly beautiful. See F. E. Hutchinson (ed), *The Works of George Herbert* (Oxford: Clarendon, 1964), p. 496.
Note: All references in the text are to paragraphs in Windsor.

Windsor urges that Anglicans seek unity through, and not in spite of, our "different traditions of reading scripture" (71). This wise exhortation points the way forward on a path that most certainly will be attended by both suffering and joy. We have a companion on the journey in the person of Paul – a fellow traveler likely welcomed with enthusiasm by some and with reluctance by others – since, as the Report notes, he lived into his own ministry only through "great pain and paradox" (56). Pain and paradox may indeed be our portion as we learn to read together in new ways. But Paul is not our only guide. Journeying with Paul, and arguing with him all along the way, are countless other witnesses who queer our efforts to establish hegemonic views of identity and guard ecclesial boundaries. Look: Tamar is there, and Ruth the Moabite, David and Jonathan, and the Ethiopian eunuch, along with faithful witnesses from later times who are less well known to us – Thecla and others whose radically subversive performances of Christian identity fit no prescribed model. May their words and ours, from every corner of our fractured and blessed Christian life, offer a powerful witness to the One who is Way, and Truth, and Life for all of God's people.

4

SCRIPTURE FOR LIBERATION

Lisa Isherwood

I want to address the way in which scripture is used in Windsor and, more generally, in the debate about same–sex relations. As a liberation theologian, I use scripture as the second act in theological praxis. In other words, once the lived reality has been assessed and liberational needs uncovered, scripture is reflected on and used as part of the liberation matrix of action and reflection, and then more action. From this perspective, I was astonished to discover that the Report appears to assume a uniform reading of scripture under the guidance of the Holy Spirit. It refers to

> the bewildering range of available interpretative strategies and results. This is tragic, since as with the Spirit who inspired scripture, we would expect that the Bible would be a means of unity and not division (30).

The implication is that we do away with contextual reading, both contemporary and historical, and simply rely on the Spirit, who will render a uniform reading mediated (one suspects) through the hierarchy. There is also an unquestioned assumption that "unity" means "uniformity". Despite talk of diverse cultures, there is a strong element of the "fresh appreciation of the riches of the Gospel" having already been determined by the Commission before the debate has even been had.

Of course, as a theologian who works in the area of gender, I am always suspicious when diversity is not embraced. As feminist scholars have shown there is power behind many seemingly "natural" aspects of gender and sexuality. With this power comes hierarchy and with hierarchy, exclusion and eventually persecution. Persecution in our day and age involves a lifetime of having to hide, and even deny, who one is for fear of social consequences. It is telling that it is accepted that scripture may be open to regional reading, but that gendered reading is not even mentioned – perhaps this remains one of the "tragic" and "bewildering" readings that are to be regretted. This hardly seems in keeping with the argument that authority in scripture is not to be understood as "a static source of information or the giving of orders ... but in terms of the dynamic, in–breaking of God's kingdom, that is, God's sovereign, saving, redeeming and reconciling rule over all creation" (28). How, one wonders, is God's redeeming rule to break out if it is held captive by restrictive and restricting readings of scripture? The Anglican Church has many logs in its eye impeding the embrace of life in abundance; gender blindness is just one of them.

In order that scripture can help shape a church to become "a foretaste of the new creation (Ephesians 1–3)" (28), we have to be clear about what it is of the world that is *not* of the new creation. There is no realization in Windsor that exclusion on the grounds of gender and sexuality belong to the old order and not the new – the fallen world and not the new creation. Windsor simply ignores feminist scholarship highlighting the message of equality in Christ declared by the early Jesus movement. In its day, this message was taken so seriously that when it did not take root women formed their own protest communities.[1] The significance of this, for the present debate, is that the life in abundance and redemptive reality of which Jesus spoke was understood as *embodied*

---

1 Jo Ann McNamara, *A New Song: Celibate Women in the First Three Centuries* (New York: Harrington Park Press, 1985). For a collection, which brings together some of the new insights from research, see Lisa Isherwood (ed), *The Good News of the Body: Sexual Theology and Feminism* (Sheffield: Sheffield Academic Press, 2000).

in every aspect of human nature. This is, after all, the message of the incarnation – that the whole created order is to be renewed – not just a heaven way beyond and in another time and space – but now on *this* earth. The Christian God, as we say, left the heavens and sought justice on the earth.

The "hermeneutic of suspicion" – as it has been called – has helped women ask important and empowering questions of scripture. Mary Rose D'Angelo, for example, has explored the likely existence of women missionary partnerships in the early church. Her interest was aroused by a funerary relief depicting two women with right hands clasped in a common gesture of commitment.[2] It is plain that others have seen it in this light also, since it has been defaced in order to make one partner look male. For D'Angelo, the existence of this relief made her wonder about the role and relationship of biblical women that may have been obscured by patriarchal bias.

The very existence of women in pairs, regardless of the physical relationship between them, is of huge significance. In a world, not unlike our own, where the energies of women are supposed to be directed towards men, to see women taking space and proclaiming a new reality is inspirational. It is also interesting to consider what kind of role and relationship the women in Jesus' immediate circle may have had since it further illuminates questions regarding his own approach to sexuality. Will we see by an examination of the relationship between Mary and Martha that Jesus was in fact a "swinger" as Rosemary Radford Ruether playfully suggested? D'Angelo reminds us that when we traditionally think of Mary and Martha as a pair they are thought to signal only two paths for women, housewife or contemplative. Mary is described as the "sister" of Martha who is usually seen as the dominant figure, and we are also told that she "ministers". That they welcomed Jesus to their home suggests that they owned it, and had some authority

---

2 See Mary Rose D'Angelo, "Women Partners in the New Testament", *Journal of Feminist Studies in Religion*, 6,1990, pp. 65–86.

within it. In John 12:2, we are told that Martha was present at dinner and "serving" (*diekonei*) which could be understood in the light of her ministry (*diakonia*), rather than as a female domestic task.[3] Mary is also shown to act as a disciple by sitting at the feet of Jesus, so we appear to have a minister and a disciple under the same roof. D'Angelo maintains that they were a missionary couple. If they owned their own house, they could well have been heads of a house church, like Prisca and Aquila, a possibility that is reinforced by the fact that they are described as "sisters", as are other missionary pairs described as "sisters" or "brothers" to this day.

What this suggests is that the early Jesus movement was more flexible than the strictly gendered relationships of the time. The early community, far from reinforcing patriarchy as exerted through the family, could have envisaged and actualized alternative lifestyles. It should be borne in mind that this was a time when the family was being used to strengthen the Roman Empire through the Augustan reforms relating to child bearing and the dominance of the husband in the family. While it may not be the case that Mary and Martha ventured further into the Empire than their own backyards, there were others who did. The choice of a woman as a partner in Christian mission may have constituted a sexual as well as a social choice.

D'Angelo concludes that by choosing the company of women, Mary and Martha were making a public statement about the value of women that would have been seen as subversive in a patriarchal context. Whether they had sex together is of course an interesting question – beyond the merely curious. The evidence from that period is that same–sex relationships were regarded as especially subversive. The example of Mary and Martha provides us with a backdoor glimpse into what may have been happening around Jesus, and suggests that the "new creation" might have been much more radical that many have supposed.

---

3 D'Angelo, "Women Partners in the New Testament", p. 77.

It may be surprising to some to realize that those around Jesus are not the only ones to have had their sexual lives put under scrutiny. Hugh Montefiore, as early as 1967, was attempting to find embodied meaning in the unmarried status of Jesus himself. Not wishing to escape into the time honored arguments about the higher value of celibacy that would not be in keeping with his own Jewish background or his adopted Anglicanism, Montefiore mused, "Could it be that Jesus was not by nature the marrying sort? This kind of speculation can be valuable if it underlies ... how God in Christ identifies himself with the outsider and the outcast from society."[4] Montefiore was quick to make it plain that he was not suggesting that Jesus sinned in any sexual way, rather that he perhaps identified as homosexual in order to complete his "outsider" status. Living outside the confines of heterosexuality, and the social order which underpins it, was understood by Montefiore to be a part of his redemptive mission.

The recent work of Theodore Jennings Jr, a Methodist biblical scholar,[5] moves the insights of Montefiore, and even D'Angelo, on even further. He proposes a gay positive reading of scripture, which is not the same as a non–homophobic reading. A gay positive reading does not assume the heterosexual orientation of characters in stories or the "normative" nature of marriage and family relations between people. The author is not concerned with establishing a gay identity for Jesus as such – but he wants to encourage us to think outside that box as well. He reads scripture in such a way as to liberate all, gay and straight, from the narrow confines of the dualistic binary opposites of male and female; binary opposites that do not necessarily lead to life in abundance and the full embrace of our rich and complex humanity.

Like many before him, Jennings asks questions concerning the "beloved disciple". Although Jesus loved all his disciples, this one

---

4 William Phipps, *Was Jesus Married? The Distortion of Sexuality in Christian Tradition* (New York: Harper and Row, 1970), p. 7.
5 Theodore Jennings Jr., *The Man Jesus Loved: Homoerotic Narratives From the New Testament* (Cleveland: Pilgrim Press, 2003).

enjoyed a special love. He was not a special disciple as such, but his intimacy with Jesus is graphically shown by lying in the lap of Jesus during the last supper – a position from which he moves forward to talk to Peter, and then lies back on Jesus' chest in order to whisper in his ear (21:20). At the crucifixion, the beloved disciple is there with Mary Magdalene, Jesus' mother and aunt, and in this company Jesus tells Mary and the beloved to take each other as mother and son (19:26–27). This is highly unusual since it was more common for women to be in the care of women, and is without biblical precedent. It seems inescapable that it signals a concern for the beloved, and not just for Mary. Jennings muses that it is as though his mother and his lover are being told to comfort each other in their common mourning. During the resurrection appearances, we have a glimpse of Peter also consoling the beloved rather than the other disciples (21:21), which suggests that there was a special relationship being mourned and a particular grief being experienced.[6]

Jennings considers the prominence of the "beloved" in John's Gospel, and suggests that the gospel is not the ascetic or spiritualized work that is sometimes supposed. It is, after all, the gospel that declares the incarnation most starkly – the word becoming flesh and dwelling among us. The drawing of people into an intimate relationship with the divine, most tellingly described in chapter 17, indicates a thoroughly realized eschatology. Far from "spiritualizing" the life of Jesus, John shows us embodiment. At the wedding feast at Cana, Jesus turns water into wine (2:1–11). When speaking to Nicodemus, Jesus says that new life requires a new birth (3:1–15) – an astonishing analogy when it is appreciated that birth was commonly regarded as a ritually impure act. In addition, the conversation with the Samaritan woman (4:7–26) who had had many men is unusually welcoming, there is no moral condemnation and she, of all people, is to act as an evangelist.

---

6 Jennings, *The Man Jesus Loved*, pp. 26–28.

Characteristically, Jesus overrides the law when it comes to purity or sexual morality.

Why then, asks Jennings, is it always assumed that Jesus would uphold a small number of Levitical texts about same–sex relationships? Indeed, Jennings, like Montefiore before him, suggests that it would be in keeping if he personally lived outside those guidelines, as he did in other ways. In the Greek world same–sex relationships were viewed as being based in mutuality in a way that cross–sex relationships were not, and Jennings believes there is a lesson here for today in relation to married Christians. Christian marriage has not traditionally been based on equality and mutuality, and Jennings urges that it should be embedded in cross–gendered relationships, just as it has been an ideal in same–gendered relationships. Jennings and Montefiore are not the first to make this suggestion, for example, Aelred of Rievaulx, maintained that John prioritized same–sex relationality.[7] There is an increasing body of scholarship, which suggests that those first brave musings by Montefiore, and others, were not mere shots in the dark, but rather insights into the way in which the radical message of Jesus may have affected all aspects of life.

Jennings leads us further into a new way of reading when he considers the nude youth referred to in the Garden of Gethsemane (Mark 14:50–52). The use of the Greek words, *neaniskos* and *gymnos*, give a strong suggestion that this boy covered only in a linen cloth may have been a boy prostitute. The use of *gymnos* is a glaring clue to those who know how to look and what to see; it is a reference to the gymnasium where a great deal of same–sex activity went on, then as now. We know from 2 Maccabees, that a gymnasium was set up in Jerusalem and caused outrage because it symbolized the cult of the male nude. The question therefore arises: is this boy in the gospels a Hellenized Jew who adopted the mores of the pederastic culture of the Greeks? Jennings suggests that with the combination of *gymnos* and

---

7 Jennings, *The Man Jesus Loved*, p. 99.

neaniskos the boy is made the focus of the homoerotic gaze – quite deliberately by the author.

Of course, where this whole issue becomes significant is in relation to Secret Mark, the gospel found in 1958 in an orthodox monastery outside Jerusalem. A letter of Clement of Alexandria (200CE) warned readers against scandalous readings of the material about the youth and Jesus. This scandalous reading is attributed to the Carpocratians, a group who rejected the ascetic and anti–erotic teaching of the growing church. Even when Clement edits the text, we are left with some material that is hard to explain. The story about the raising of a young man who was in the tomb emphasizes the exchange of looks of love between Jesus and the youth, after which the youth begs to be with him. Jesus goes to his house where he stays for a number of days, and in the evening of the sixth night, the young man goes to him wearing only a linen cloth "and remained with him that night for Jesus taught him the mystery of the kingdom of God ... arising he returned to the other side of the Jordan." Clement edited the text that read that Jesus and the youth were in this instruction "naked man to naked man."[8] There may be links here with what appeared to have happened at Gethsemane. Could this be the same lad, and is he so connected to Jesus that he remains loyal? In order to fully emphasis the erotic elements of this account Salome is mentioned in the story as the sister of the youth, and she is the alleged apostle of sexual freedom for the second century Carpocratic Christians.

Morton Smith who discovered the gospel suggests that freedom from the law may have meant that spiritual union may have involved physical union as well. This was possibly the case for some Gnostic Christians, but we have no way of knowing where their ideas originated. Is it beyond the bounds of possibility that they had a scriptural base, even if that scripture was relatively quickly excised from the canon? Do we see a battle between Clement who was the champion of asceticism

---

8 Jennings, *The Man Jesus Loved*, p. 116.

and who has been widely credited with introducing homophobia into the Christian tradition, and a much older and more body friendly form of Christianity? If the story of the disciple Jesus loved had not remained in the canonical literature then these new texts would not cause us to ask questions and one guesses they would not have caused problems for Clement.

Jennings makes a persuasive case that the way in which Matthew employs the story of the Centurion's Lad (8:5–13) is deliberately provocative. Matthew uses the word *pais* not *doulos* as is used by Luke; the former means "boy–lover" or "boyfriend", while the latter means "slave". Is this a mistake? Jennings does not think so, and points to various, hitherto insufficiently realized, radical elements in the gospel. He argues, for example, that when Matthew refers to the magi (see chapter 2), he is defying Jewish custom, which demands that such sorcerers be scorned. Far from despising them, they are placed centrally as those who recognize and pay homage to Jesus. Similarly, when he introduces the reader to the Syrophoenecian woman she is referred to as a "dog", *kunariois*, a cultic prostitute, a person connected with a sexual irregularity (15:21–28) yet, it is this woman who is shown as the one with insight. So to also include a reference to pederasty, through the introduction of the Centurion's boy, would complete the trio of things that the orthodox Jew would shy away from. And, the point is, that in shying away, they are foregoing participation in the new creation. What a lesson there is here for the Anglican Communion: what is placed outside communion might in fact be the stuff of the new creation.

The readings that Jennings suggests are obviously troubling to those who hold fast to gender roles that underpin patriarchy, heterosexism and masculinist understandings. It is far too simple to suggest that Jesus was gay, since that reading is a way of falling back into the very binary opposites that need to be questioned. However, we do see that Jesus had close and affectionate relationships with men, particularly the beloved disciple, that challenges standard masculinist understandings of gender. There are only six verses in the Bible that read as opposed to homosexuality, while there is a significant amount of gospel material that can be seen as containing homoerotic elements. These readings fundamentally challenge the assertion of the Lambeth Conference of 1978 that "affirm heterosexuality as the scriptural norm" (73).

Windsor asserts that, "We can no longer be content to drop random texts into arguments, imagining that the point is thereby proved, or indeed to sweep away sections of the New Testament as irrelevant to today's world, imagining that problems are thereby solved" (30). But why then does it only select the "clobber texts"[9], even to the point of reading those out of context and refusing to see what is before their eyes? And what is it that is before their eyes? In my view, a much more complex picture than we could ever have imagined. A world in which the construction of gender and the sexual relationships that sprang from them held in place an unjust and, at times, crippling reality for women and men. We know through contemporary gender studies, and recent work in theology, that the way in which we understand our sexual arrangements, as well as the permissible boundaries of gender performance, affect virtually everything in our lives from personal safety to educational, career and economic access. Even in our comfortable western world there is not an area untouched by the creation and maintenance of gender.

Christians declare that what the life of Jesus showed was a "new way", a way to experience heaven on earth. Gender has always played a role in this even in the writings of the Church Fathers who could not conceive that women, unmanipulated bodily could enter heaven, and were concerned that women's bodies should be highly controlled while still on earth. As we saw earlier, McNamara puts forward a persuasive case that these women did not live in community in order to flee from, or subdue, the body, but rather to live *outside* the constraints of the

---

9 Those texts in both the Hebrew Bible and the Christian scriptures that appear to condemn homosexuality, but which have been shown to involve a much broader and more complex picture.

patriarchal world they understood Christianity to have declared over–turned.[10] From within these communities, which were engaged with the world, not ascetic as once thought, they wrote against original sin as they saw it – the sin of the arrogance and domination of men.[11] They did not deny their womanhood, but they were not willing to be enslaved to narrow gender understandings.

There are parallels with the present debate. In asking why the women acted as they did, and, in searching for an answer, we come to realize that the insistence on rigid binary opposite gender construction cannot be truly "Christian" if only because it serves power–laden hierarchies. Far from insisting on narrowly constructed heterosexuality, the Anglican Communion should be expanding understandings of gender and role performance in order to destabilize many aspects of the social order that do not signal the new creation.

Disturbed as I am by Windsor, I am not suggesting that Anglicans should move beyond the Bible or the Christian tradition to find more liberating outcomes. I am suggesting that the homophobia that stems from culture and ecclesiastical habit be challenged by bolder readings of both scripture and tradition. The Spirit – so freely spoken about in this Report – should be allowed to blow away the veils of gender, sex and orientation prejudice, that have no Gospel basis, yet hang so accusingly over the Anglican Communion.

---

10 McNamara, *A New Song*, p. 41.
11 McNamara, *A New Song*, p. 78.

5

Harmonious Dissimilitude

Vincent Strudwick

The Windsor Report, and the meeting of Anglican Primates at the Dromatine Center near Newry in February 2005, had a laudable and common objective, which was to provide a way of holding the Anglican Communion together while the issues that had caused disagreement within the Communion were examined and worked at. The immediate issue was that of the human rights of gay Christians in the church; and the "Communion" being held together was that which had evolved since the setting up of the first Lambeth Conference in 1867 by Archbishop Longley.

    The Communion with which we are familiar has been in a state of continuous evolution. Its genesis in the history of sixteenth–century England, its expansion in the nineteenth century, and its transformation in the twentieth, all were accomplished with attempts to define a common theological basis but without success. This lack was bound to disrupt the Communion at some point, and this disruption occurred not with the episcopal ordination of Gene Robinson, but earlier, when the Lambeth Conference of 1998 declared that homosexuality was "incompatible with scripture" and assumed a common theological basis for this dictat.

The underlying issues

Two questions must be asked: "Is the gay issue the one that should be tackled?" and "Is the Communion in its present shape that which should be preserved?" In my view the gay issue, though vitally important, is not the root issue. When Bill Clinton was asked before an election what was the root issue that would decide the outcome, he replied, "The economy, stupid". In our case, it is "biblical authority, stupid". While the substance of the current debate on human sexuality is pressing and important, and must not be side stepped or blurred, the reason that it has caused such a passionate split within Anglicanism is because of differences in understanding the nature of biblical authority. Biblical authority has been acknowledged consistently by all shades of opinion within Anglicanism, but what has been obscured is the fact that this authority has been differently conceived and differently used by those who cite it as a common reference.

If Windsor and Newry have been successful in "buying time" then that time will be well spent in initiating two simultaneous educational studies at all levels throughout the Communion. One of these should be on the nature of biblical authority, and its role in the unfolding life of the church, and the second on the future shape of the Communion in the modern world. In the course of this agenda, a host of difficult issues will surface and need resolution; but in my view they should be dealt with as sub–items of this main agenda. It is as a contribution towards initiating these studies that this essay is offered.

Gray areas: the nature of biblical authority

In the thought of the sixteenth–century reformers, the source of authority for Christians was defined as scripture alone (*sola scriptura*). Here is a message from God himself: a message, which is apart from the church and by which the church is judged. So, in the case of homosexuality, to those who regard scripture in this way God's message seems clear. Romans 1:26–27, 1 Corinthians 6:9. 1 Timothy 1:10 contain texts that combine to send a message that gay relationships are contrary to God's will and purpose for humanity. It was this kind of interpretation of the role of scripture that carried the day in the 1998 Lambeth Conference.

However, from the very earliest days of the church of England, the nature of biblical authority was a gray area. When Henry VIII ordered the English Bible to be placed in all churches in 1536, Archbishop Cranmer found it necessary to write a preface that required people to "ask thy curate" if they wished to know the meaning of a passage. It was to be a matter for the church to interpret, not the individual. On the continent of Europe, Calvin's *sola scriptura* became the norm for evangelical Christians, but was disputed in England. The theologian who pre–eminently developed Anglican thought in a biblical and philosophical framework was Richard Hooker. In his main work *Of the Laws of Ecclesiastical Polity*, he opposes Calvin's argument (which was being pressed by evangelicals – puritans – within the church of England) that the scriptures must be literally and absolutely followed. The scriptures are "the oracles of God" writes Hooker, but the authority on which they are to be accepted and acted upon is, according to Hooker, the authority of the church. He challenges the idea that scripture is its own interpreter, and holds that in practice the outcome of such a view is that all can use scripture to their own ends. The church is the guardian of scripture, and it is interpreted by the church in the light of the tradition of our predecessors, and the testing out of its validity by experience and reason. For Hooker reason is of prime importance. "The light of natural understanding, wit, and reason is from God; He it is which thereby doth illuminate everyman entering into the world" (*Laws*, Book III, Chapter ix. 3). He goes on to say that the general laws of nature and the moral laws of scripture "are in the substance of law all one", and some of these are turned into positive law in scripture.

In Hooker's thought, it is the duty of the church to weigh the nature of the different kinds of material in scripture, to consider the variety of judgments that might be made and, on the basis of this, to settle controversial matters and to end disputes by a definite decision, even if that decision sometimes proves later to be erroneous.

It is part of Hooker's thesis that the church in its teaching and practice must be open to change as it is guided by the Holy Spirit. He points out that such change must not come about simply by reason of a development in the culture alone because we must beware that "the looseness and slackness of men may not cause the commandments for God to be unexecuted", and he reasons "laws human must be made according to the general laws of nature, and without contradiction unto any positive law in scripture. Otherwise they are ill made" (*Laws*, Book III, Chapter ix, 3).

But Hooker then argues for two caveats to the above. Firstly, that the laws of nature require interpretation and the regulative principle in this interpretation is that of "purpose". If we were to take the example of the inclusion of gay people on equal terms with everybody in the church, a challenge would be required to the view that in nature and in scripture sex is designed solely for procreation. While this is a view that has been held, it is difficult to justify by experience or reason. From the point of view of natural law, is not one of the underlying "purposes" of being human to engage in loving relationships through which our humanity is fulfilled? Further, there are questions as to whether the "positive law of scripture" (as expressed in the biblical quotations referred to above) are *per se* against homosexuality, or against homosexuality in the religious and cultural environment in which they were being experienced at the time. A sexual hierarchy, in which men dominate, was deeply ingrained. Women were regarded as "possessions". Such a hierarchy was embedded in Anglican life and liturgy well into the twentieth century, and persists in parts of the Communion today, as expressed in the telling question in the marriage ceremony: "Who giveth this woman to be married to this man?" Sex between men, and between women, upsets this "natural" hierarchy, and may well have been the cause of early Christian disapproval.

Secondly, Hooker argues that, even if there is a positive law in scripture, it can be changed. In a rather gnomic paragraph Hooker writes:

> God never ordained anything that could be bettered. Yet many things he hath that have been changed, and that for the better. That which succeedeth as better now when change is requisite, had been worse when that which now is changed was instituted. Otherwise, God had not then left this to choose that, neither would now reject that to choose this, were it not for some new grown occasion making that which hath been better worse. In this case therefore men do not presume to change God's ordinance, but they yield there unto requiring itself to be changed (*Laws*, Book III, Chapter x, 5).

In my view, the gay issue comes under this precept. In 1988, I recall, a request was made by some African bishops that polygamy should be regarded in a similar light. In this case, converts who became Christian, and brought two or three wives with them, should be allowed to keep them, while not being allowed to add more. Here was an example of inclusive thinking contrary to the letter of scripture. In the less confrontational atmosphere of Lambeth 1988, this did not precipitate an ecclesial crisis.

But that which underlies all such reasoning is the need to develop an understanding of the ways in which scripture may be interpreted and held authoritative in the twenty–first century, and hopefully, a common acceptance of the varieties of practice that this may engender. The "time brought" for the North American provinces to reflect on their actions will be wasted unless the whole Communion reflects together in the listening, trusting mode that the Archbishop of Canterbury has recently described happening at Newry. The place for this reflection to begin is surely with a Communion–wide, cross–cultural study of the nature of authority in the church, in its theology and practice. This must be undertaken in the light of the work on biblical criticism that has taken place over the last two hundred years, for that is a task yet to be accomplished.

As I write of a "Communion–wide study", I can almost hear the cries of despair from those who will think it impracticable and a recipe for confusion. Yet, I do have some experience of this. At the Lambeth Conference of 1988, I was the education process consultant and was able to observe the effect of the corporate Bible study throughout the conference, prepared by Bishop John Taylor. It was (of course) unevenly performed and imperfectly accomplished, yet, I was impressed by its illuminating quality, and the way in which it strengthened the corporate understanding of the episcopal participants. The second thing I recall from that experience was my task of preparing the assembled bishops to "take Lambeth back to their dioceses". I am sure that what was taken back was not in most cases a form of the printed resolutions that were produced in the post–conference booklet, but rather a selection of issues and (more importantly) a personal episcopal warmth about the process of the conference in which they had been involved, which they wished the faithful to share. The "feed–back" was positive. It is on this basis that I believe a careful inclusive study program could be devised and implemented.

The Communion come of age?

In the nineteenth century the church of England, which had already spread beyond the shores of its birth, experienced an immense growth as the colonial and missionary movement took the Anglican form of church polity to many parts of the globe. The inevitable emphasis on preaching and teaching underlined the unresolved differences within the church of England concerning the authority of scripture and the nature of doctrine, particularly at a time when scientists like Darwin were challenging the sense in which many had held the scriptures to be authoritative. As the church grew and controversies multiplied, so the necessity for a better organization to manage this expanded Church of

England was called for. A doctrine commission was proposed but its composition and role could not be agreed, and instead the Lambeth Conference was called, and from 1867 has served the Communion as an important ingredient in its expansion and development. Following the end of empire, churches of the Communion in independent countries have ordered their own affairs while remaining part of a world wide family, now numbering 78 million people. Recently, there have been moves to respond to a perceived need to improve communication and structures in an increasingly complex organization in which, for example, the number of bishops attending the Lambeth Conference doubled between 1978 and 1998, and the variety of languages and cultures represented at these conferences presented an increasingly difficult task in communication, let alone theological understanding and agreement. The Primates' Meeting and the Anglican Consultative Council have both played essential roles in maintaining the unity and servicing the mission of the Communion.

There is a temptation for such a complex organization to try to become more centralized and "authoritarian". While there is constant insistence that the Archbishop of Canterbury is not a mini–pope, there is an increasing expectation that he should act like one in times of crisis such as we are currently experiencing. Puzzlement from other churches, and pressure from the media, adds to the conviction that the Anglican theory and practice of dispersed authority has had its day; yet, it is my conviction that the Anglican experiment is still in its early stages. Those who practice a strict hierarchical authority are in constant danger of having authority disregarded, as Lewis Carroll amusingly demonstrated in *Through the Looking Glass.* "'Off with her head', said the Red Queen. Nobody moved." What the Communion needs to work on is the *consensus fidelium,* which is a feature of dispersed authority, outside the shaping of the international structures that have evolved; for the real heart of the Communion is in the parishes and congregations throughout the world, worshipping, learning and living the Gospel. Here is our "authority"; and when this network is in a process of learning together, in charity, it is a powerful example of what "being the church" means. Study of the Bible, and argument about its meaning, lies at the heart of the life of the church. We need a "shape" for the church that enables us to do this better. For only then shall we learn to worship, teach and engage in Christian mission at the same time as we argue our way through difficult problems.

Towards harmonious dissimilitude

The alternative to more authoritarian and tighter structures in the Communion is to re–imagine the Anglican Communion honoring our heritage of faith, fostering a unity in spirit and purpose, yet, allowing within the Communion a variety of expression, not only in "adiaphora" but in matters about which we care passionately but disagree. We might call such issues "eudiaphora". As Bishop Stephen Neill wrote "we are a learning church as well as a teaching church" and in that spirit we should be continually listening to each other and learning from each other.

To some, the vision of such a Communion may seem messy and unsatisfactory, as well as perpetuating the very weaknesses that were evident as the organization of the Communion formed in the nineteenth century. Yet, this may well be the reality of the future, which carries its own authority, if it allows the work of Christ to go forward without being blocked by bitter feuding and disagreements. Father Vincent Donovan who ministered among the Masai of Tanzania wrote: "Historically, a single form of this response to the Christian message has grown and thrived … what we are coming to see, now, is that there must be many responses possible to the Christian message, which have hitherto been neither encouraged or allowed. We have come to believe that any valid, positive response to the Christian message could and should be recognized and accepted as church. That is the church that might have been and might yet be". Such a "valid" response would mean moving beyond the concept of "adiaphora" envisaged in Windsor to include things which matter, but on which we differ, as members of a family – "eudiaphora".

To move from a concept of church that has been meticulously defined to a church with less clearly defined boundaries will be a difficult task, but the alternative may well be the break up of the Communion and a frustration of its corporate mission to preach the Gospel in the world. Even this bold concept was foreshadowed by the good Richard Hooker: "A more dutiful and religious way for us were to admire the wisdom of God which shineth in the beautiful variety of all things, but most in the manifold and yet harmonious dissimilitude of those ways whereby his church of earth is guided from age to age through all generations of men" (*Laws*, Book III, Chapter xi, 9). If we dare to embrace this "more dutiful and religious way", it will require restraint all round: from those whose opinions on the nature of biblical authority differ, from those who in pursuit of what they perceive to be truth and justice have moved apart from the others, and (most costly of all) from those gay Christians who painfully suffer from humiliation and exclusion. But my thesis is that if the period between now and Lambeth 2008 is to be anything other than a period of delay, then, the participation of all is required, as we seek to become the church – better. In all sorts of ways, the Council of Trent in the sixteenth century lost the opportunity to be inclusive. Let us not lose this one, for the process towards Lambeth 2008 is what will determine its outcome – a process which may strengthen our Communion and deepen our understanding of what God would have us do, as we preach and live the Gospel of Jesus Christ.

Note: *Of the Laws of Ecclesiastical Polity.* Quotations from Hooker are from a text printed in Oxford at the University Press MDCCCL and based on the Keble edition of 1836.

PART II

THE NATURE OF
COMMUNION

6

FAITHFULNESS IN CRISIS

Marilyn McCord Adams

I. Current contexts

Windsor was supposed to define a way through a "crisis", whose presenting issue was human sexuality, especially the acceptability of non–celibate homosexual lifestyles among the clergy and leaders of the church. Its approach is to forward a new polity for the Anglican Communion, one that translates the poetry of mutual affection and nostalgia for Canterbury into institutional structures that move in the direction of international canon law. What was formerly a loose federation of legally independent churches would now be bound together by a covenant, which would be given legal status by each of the member churches passing a canon to observe it. Just as the United Nations uses the doctrine of human rights to critique the legal practices of member states, so the covenant would hold member churches to "essentials" while allowing them autonomy over matters of indifference. The covenant would oblige members to submit innovations in theology or ethics to the "instruments of union" (the Archbishop of Canterbury, the Lambeth Conference, the Anglican Consultative Council, and the Primates' Meeting). It also implies that the selection of bishops would be subject to the approval of these communion–wide authorities. Compliance would be enforced on pain of excommunication from the Anglican Communion.

Windsor's proposal focusses on giving the Anglican Communion – notorious for its fuzzy boundaries – sharper definition. Archbishop Robin Eames spoke of the desire – perhaps even felt need – to draw a line in the sand, the crossing of which would count member churches out. Windsor's appeal to the distinction between what is core and what is indifferent (what churches can disagree about and still be members of one communion) is marked by two key moves. Structurally, the Report lodges authority to discriminate the essential from the indifferent with the instruments of union. Its criterion for what violates essentials is what disrupts the union and/or compromises the common good of the Anglican Communion. Thus, what counts as essential becomes a function of what international bodies can or cannot tolerate. So far as content is concerned, Windsor widens the core beyond theological doctrines (such as are mentioned in the creeds) to ethics and mores.

Religion is always conservative. But the effect of Windsor is to define the Anglican Communion in such a way as to make it a bulwark against cultural change. In particular, it allows church members in societies where institutions are in flux, where taboos are unraveling, to appeal to member churches in more conservative societies where the taboos are still in place, to keep the changes from affecting the church. These ecclesial structures have been designed for immediate application to the presenting issue of human sexuality: to the consecration of a coupled gay man as bishop by the Episcopal Church of the United States (ECUSA), and the authorization of rites for the blessing of same–sex unions by the Anglican Church of Canada. Windsor does not concern itself with comparable provision for searching out and uprooting systemic evils entrenched within and across many societies.

The polity outlined in the Report was already circulated and discussed in a variety of proposals. But even the original document has a tendency to speak as if the polity were already accepted and in force. It talks as if ECUSA and the Anglican Church of Canada had failed to meet their *obligations* – which would exist if there were an Anglican covenant to abide by the instruments of union to which ECUSA and the Anglican Church of Canada had subscribed, sealing the deal with provisions in their own canon laws. As with *Issues in Human Sexuality* in the Church of England, the slide from the status of discussion document to official norm, seems all too easy.

The communiqué issuing out of the Primates' meeting in Ireland (in late February 2005) bears out this analysis. The Primates show a surprizing willingness to concede that the authoritarian structures outlined in sections A, B, and C of Windsor are accurate if sometimes "idealized" *descriptions* of how the Anglican communion does and/or should work (*communiqué* paras 8–9). To be sure, they express caution lest we elevate the Archbishop of Canterbury to the status of pope (*communiqué* para 10) and acknowledge that creativity will be needed to find a way to elicit appropriate cross–communion feed–back in episcopal elections (*communiqué* para 11). But their statement does not protest Windsor's thrust towards more centralized control with an emphasis on gate keeping. The communiqué pays more accurate attention than did the Report to differences in polity (in the procedures for episcopal selection and in where the authority to take decisions on behalf of the ecclesial body rests) (*communiqué* para 6). But where gate keeping is concerned, it does not matter that ECUSA and the Anglican Church of Canada acted in accord with their own canon–legal procedures. What is decisive is whether the results accord with what the majority of member churches and/or the instruments of union can accept.

The communiqué explicitly assigns creedal status to positions on controversial ethical issues, with its remarkable declaration that unless ECUSA and the Anglican Church of Canada "accept the same teaching on matters of sexual morality as is generally accepted elsewhere in the Communion" – "the underlying reality of our communion in God the Holy Trinity is obscured" (para 12). The communiqué "pledges itself afresh" to 1998 Lambeth Resolution 1.10 "in its entirety" (para 17). The communiqué explicitly presents ECUSA and the Anglican Church of Canada with a "take it or leave it" choice: accede to the majority–report on non–celibate homosexual lifestyles – put yourself in full alignment with 1998 Lambeth Resolution 1.10 on human sexuality

– or count yourself out. The communiqué puts ECUSA and the Anglican Church of Canada on probation, by asking them to voluntarily withdraw their representatives from the Anglican Consultative Council until Lambeth 2008 (*communiqué* para 14). It asks for *de facto* conformity to 1998 Lambeth Resolution 1.10 with moratoria on consecrating coupled homosexual bishops and public blessings of same–gendered unions (para 18). It recognizes that the provisions of 1998 Lambeth Resolution 1.10, have been unevenly emphasized. So far as its pledge to listen to homosexuals is concerned, it proposes to make up for lost time by inviting ECUSA and the Anglican Church of Canada to a meeting in June 2005 to "set out the thinking behind the actions of their Provinces," in accordance of paragraph 141 of the Report, which specifies that innovating churches

> must be able, as a beginning, to *demonstrate* to the rest of the Communion why their proposal meets the criteria of scripture, tradition, and reason. In order to be received as a legitimate development of tradition, it must be possible to *demonstrate* how public Rites of Blessing for same–sex unions would constitute grown in harmony with the apostolic tradition as it has been receive (italics mine).

Windsor goes on to comment that while "there have been the beginnings of such demonstration," these have proved so far unconvincing, because many would see the development as "surrendering to the spirit of the age" (142).

The Primates' communiqué recognizes that different member churches have acted in accordance with their own discernment: African and Asian bishops, in stepping in to function as bishops for North American congregations and clergy who believe their bishops have counted themselves out of the communion; and ECUSA and the Anglican Church of Canada in consecrating Gene Robinson and blessing same–sex unions. The Primates' communiqué calls for a moratorium on both sides to allow space for healing and reflection. It also calls on the Archbishop of Canterbury to create a panel to oversee the pastoral needs of congregations and clergy who believe their bishops to have transgressed the essentials, while bringing uninvited intrusions by foreign bishops to a halt. Despite this balance, the presumption of the communiqué is that if ECUSA and the Anglican Church of Canada do not decide to conform to majority views about sexual morality, if they do not decide to make these moratoria permanent, they will excommunicate themselves from the Anglican Communion.

II. The ineptitude of the Windsor Report

Like all parties to the debate, I value the Anglican Communion. Nevertheless – the primates to the contrary, notwithstanding – I find Windsor radically off–course, both as to what the Anglican Communion should be and how we should get there.

It offers a *Pernicious Polity*. Nineteenth and twentieth century Anglicanism seated itself on the three–legged stool (scripture, tradition, and reason) and prided itself on being able to hold together without the authoritarian structures of Rome. Alternatively, the 1888 Lambeth Quadrilateral – scripture, the Nicene creed, the dominical sacraments, historic episcopate – was sufficient to achieve collegial unity while allowing the Spirit room to move in the various member churches in different ways. "If it ain't broke, don't fix it!" It violates the spirit of post–wars–of–religion Anglicanism to want to get one another very much under control.

And a *Narrowed Indifference*. Likewise wrong–headed is Windsor's remodeling of the distinction between essential and indifferent. First, the Report's move to promote ethics to creedal status is idolatrous. No serious Christian would deny that response to God's love is life transforming. But to give majority–report sexual mores – "the same teaching on matters of sexual morality as generally accepted elsewhere in the Communion" (*communiqué* para 12) – the same status as the doctrine of the Trinity is to promote human social arrangements to the status of the sacred. This is understandable because it is a fallen–natural human tendency. But sober theology would insist that *all* human social arrangements – whether *entrenched* by long tradition (as are racism, sexism, slavery, polygamy) or *innovative* – fall short of the Reign of God because they reflect limited human social competence. Human beings have never been smart enough or good enough to organize utopia. That's one big reason why we need the Reign of God.

Second, such promotion of ethical norms to creedal status is untimely, because all human cultures are in transition. Colonialism and missionary work disturbed traditional social patterns. Emerging from these, Africa finds itself caught up in global economic developments. Its peoples – as much as North Americans – are at work sifting and reclaiming, reaching for fresh integration. Archbishop Akinola is right: it is a season for Africans to think and speak for themselves, for Africans to discover their own distinctive voices (which are different from one another as is illustrated by the contrast between Archbishops Akinola and Tutu regarding homosexuality). The Gospel needs to speak into the flux of cultural change worldwide, but we shouldn't expect the same social patterns to emerge in all cases. Look at the variety of institutions that count as marriage in the space–time of the bible story itself.

Third, Windsor's demand for "demonstration before innovation" is naive and unreasonable. Historically, gender roles and institutions for managing sexual expression are seen to vary in nomadic versus agrarian versus urban contexts and to change with altering economic and social patterns. In the best of circumstances, even among those of similar backgrounds, fresh consensus is the work of decades. Because we have individually and collectively defined ourselves in terms of now–challenged ways of life, their maintenance can seem like a matter of life and death. Since existing institutions are protected by taboos and sanctions, attempts to uproot them are bound to meet with virulent resistance. Not all changes are salutary. But equally, wholesome changes will not win majority consensus until the upheaval is over and things once again settle down. Not only do such social–psychological factors prevent people from being persuaded in advance, what later comes to be regarded as the side of the angels can seem – for a long time – to be losing the argument. Pro–slavery advocates made a better case from the Bible than abolitionists before and during the American civil war. Jesus' opponents appealed to scripture and tradition to conclude that his Sabbath healings and other taboo violations were demonically empowered. St Paul's inclusion of Gentiles met with many objections and called down the same ire. We can join Presiding Bishop Griswold in welcoming the June 2005 opportunity "to speak from the truth of our experience" as Paul did before King Agrippa. But *demonstration* will not be in the "offing," and many will remain unconvinced because the burden of proof – laid down by their particular way of reading scripture – is too high.

All of this suggests that we should agree to differ, not only where the issue is unimportant (the Report instances the direction in which the pious cross themselves), *but also where the question is momentous yet not decidable by us with enough clarity to convince one another.* Instead of demonizing one another, we should follow Gamaliel's advice: let others run their experiment and wait to see whether the Lord prospers it.

III. The costs of discipleship

Within the Anglican Communion, North American and European member churches are under considerable pressure to be conciliatory. Many African and Asian dioceses have joined some North Americans in identifying the legitimacy of non–celibate homosexual lifestyles as *a church–dividing issue.* They point out that the church is vibrant and growing in their regions, while in Europe and North America, religious institutions appear to be losing ground. Theologically, they present this fact as evidence that the Spirit is with them. Politically, they remind Northerners that there has been a seismic shift in the balance of power within the Anglican Communion, away from old–fashioned (British empire) and new–fangled economic (American and EU) colonialists in favor of the very people they have oppressed.

History intensifies this pressure to "go along to get along." The record of colonial oppression, of continuing economic exploitation and indifference to developing–country needs, of paternalistic and patronizing engagement of local leadership – all of this cuts northerners to the heart, weighs us down with guilt, and makes us eager to show works meet for repentance. As Archbishop Andrew Hutchinson of Canada reports, African and Asian bishops made it clear, they needed to be able to show that their concerns had been taken seriously, if a way forward was to be found.

It is meet and right that member churches should treat one another respectfully, as peers, from whom one might expect to learn. But *to listen carefully and to treat with dignity, are not the same as to agree,* to do only what the other can recommend you to do, or say only what the other can approve you to say. Spiritual discernment is not certified in the short run by majority rule. *Northern member churches* – not only ECUSA and the Anglican Church of Canada, but also the Church of England – *are not entitled under God to delegate their own discernment within their own cultural contexts to the now–majority African and Asian churches.* To do so is not to behave as fellow adults, as mature bodies in relation to one another, but to regress to the child's role. Before God, northern member churches – particularly ECUSA and the Anglican Church of Canada – have a responsibility and (in June 2005) will have the opportunity to bear witness (in Presiding Bishop Griswold's words) "to speak out of the truth of our experience."

Notoriously, American Episcopalians aligned with the Network agree with Archbishop Akinola about homosexuality. But *those of us, who have thought gay and lesbian, bisexual and transgendered persons to be treasures of the church, should not mollify our message. We should seize the initiative and take the opportunity to clarify just how opposed our discernment is to theirs.* I agree that northern Anglicans owe apologies to African and Asian member churches for being insufficiently respectful. *And* in my judgment, the Anglican Communion, the Church of England, my own ECUSA need equally to beg the pardon of gay and lesbian, bisexual and transgendered persons for ecclesiastical complicity in centuries of abuse.

So far from repenting of consecrating Gene Robinson or approving rites for the blessing of same–gendered unions, we should call on the Anglican communion, the Church of England, my own ECUSA to repent of not contradicting the Levitical language of abomination, for – by turns – sponsoring and acquiescing in the judgment that who gay and lesbian, bisexual and transgendered persons are, and what they do is an abomination to the Lord. Our Communion needs to apologize for setting its seal of approval on the centuries–long criminalization of homosexual activity and on the consequent curtailment of civil rights. For doing little or nothing to quench the sentiments behind gay bashing and hate crimes, so grotesquely expressed in the murder of Matthew Shepherd, and the fundamentalist picket sign "God hates fags!" For alienating many gay and lesbian, bisexual and transgendered persons from God by making God guilty by association with the church.

So far from repenting of consecrating Gene Robinson or approving rites for the blessing of same–gendered unions, we should call on the Anglican Communion, the Church of England, my own ECUSA, to own up to the spiritual violence we have done to gay and lesbian, bisexual and transgendered persons. For how long, in how many and various ways has the church enforced closeting on the outside? Yes, especially in an established church, everyone is welcome, but only if you don wedding garments of respectability, only if you can "pass" as sexually conventional, celibate or married. Whatever else may be true about you sexually, "don't ask, don't tell."

Closeting on the outside fosters spiritual fragmentation on the inside. If God is so revolted by homosexual expression – maybe sexual activity generally – better to split it off and lock it in a separate psychospiritual cupboard, from the part of the self that trafficks with God, lest God see and reject us altogether. We should call on the church to do penance for making it harder for gay and lesbian, bisexual and transgendered persons to win through to integrity, for encouraging the repression that dampens creativity. We should warn the church to stop setting up stones of stumbling that trip up its own children, that bruise and skin the knees of their attempts to stand up to their full stature in Christ.

So far from repenting of the consecration of Gene Robinson or approving rites for the blessing of same–gendered unions, we should call on the Church of England to apologize for the clumsiness of its so–called "pastoral" accommodation, which allows stable same–sex couplings for laity who can't control themselves, but enjoins celibacy as a counsel of perfection to which homosexual clergy must conform. Besides invoking a double standard that betrays the priesthood of all believers, it forgets that celibacy is a calling, not obviously correlated with sexual orientation. It neglects to note how – in the vast majority of cases – celibacy can flourish only where there are institutions to reinforce and support it. Shirking its responsibility to furnish such social structures, the church imposes celibacy as a punitive consequence of being statistically abnormal rather than as a viable life–style alternative. Its judgment bears down in the spirit of amputating the offending right hand.

So far from repenting of the consecration of Gene Robinson or approving rites for the blessing of same gendered unions, we should call upon the Anglican Communion, the Church of England, my own ECUSA to repent of its rude reception of gay and lesbian clergy. "Don't ask, don't tell" what most people know: some of our ablest clergy are – like some of our most prominent members – lesbian or gay. The church stands ever–ready to gobble up their gifts, even demand their services, while insisting that they can have a place at the table only if they trim and tailor their *personae* to the corporate profile, only if they pretend to be someone at least slightly different from who they really are. The church remains mostly unwilling to celebrate the partnerships that fuel their creativity and give them strength for ministry. While on–the–job–effectiveness may promote them to positions of responsibility and influence, the church roofs them in with the stained–glass ceiling, limits their scope for leadership, and deprives itself of excellent bishops.

So far from repenting of the consecration of Gene Robinson or approving rites for the blessing of same gendered unions, we should call upon the Anglican Communion to apologize for the harm caused by the passage of 1998 Lambeth Resolution 1.10, and to express regret by repealing it at the earliest available opportunity.

Evidently, the majority of primates could not honestly accede to our exhortations, because their discernment is different. Archbishop Rowan Williams warns, "North Americans may have to back down, because the cost of carrying on with this sort of unilateral development will be very high." Doubtless, he has in mind, the fracture of the Anglican Communion and the necessity for ECUSA and the Anglican Church of Canada to walk separately. For us who recognize gay and lesbian, bisexual and transgendered persons as treasures of the church, backing down would carry a different cost that we cannot afford to pay: a failure of faithfulness, a betrayal of our own honest and prayerful discernment.

Yet, the current crisis puts not only ECUSA and the Anglican Church of Canada on the spot, but also the Church of England. For She is the mother of the churches in Britain's former colonies and other realms of the United Kingdom, now national churches that join together in the Anglican Communion. I close with a simile. What happens if some of the adult children of a family come to have values and lifestyles of which the others vehemently disapprove? What if some tell the parents, "we will not come to Christmas dinner, if you invite those others"? It is appropriate for the parents to try to mediate, to reason with all their children to try to restore relationships. It is fitting for the parents to express their own views on the issues, to have honest discussions, to exert themselves to convince, to open themselves to being persuaded. But it is undignified for the parents to capitulate to the demands by some of their adult children to excommunicate the others. Their response should rather be, "you are all welcome in my house, even if you are not willing to come at the same time!"

7

A REASONABLE DEVELOPMENT?

Charles Hefling

It seems the first question many people wanted to ask about the Windsor Report was: has it got teeth? A better question might be: has it got brains? Even if nothing much changes, practically speaking, as a result of the Lambeth Commission's recommendations, it makes them in a theological context. Doctrinal development, biblical authority, the gospel and culture, the foundations of ethics – on these and other topics, what it has to say is worth serious and thoughtful attention. Given the constraints under which the Commission had to work, it was not to be expected that they would produce a seamless, comprehensive document, and Windsor is neither. My comments here, however, are for the most part meant to make the best of what the Commission did accomplish, and to follow up possibilities to which I think the theological position they present is open. I am going to propose that those who consider Resolution I.10 of the 1998 Lambeth Conference a mistake, and who in principle support the actions of the Canadian and American churches to which Windsor has responded, have in its response some grounds for hope. Ample grounds they are not. But that was not to be expected either.

The Report delivers three broad evaluative judgments with respect to the situation Anglicans find themselves in. These can be stated very schematically as follows:

1. What might have happened, and ought to have done, did not.
2. What happened instead must be prevented.
3. But what might have happened still might, and it still should.

It is the third of these judgments that I find hopeful. The second, however, the one that may or may not bite, has drawn more attention, and something should be said about it first. Windsor recommends what has been called, fairly enough, a policy of containment. This policy is to be implemented by strengthening institutional structures that already exist and by adding new ones. In turn, it corresponds to one aspect – not, I will suggest, the only one – of the way the Report sees what might and ought to have happened. If, we are given to understand, things had been handled *this* way instead, the present difficulties need not have arisen.

"*This* way" is specified by example, and the example chosen is likewise an innovation and likewise controversial, namely the ordination of women. The exemplarity of this episode lies in the "mutual discernment" that took place, and most especially in the "co–operation" of the Instruments of Unity. Those who experienced the controversy as it was unfolding, ordained women particularly, may find this interpretation of what happened less than satisfactory. It downplays the rancor, the schisms, and the very real impairments of communion that have resulted within and between provinces. There might also be some doubt as to whether "co–operation" really describes the Instruments' part in inaugurating the ministries of women presbyters and bishops. These reservations are worth mentioning in themselves, but also and especially because Windsor clearly wants women's ordination to be seen as a prefiguration of the role it envisions for the Instruments hereafter. It tells the story of one innovation in such a way as to lend support to another one, a fairly recent development of church polity which, like every such development, is at the same time a development of church doctrine as well.

The doctrine of a transprovincial episcopate (see para 65),

organized around a college of primates – "meeting" will no longer be an adequate term – may be one that Anglicans would do well to embrace. It may not. The very fact that Windsor has proposed it, however, raises the question why *any* development, any innovation in teaching and practice, ought to be received, welcomed, and integrated into the church's common life. On that question the Report has a good deal to say, and what it says is arguably more important than the rather juridical, not to say Romanizing remedies it proposes on the pragmatic side. Those remedies, I have said, correspond to one aspect of Windsor's diagnosis: the American Episcopal Church, in particular, went wrong in failing to secure the cooperation of the Instruments of Unity before its own General Convention took the actions it did in 2003. But there is another aspect of the matter, less formal and more substantive. ECUSA ought to have given reasons to explain why the Instruments, or anyone else, *should* cooperate, if not by approving of what went on to happen, at least by acquiescing in it. Such an explanation is part of "what might have happened, and ought to have done." It is also part – the more hopeful part – of Windsor's assessment of what might still happen, and should.

The assessment is hopeful inasmuch as the Report recognizes that consulting the requisite number of prelates does not by itself constitute "mutual discernment" and that communion in the relevant sense depends only incidentally on institutional structures, canonical procedure, enforceable policy, and so forth; in other words, on power. Essentially, communion is a matter of common *meaning*. To be in communion is to be at one in heart and mind, first of all on the basis of common prayer – which one could wish was more prominent in Windsor – and so also on the basis of common understanding and belief, common intention and purpose, common judgments about what is true and good. Communion in this intentional sense is a function of consensus arrived at by intelligent persuasion, which is the way in which meaning, unforced, becomes common to many. Its "instruments" are conversation, discussion, argument, reasoning.

This mindful side of Windsor, not its attention to mechanisms or its teeth, is the one I take to be most authentically Anglican. Ever since the English church abjured the extrinsic authoritarianism of papal Rome, Anglicanism has characteristically commended its belief and practice as intrinsically reasonable. Hence, the high esteem for learning and scholarship that informs so much of Anglican tradition. Windsor exemplifies this tradition inasmuch as it looks to reasoning as the indispensable means to consensus, and therefore to communion in the most serious sense. The Report does aim to rein in certain changes, but it does not rule them out – if there are reasons for making them.

More specifically, Windsor rightly insists that for Christians ethical matters, norms of character and conduct, must be grounded in theology and doctrine (para 36). At the same time, it acknowledges that Christian doctrine and its theological exposition develop. Their development is a corollary of Christianity's missionary imperative and the consequent enculturation of its message (para 32). To develop, however, is not simply to change: development in the relevant sense consists in harmonious change that maintains continuity together with innovation (para 141). Nor, therefore, can the harmony intrinsic to genuine development simply be asserted. It has to be shown, demonstrated, argued for; and the responsibility for doing this is not to be avoided by peremptory claims that the Holy Spirit has acted. There needs to be intelligent, intelligible explanation. Theological reasoning thus belongs inherently to the process of development itself, properly so called, and consequently it belongs as well to the acceptance of what develops, to the process of being welcomed into the common mind that constitutes ecclesial communion.

Accordingly, it was incumbent upon ECUSA to have a sound theological rationale for the significantly innovative steps it took, and to make its reasoning known to the Communion at large. Absent such a rationale, the sequence that constitutes the "doctrine of reception" as Windsor construes it has not even begun. In effect, then, the Report recommends that ECUSA be invited to start over, at the beginning, and do what it ought to have done in the first place, by supplying an argument that explains how actions which a great many Anglicans see as disharmonious are, on the contrary, justifiable as an instance of authentic theological development. To raise some questions that might contribute to such an argument is the main purpose of this essay. But before they can be raised, some observations on the invitation to present an argument will be in order.

First, there is nothing in Windsor's invitation to object to in principle. The Report is simply saying that in the same way it behooves an individual to take thought before embarking on a course of action, so too it behooves a church, all the more when the proposed action departs significantly from traditional norms.

The second observation, however, is that this priority of thinking over acting does not always work itself out in a corresponding temporal sequence. The history of actual developments in Christian teaching shows, often enough, that theological explanation has been arrived at *ex post facto*. For example, there was no explicit doctrinal justification for the new devotional practice of referring to the Virgin Mary as Mother of God. The practice itself was what set off the theological disputes that led to the Chalcedonian definition of Christ's single, two–natured person, from which follows the propriety of the novel language about his mother. Closer to home, it was only when Samuel Seabury had been consecrated by nonjuring Scottish bishops, themselves in "impaired communion" with the Church of England, that Anglican thought began to find a place for the idea of a historic episcopate with no constitutional ties to an established national church. Closer still, at the time when the American women deacons known as the Philadephia Eleven were made presbyters, and their orders were formally accepted, there was not yet much in the way of a theological rationale for the ordination. Rather, it was the pragmatic fact that there now existed priests who were women, and women who were priests, which elicited arguments to explain how this could *be* a fact.

A third observation follows. Given Windsor's acknowledgment of the *sensus fidelium* as a theological criterion, it cannot be irrelevant that for many of the faithful, experiencing priestly ministry exercised by women has been the evidence that settles the question whether a woman can be a priest. With perfectly sound logic, such persons infer the possibility from the fact. Similarly, one way to address the question that Windsor puts to the American church – "how a person living in a same gender union may be considered eligible to lead the flock of Christ" (para 135) – would be to send an investigative team to the diocese of New Hampshire.

That is probably not what the Lambeth Commission had in mind. Perhaps it should have been. For a final observation about Windsor's invitation is that the question about eligibility it poses is posed in the abstract. It regards not *this* leader or *this* flock but "a person," unsituated and unspecified. The assumption, evidently, is that leading the flock of Christ is the same thing always and everywhere. That bishops are bishops for the whole church is true and important; but Windsor takes this to mean that bishops, like bureaucrats, are interchangeable – "translatable" to any diocese, wherever it might be. On the other hand, if the office and work to which a bishop is ordained vary with the cultural context in which they are exercised, then it could very well happen that some particular person, leading some particular flock of Christ in an altogether admirable way, might nevertheless be prevented by any number of circumstances from doing the same in a different setting. Requiring this person to be "translatable" makes sense only in so far as all cultures are the same and all flocks identical. But that is just what they are not, as Windsor itself acknowledges elsewhere. History makes a difference. Enculturation is therefore an imperative of communicating the Gospel. On its own showing, then, the Report would have done well to frame its question about episcopal eligibility more concretely: by whom, for whom, should an eligible shepherd be eligible?

Much the same point was made in a different way by the Presiding Bishop of ECUSA in his initial response to Windsor: "in the Episcopal Church we are seeking to live the gospel in a society where homosexuality is openly discussed and increasingly acknowledged in all areas of our public life." That is not the culture which informs some other societies within which Anglican bishops do their shepherding. It does inform the social milieu of the Episcopal Church and its clergy today. There was a time when anomalous sexuality could be, and was, accommodated by exercising Anglican reticence. That time is past. The policy of "Don't ask, don't tell" is less and less acceptable to people who are gay, and more and more pointless in the judgment of people who are not. Nor is it at all likely that "coming out," to use the gay vernacular, is a trend that is going to reverse itself, at least not in the "global North."

I have been suggesting that it would be possible to respond to Windsor's call for a theological rationale by developing the Report's own suggestion that different concrete circumstances, different cultural contexts, can and do condition the acceptability of innovations in religious practice. But clearly such an argument goes only so far. It *may* be that the North American churches, in responding to an undeniable cultural shift with respect to gay people, have been engaged in what can truly be called enculturation. They may, that is, have been effecting a development appropriate to their own culture, though not necessarily to any other. But they may, on the other hand, have been duped by the *Zeitgeist.* Cultural multiplicity is a fact. From that fact it does not follow that every culture, or every aspect of any culture, is just as good as every other.

Sooner or later, therefore, a response to the questions Windsor pointedly raises will have to enter the debate it pointedly avoids – the debate about the morality of sexual intimacy between two women or two men. To put the matter starkly, if the correct moral description of a person living in a same–gender union is "unrepentant sinner," then ECUSA has erred, and what it has to apologize for is not just a breach of etiquette, however painful, but connivance in wrongdoing. On whether that description *is* correct, the Lambeth Commission kept deliberate silence; but its Report plainly lays on ECUSA the burden of proof that some other description would be better. Implicit in that church's actions was an ethical judgment that could be responsibly acted on only if it had been shown to have a convincing theological justification. The Lambeth Commission has said, in effect: "We are willing to suspend judgment on the substantive ethical issue, which does not fall within our remit, but we do insist that it ought to have been settled before any action was taken, and that before any further action is taken a theologically sound argument for taking it will have to be produced."

Now, as the Commission must have been aware, there is no dearth of theological arguments to support the judgment that same–gender unions, as such, do not merit the condemnation that Christianity has traditionally laid on them. Such arguments have been piling up for years. Presumably they influenced, directly or indirectly, the deliberation and discernment of those responsible for the actions now at issue. On the other hand, not only are the available arguments many: they are bewilderingly various. If they all point in the general direction of revising what has long been the church's stated teaching on gay sex, still they point in different ways, and on different grounds. The variety is no greater than it is with any other issue in theological ethics, but it is symptomatic of a serious problem that affects every aspect of theology. There simply is not, at present, a generally accepted method or mode of proceeding. Theologians do not agree on what constitutes a sound theological argument and moral theologians in particular do not agree on how to arrive at sound judgments of moral value.

Perhaps that is why Windsor's request for yet another argument comes with a methodological proviso of its own. Having stated three criteria for ascertaining the legitimacy of Christian theological and doctrinal development, the Report stipulates that the same three are to be employed in ECUSA's defense of same–gender unions (paras 135, 141). The criteria are scripture, tradition, and reason – the "three–legged stool" that has come to be regarded as particularly

Anglican. Short of offering its own disquisition on theological method, appealing to this conventional triad was probably the best that Windsor could do. What it does not do is explain how the three criteria are related, or how all of them, together, are to be applied. The admirable paragraphs on scripture, its authority, and its interpretation do ask the methodologically relevant question of what scripture is *for*, and the answer given – that scripture is for mission, for making the Paschal mystery operative in the world (para 55) – does ground the possibility of what Windsor calls a re–evaluation of scripture in use, scripture as means to an end, scripture as requiring to be read, marked, learned, and inwardly digested (para 61). But to actualize this possibility by presenting its own re–evaluation was more than the Commission could attempt. Among the issues it would have had to take up is this very basic one: Granted that the criteriological stool does have other legs, what part does "reason" in particular – human intelligence in act, raising and answering questions – play in Christian moral theology, in relation to the Bible?

In some sense that was the issue which gave rise to a distinctively Anglican theology at the time of the Elizabethan settlement. Granted that scripture is *for* something, that it functions as a means, the next question is whether its function is specific or general. For Hooker, and the Anglican tradition that followed his lead, scripture has a specific function, which, stated in its own words, is to make us wise unto salvation. As far as attaining that supernatural end is concerned, it containeth all things necessary. This classically Anglican position stood, and stands, opposed to the position that scripture has a general function, that it bears on every end, that it makes us wise in all things, so that beyond what is scripturally warranted we dare not venture in thought, word, or deed. Such was, and is, the Puritan position. Its corollary is that reason can in no way supplement or correct the all–sufficient guidance that scripture provides. The stool has just one leg.

By no means is this a historical issue only. The scripturalism of the Puritans, to which Hooker provided a more reasonable alternative, has had its proponents ever since. In the middle of the twentieth century a massive effort to reinstate it began in Europe, the effects of which are still being felt. They can be felt strongly, brought to bear on the question at hand, in the "St Andrew's Day Statement" (SADS). Both the form and the content of this document rest on a straightforward precept: no constructing allowed. Specifically, what it is to be human, and what it is to be oneself in particular, are not to be grasped by intelligent inquiry and insight with respect to experience. The exercise of reason pertains merely to "phenomena," appearances, and never gets beyond them. Human being, general and particular, *really* exists only in Christ. Only in Christ, therefore, can it be known. Accordingly, knowing it is no achievement of human intellectual reasoning; that is, no "construction." It is given. Human nature comes to be known only inasmuch as Christ's Spirit "directs us in the task of understanding *all* human life and experience through the Scriptures."[1] How we are to think about sexual desires and activities falls under this rule, like everything else. These too are but phenomena. In the case of "homosexual" persons, so called, they are to be construed under the general heading of idolatry (following Romans 1) and regulated in either of two categories, marriage or "singleness" (following 1 Corinthians 7). It is thus a fairly simple matter to settle the moral and ontological status of what gay people might have thought was their sexuality. Having settled it in accordance with scripture, the church can go on to learn from other lines of inquiry. Anything it learns, however, will be subject to correction that brings it into line with human nature as given in Christ—that is, in the gospel—that is, in the Bible—that is, in letters written by Paul, mostly. For those who understand themselves as gay, the good news is that they are not: they are human beings, male

---

1 "An Examination of the Theological Principles Affecting the Homosexuality Debate" (St. Andrew's Day Statement), pp. 5–11 in *The Way Forward? Christian Voices on Homosexuality and the Church* (ed), Timothy Bradshaw (London: SCM Press, 2nd ed., 2003); quotation at p. 6; emphasis added.

and female, and like everyone else they are called to friendship in singleness if not in marriage.

Thus says SADS. One of its authors has complained that although its purpose was to initiate fruitful discussion and debate, no shred of answer has been forthcoming from the side of those who disagree with its conclusions. But SADS really allows of only two responses: take it or leave it. As the same author acknowledged, it is a confessional document. Like Karl Barth's Barmen Declaration, to which its resemblance is probably deliberate, SADS asks no questions and leaves none open. Its content is likewise Barthian, modeled fairly closely on a chapter of the *Church Dogmatics*.[2] If this is an indication of the doctrinal horizon within which the discourse of SADS has its meaning, we should ask whether it is necessary to stand within that horizon in order to have any conversation at all with the statement's authors. If so, we should ask further whether the conversation depends on holding as true such doctrines as that the created universe has neither goodness nor intelligibility of its own, that human action involves no initiative of its own, that the human mind discovers nothing real on its own, that it apprehends realities (as contrasted with phenomena) only as a passive receiver of divine speech, that this receiving happens in and as commentary on a set of texts, the Bible, and that these texts are somehow the same Word of God who was incarnate in Jesus.

Otherwise stated, my point is that what SADS has to say about gay sex is the tip of an iceberg. Christian ethical discourse has, or ought to have, theological underpinnings, as Windsor rightly maintains. But what is true of particular ethical questions (Is such–and–such to be done?) is no less true of meta–ethical questions (How do we arrive at judgment as to whether such–and–such is to be done?). They too depend for their answers on the questioner's theological commitments. Since theology aims at making intelligent statements about God and

---

2 See Karl Barth, *Church Dogmatics* III.2, ch. 10, "The Creature," esp. §44 on "Phenomena of the Human."

about all things in their relations to God, how it is possible to know what those relations are and what they are meant to be is a question of enormous importance. The answer I have called the Puritan answer, of which I take SADS to be a fair specimen, is that we are *told* what these relations are, all of them, so that we have only to listen. The answer I take to be more centrally Anglican, as represented by the likes of Hooker, Sanderson, and Taylor, is different, for reasons mentioned a moment ago. We read, mark, learn, and inwardly digest what we are told in scripture inasmuch as it concerns our *ultimate* end, the salvation through faith in Christ Jesus that God wills for all. Without being told, we could not even know this "supernatural" end exists, because it completely surpasses every capacity we have as humans. But the ultimate end is not the only end. There are others. There are "natural" human goods that we do have the capacity to bring into being. To bring them into being, we have to discover what they are, and that too we are capable of doing. It belongs to the constitution of human nature to apprehend the human goods that pertain to this present life, by exercising human intelligence. Because this exercise is intrinsic to actualizing the goods apprehended, intelligent deliberation and rational judgment are constituents of right decisions about what is to be done. Thus, reason has something to do in the sphere of ethical conduct, beyond attending to an authoritative text. There is an ordered universe of concrete beings to be understood, within which there are reasonable judgments to be made by beings who, being rational by nature, have the responsibility of ordering their own doings.

The position I have just pointed to belongs to the tradition commonly if misleadingly called "natural law" ethics. However it is named, its premise is simply that what humans are good for and what is good for humans can be humanly known, and that to know them is what God gave humans reason for. To say there is such a thing as natural law is to say, with Hooker, that all things participate in the eternal law which is the intelligence of God. For humans, that participation consists partly in discovering their own participation, their place and duty in the order God appoints by creating it. In so doing, they are fulfilling their natural end, which is to be and to act intelligently and reasonably. As a criterion, then—one leg of a stool—reason plays its part by shedding light on whatever other ends there are to choose between. We choose responsibly in so far as we understand the nature of what there is to be chosen.

My suggestion, then, is that in meeting Windsor's request for "reasoned reflection" on the ethical aspect of the innovations that sparked the current firestorm, it would be best to begin with description, not prescription. Understanding the good about which there are decisions to be made comes before judging what it would be good to decide. In this regard it might be recalled that nearly thirty years have passed since a Lambeth Conference recommended a Communion–wide study of sexuality. The recommendation has yet to be acted on. There are, of course, those who maintain that "more study" is just a cloak for smuggling in yet more unapproved change. It remains that unless Anglicans are willing to sell their birthright for a mess of juridical pottage, decisions about their common life will have to rely on whatever common meaning they can achieve. And common meaning cannot be achieved otherwise than by raising and answering questions.

There are, I think, three broad questions which it would be well to answer as fully and dispassionately as possible before any attempt is made to pass judgment, one way or the other, on same–gender unions and the persons who have chosen to live in them. To answer these questions adequately is too much for one essay or one author. They call for collaboration. But after listing them I will add some comments by way of clarification. They are:

(1) What good is sex?

(2) What good is celibacy?

(3) What difference does gender make?

What good is sex?

Anything that is good is concrete. It actually exists or can exist, actually happens or can happen. Now sex, as the word is used today and is being used here, is something that happens. People "have sex." Exactly *what* happens when they have it is not at all a superfluous question. Quite a lot of ethical and theological discourse about sex is carried on in colorless abstractions and squeamish circumlocutions, as though it can be taken for granted that everyone already understands all there is to be understood. Perhaps they do understand it; but even so, what is understood had best be made explicit. Having sex, it would seem, consists in certain actions and responses that involve human bodies and in particular certain bodily organs. True enough. But for one thing, these perspicuous events are many and various. For another, what happens when they are happening does not happen to organs or organisms without happening to persons. There are mental, emotional, and psychological dimensions as well as physiological. And for a third, what happens does not consist in discrete, isolated occurrences. Every instance of sexual activity belongs to, and in part constitutes, a history – the narrative trajectory of becoming that defines the character and identity of a concrete human being in his or her relations with other human beings and their lived world.

All this, in its enormous variety and complexity, is "what happens" in, as, and because of having sex. It all needs to be articulated. To ask what good sex is or can be is to ask about what, as a matter of ascertainable fact – biological, psychological, intersubjective, developmental, social, historical fact – sex *does*. If it is good to have sex, sometimes anyhow, the value lies in some intelligible trend or pattern or vector of human becoming, some order or orders for which there is empirical evidence. It follows that if the question of what sex is good for is to be answered intelligently, by appealing to reason, all the available evidence will have to be taken into account. Deciding in advance what does and does not pertain to the "finality" of sex, its for–the–sake–of, is either prejudice or begging the question. Either way, it is unreasonable.

What good is celibacy?

In so far as sexual events are not automatic reflexes, they may be both subjectively desirable and objectively possible, without becoming actual. Something else happens instead, because someone has chosen it as preferable. Celibacy may be defined as a consistent series of such choices not to engage in sex. Christian tradition has consistently maintained that a way of life characterized by such a series of choices is itself choiceworthy, and has sometimes added that it is more choiceworthy than any alternative. *Why* celibacy is good, and exactly what it is good for, are questions worth asking, because any answer will both imply and be implied by judgments as to the value of sex.

On the one hand, celibacy might be good *despite* the activities it omits and the developments it precludes. In that case, its value would be analogous to that of other ascetic practices, like fasting. On the other hand, it might be good *because* of what it omits and precludes. In that case, some negative judgment is at least implicitly operative, which ought to be made explicit and grounded, if it can be, in evidence. This might be a judgment to the effect that nothing sex is good for outweighs the good of abstaining from it altogether. Such judgments have been pronounced by Protestants, Catholics, and Anglicans throughout the church's history, for reasons that should not be unquestioningly dismissed or unquestioningly accepted. Alternatively, the judgment that celibacy is good because of what it does not involve might regard, not everything that counts as sex, but particular directions that having sex in particular ways can take in particular circumstances. The good of celibacy would then be conditioned by those ways and circumstances, whatever they are. Specifying them, and explaining why they make it valuable to prevent from happening something that happens in having sex, is a further aspect of understanding what sex is good for.

What difference does gender make?

All three questions I am posing aim at an intelligent, reasonable account of sex as a natural human good. The first asks about sex as something that human persons do; the second, about sex as something that human persons may refuse to do. The third asks about the persons who do it. They are either male or female. How does that distinction affect what sex is good for?

As with the first question, there are obvious answers available. As with the first question, the obvious answers are not correct by reason of being obvious. They may be true, as far as they go, yet incomplete or simplistic. As it would be worthwhile to specify what having sex does in all its complexity, so too it would be worthwhile to specify exactly what distinction is meant when the terms "male" and "female" are contrasted. No one doubts that women and men differ with respect to their chromosomes, their hormones, their anatomy, and their physiology. It is a further question how far these differences are correlated with different psychological patterns, different affectivities, different ways of knowing and loving, different desires and expectations in regard to personal relationships and social roles.

That further question is of course a matter of debate – a debate, it needs to be remembered, that has been inaugurated, widened, and deepened primarily by women. Theirs has been the project of setting out to understand what it is to be a woman, not on *a priori* grounds, but by raising and answering questions about themselves, their own bodies and feelings, their own mentalities and spiritualities. As a result, it is more and more widely recognized, at least in the "global North," that gender issues are not adequately addressed so long as only men address them. Similarly, it would seem that a reasonable approach to sexuality issues – an approach which does not beg the question of what sex is and does – would do well to take account of what in fact happens when the otherness of sexual partners does not include the biological otherness of anatomical parts and their physiological operations. In other words, it would be reasonable to acquire some understanding of gay sex, before determining what difference it makes whether sexual partners are or are not persons of the same gender.

No doubt, it makes *some* difference. Same–gender unions are not interchangeable with mixed–gender unions. But then, not all mixed–gender unions are interchangeable either. Any such union, any marriage in the traditional sense of the word, is a multifaceted compound. To ask the third of my three questions in a serious, empirical way would include asking which facets depend on the communion – the common meaning – of two entire persons, and which of them depend only or also on the interaction of differently gendered organic bodies. That question is ruled out in advance when everything that makes for what the American Prayer Book calls "union ... in heart, body, and mind" is conflated under the catch–all term "complementarity." A more concrete approach would begin from the fact that not all the ways in which sex can happen are possible for two women or two men. Nor, for that matter, are all of them possible for a man and a woman. How do these differences affect what having sex does?

At this point, but perhaps not before, it becomes appropriate to turn to the characteristic of same–gender unions, male or female, that tends to pre–empt all others. No such union, in the nature of things, is constituted by the act that is the most common means to the end of conception. The absence of what is referred to in some discussions as PIV, penis–in–vagina intercourse, presumably affects the character and quality of those unions. How, exactly, does it affect them? What difference does it make? To be sure, PIV can be constitutive of human goods that are eminently choiceworthy. But it has never been a sufficient condition of human reproduction, and it is certainly not a sufficient condition of any two–in–one–flesh unity, or any mutual self–donation, that is humanly valuable. Is it nevertheless a *necessary* condition of such reciprocity – a *sine qua non* of the Two that in Chesterton's phrase is not twice one, but ten thousand times one? Or are there other means, specifically sexual means, to that beautiful end?

If there are other means, then by the canons of reason that I have been invoking all along, there will be evidence in same–gender unions for what is usually called the "unitive" good of sex. That good is historical. It takes time. If it is to flourish, it needs the support of other persons – neighbors, families, communities, society at large. Not only has such support been withheld (to say the least) in the case of gay couples, but the evidence which, in spite of that, their unions might have provided has been for the most part hidden, or overlooked, or ignored. Only lately has it started to become public. "Reasoned reflection" on sexual ethics cannot responsibly leave it out of account. In this regard, if no other, it is appropriate that Windsor's request for a reasoned statement on same–gender unions is directed to Anglicans in America, where there is at least some possibility of finding out what good sex can be for two people of the same gender, when at least some of the legal and cultural restrictions on the historical working–out of that good are loosened.

My three questions have one premise. Some people find themselves to be gay. Whether it is possible for them to make something good of what they find is a matter of fact. It can be settled by an appeal to reason, weighing the evidence for what actually happens. As will be evident, my own notion of what would be settled is that Lambeth 1998 was in error when it set before gay people two possibilities and two only – sin and celibacy. There may be excellent reasons for choosing the celibate life, and avoiding sin may be one of them. But on the position I have argued for, "incompatibility with scripture" is not enough to warrant assigning the terrible name of sin to everything gay people do inasmuch as they are gay. Sin is a theological term. It refers to what offends God. But "God is not offended by us," as Thomas Aquinas declared, "except by what we do against our own good."[3] If the sex gay people have does, always and inevitably, go against the human good, if it is by its very nature the abomination that the biblical writers, Paul included, thought it was, let the evidence be produced that confirms their judgment. Absent such evidence, it is a judgment that can and

---

3 *Summa contra Gentiles*, III, §122.

perhaps should be set aside, as Christians have done with any number of biblical prohibitions and condemnations.

The sort of argument my three questions envision, however, would be more positive. It would endeavor to show that persons living in same–gender unions are not necessarily setting themselves *against* their own good or anyone else's; but it would do this because it would show – what is far more important – that what sex is good for can be effected by two women or two men no less really and concretely than it can by a man and a woman. And the core of the argument that this can happen would be that, as a matter of fact, it does.

8

NO EASY PATHS:
WAS TROLLOPE RIGHT?

Rowan A. Greer

In chapter 21 of *Barchester Towers*, Anthony Trollope recounts a conversation between Mr. Arabin, who has narrowly escaped the fate of being an Oxford Apostle, and his wife–to–be, Eleanor Bold. Eleanor rebukes Arabin for the bitterness of ecclesiastical wars about trifles, but Arabin points out that quarrels among neighbors are always bitter. "What combatants are ever so eager as two brothers?" He continues by arguing that the only way to avoid such contentions would be "that of acknowledging a common head of our church, whose word on all points of doctrine shall be authoritative." He confesses that such a dream has been almost irresistible to him, but delivers his considered opinion by saying: "Had it pleased God to vouchsafe to us such a church our path would have been easy. But easy paths have not been thought good for us." In his Foreword to the Windsor Report, Archbishop Eames suggests that the present controversy regarding homosexuality "has on occasion introduced a degree of harshness and a lack of charity which is new to Anglicanism" (5). Perhaps I may be forgiven for wondering whether this is true, and for remembering Jeremy Taylor's lament for times in which faith is made to cut the throat of charity.[1] More to the

---

1 Jeremy Taylor, *The Great Exemplar: Discourse VII Of Faith*, Section 12 (first published 1649) from *Jeremy Taylor: Selected Works*, Classics of Western Spirituality, (ed) Thomas K. Carroll (New York: Paulist Press, 1990), p. 286.

point, despite my recognition that the Lambeth Commission in issuing the Windsor Report has completed a difficult, if not a thankless task, I wonder whether they have not sought an easy path.

The Report attempts to deal with the present controversy without directly addressing the controversial issue itself (26, 43). It is possible to find fault with this decision, but I should prefer to respect it for several reasons. Since the Report and its recommendations are purely advisory and since the Commission has attempted to honor widely differing views, it seems to me reasonable to raise the prior question of how the Anglican Communion can address controversy. Archbishop Eames insists that the Report is "not a judgment," but "part of a process" (6). We are asked to reflect upon the question of what communion means for Anglicans. In what follows, I wish to accept that implied invitation and to focus attention on the Report's articulation of a theoretical understanding of communion, including the proposed Anglican covenant appended to the Report. My own thinking about the issues revolving around human sexuality is far too confused to be helpful. I hold only two opinions with confidence. First, what could be called the traditional view no longer compels widespread assent, not only with respect to homosexuality, but also in reference to issues such as the remarriage of divorced persons, heterosexual cohabitation outside marriage, and childless marriages of those capable of bearing children. It does not seem to me reasonable to treat the gay issue in isolation from other aspects of human sexuality. Second, granted that moral norms should not be severed from doctrinal considerations, I find it difficult to think of them as quite the same, and remain unconvinced that a particular view of human sexuality must be held necessary to salvation.

The Bible and its authority

With this apology – or better this confession of my incompetence to address the underlying controversy – let me turn to the Report's theoretical understanding of communion by considering, first, what it says about scripture and the authority of the Bible. The opening five sections of the document have the heading: "The communion we have been given in Christ: Biblical foundations." Passages from Ephesians and 1 Corinthians undergird the discussion, and it is possible to examine the use made of Paul's advice to the "weak" and the "strong" (Romans 14–15, 1 Corinthians 8–10) elsewhere in the Report (36, 87, 92). The Report recognizes that these Pauline passages, which do affirm the unity of God's people in Christ, nonetheless celebrate "the diversity within that unity." What is not entirely clear is whether diversity, if it is to build up the body of Christ in love, can be an agreement to disagree. The Report does appear to recognize that Ephesians treats unity in Christ as "an *anticipatory* sign of God's healing and restorative future for the world" (2) and, consequently, as imperfect in this life. But it is possible to go further in insisting that our present unity in Christ cannot be identified with the eschatological unity that is our hope. In Galatians 3:28, Paul repeats what seems to be a baptismal tradition: "There is no longer Jew or Greek, there is no longer slave or free, there is no longer male and female; for all of you are one in Christ Jesus." It is instructive to examine Paul's letters in order to understand *how* he supposes these divisions disappear for those baptized into Christ. Outwardly the divisions almost certainly remain. The "gospel for the circumcision" (Galatians 2:7–8) probably implies that Jewish Christians may continue to be law–observant. Paul returns the runaway slave Onesimus to Philemon. The Corinthians are wrong to suppose that marriage has been abolished, though Paul's specific advice is sometimes his own, sometimes the Lord's (1 Corinthians 7). At any rate marriage remains one way of anticipating the age to come, when there will no longer be marrying or giving in marriage (Mark 12:25). The outward divisions, then, remain; but they no longer have any final say. The point I wish to make is that I should not want to dispense with what can be called Paul's "eschatological reservation." However much Christian unity in the present must point towards and be informed by the Christian hope, it necessarily remains imperfect. Does the Report sufficiently recognize this?

The opening section of the Report presupposes scriptural authority, and we are told that the "Anglican Communion has always declared that its supreme authority is scripture" (42, cf. 70). But it is only later (53–62) that we find an extended discussion of what this means. Section 53 runs the risk of suggesting that Anglicans have been consistent in their understanding of scripture's "supreme authority" and that even "the early Anglican reformers" insisted on "the importance of the Bible and the Fathers" as "part of their appeal to ancient undivided Christian faith and life." I find myself doubtful of these claims, not least because they seem to me to reflect Restoration Anglicanism and what could be called a high church perspective. To speak of the supreme authority of scripture in early Anglicanism it is necessary to consider the sixth Article of Religion:[2] "Holy Scripture containeth all things necessary to salvation: so that whatsoever is not read therein, nor may be proved thereby, is not to be required of any man, that it should be believed as an article of the Faith, or be thought requisite or necessary to salvation." The distinction made by the article is one between what is necessary or essential and what is a matter of indifference (the *adiaphora*), and it resembles the distinction Luther makes in order to secure the perspicuity of scripture, that is, its sufficiency to reveal the gospel to the simplest reader. The Windsor Report recognizes this distinction, even though it reinterprets it as one between essential and non–essential matters (36–37, 87–95). But what is quite surprizing is that it does not associate the idea with scripture. It does, however, point out that the real difficulty has to do with *how* we are to make the distinction. The early Anglican divines by no means resolve the problem, but their concern can be understood as a refusal to replace an ecclesiastical infallibility with a scriptural one. Hooker, for example, in the *Laws of Ecclesiastical Polity* speaks of two opposite views.[3] Rome

---

2 The text is printed in the 1979 *American Prayer Book* under the rubric "Historical Documents." See p. 868.
3 References are given in the text by book, chapter, and section. See *The Folger Library Edition of the Works of Richard Hooker*, (ed) W. Speed Hill. Vol. 1, *Of the Laws of Ecclesiastical Polity*, Books I to IV; Vol. 2, Book V (Cambridge, Mass., and London: Harvard University Press, 1977).

regards scripture as insufficient, whereas his Puritan opponents make the mistake of assuming the Bible is omnicompetent (II.8.7). The sufficiency of scripture is restricted to its purpose, namely, to reveal what is necessary to salvation.

Granted this basic point, we find in the reformers both a reluctance to supply any catalogue of necessary beliefs or norms, and an ambiguity as to whether what is necessary is plainly revealed in scripture or must be deduced and proved from it. In the earlier books of the *Laws*, Hooker's emphasis is upon the necessity of making deductions from scripture; and the primary tool for doing so is reason, "a necessary instrument, without which we could not reape by the scriptures perfection, that fruite and benefit which it yieldeth" (III.8.10). Later, however, he argues that the plain passages in scripture are so sufficient that even children can understand what is "plaine and easie" without an interpreter. "Scripture therefore is not so harde but that the onlie readinge thereof may give life unto willinge hearers" (V.22.14).

Bishop Joseph Hall (1574–1656) largely identifies what is necessary with the plain passages in scripture. Following Gregory the Great, he argues that there are shallows in scripture where even lambs can wade and great deeps where only elephants can swim. In all essential matters, scripture explains itself. Worrying about the hard passages is "a disease in our appetite, when we have wholesome provision laid before us, to nauseate all good dishes; and to long for mushrooms, whereof some are venemous, all unwholesome."[4] William Chillingworth (1602–44) in *The Religion of Protestants, A Safe Way of Salvation*, published in 1638, agrees with Hall about the plain passages, but makes explicit Hall's failure to say what they are by refusing to give a list. In his view, it suffices that there are such passages, which may differ somewhat from person to person. Yet, taken together, the plain passages secure Christian concord. All religious controversies concern matters of

---

4 Joseph Hall, *Christian Moderation*, Book 2, Rule 4, (ed) Josiah Pratt (London: 1808), Vol. 7, p. 444 (first published 1639). For the tag from Gregory the Great, see *Select Thoughts* XLIV (Pratt, Vol. 6, pp. 270–1) and *The Devout Soul* 4.2 (Pratt, Vol. 7, p. 505).

indifference and need not be resolved. There is concord at one level and a tolerant liberty at another.[5]

Much more would need to be said, but my argument is that even in early Anglicanism it is impossible to find any one clear understanding of biblical authority. There are differing views not only about what is necessary to salvation, but also concerning the relation of practice to belief and the method to be employed in interpreting scripture. For this reason, I am uncomfortable with the Report's appeal to that shibboleth of contemporary Anglicanism, "scripture, tradition, and reason" (53, 141–42, and Article 4 of the proposed covenant). It seems to me that Hooker treats tradition positively only as the persuasive work of the church that leads people to scripture. Induced to consult the Bible, they will find its authority (III.8.13–15). Negatively, tradition cannot be lightly abandoned despite the fact that it has no authority apart from scripture. Jeremy Taylor, on the other hand, argues that the Apostles' Creed is what enables us to discern what is necessary in scripture.[6]

Tradition, then, can mean a number of different things. If we distinguish the apostolic tradition from the ongoing tradition of the church, what would we mean by "apostolic"? Indeed, was there ever such a thing as the ancient undivided church? "Reason" is an even more slippery term. Are we to think of it in Thomistic categories? Or is reason some innate principle as the Cambridge Platonists presumed? Or is reason a faculty of judgment by which we separate true from false and good from evil? Even if it is the case that the early Anglican divines endorsed the triple cord, it is hard for me to see that they do so in any clear or consistent way.

If section 53 of the Report arguably raises more questions than it solves, and runs the risk of thinking of Anglicanism as a more unified

---

5 I have used the text printed in London by Thomas Tegg in 1845. See, e.g., 2.5 (pp. 88–89), 2.85 (p. 135), 2.104 (p. 149), 3.81 (pp. 267–8), and 4.84 (p. 325).
6 Jeremy Taylor, *A Discourse of the Liberty of Prophesying* (London: 1836; first published 1647), Section XVI, pp. 304–5.

phenomenon than seems to me realistic historically, the sections that follow articulate a persuasive view that appears widely held in contemporary Anglicanism. I suspect that this account reflects two developments that can be discerned in Coleridge's *Confessions of an Inquiring Spirit* (published posthumously in 1840) and in F. D. Maurice's review of Newman's *Essay on Development* (in *The Letter to the Hebrews*, published in 1846) and his *Kingdom of Christ*. The first of these developments is the repudiation of any view of the verbal inerrancy of scripture. For Coleridge such a view makes God a ventriloquist; it "petrifies" scripture and turns the Bible's "glorious *panharmonicon*" into "a colossal Memnon's head, a hollow passage for a voice, a voice that mocks the voices of many men, and speaks in their name."[7] Maurice treats the Bible as "the testimony of different witnesses" to the revelation of the Kingdom of Christ. The idea of dictation substitutes the Bible for the living God and is, consequently, a form of idolatry.[8] It would be possible to trace this conviction as it appears in the writings of Charles Gore and William Temple. The Bible becomes the inspired response to revelation, but the response is a human one and not simply identified with the revelation. Similarly, the Windsor Report concludes that the authority of scripture "must be regarded as a shorthand, and a potentially misleading one at that, for the longer and more complex notion of "the authority of the triune God, *exercised through* scripture'" (54).

The other theme found in the thought of Coleridge and Maurice is the insistence that the Bible is the church's book. The Report underlines the theme by saying that the New Testament was not intended to be "a repository of various suggestions for developing one's private spirituality, but as the collection of books through which the Spirit who was working so powerfully through the apostles would

---

7 Samuel Taylor Coleridge, *Confessions of an Inquiring Spirit*, Letter III, (ed) H. StJ. Hart (London: Adam & Charles Black, 1956), pp. 52–3.
8 F. D. Maurice, *The Kingdom of Christ*, Part II, Chap. IV, Section VI (London: Macmillan & Co., 1891; first published 1838), Vol. 2, p. 195.

develop and continue that work in the churches" (56). Since it belongs to the church, "the authoritative teaching of scripture cannot be left to academic researchers, vital though they are" (58). The historical critics have an important role to play, since they can prevent us from hearing in scripture "simply the echo of our own voices ... or the memory of earlier Christian interpretations" (59). What seems implied is that historical criticism can go only so far in interpreting the Bible for the church. Perhaps the point could be made by suggesting that the umpire ought not to play the game. The church reads scripture, not as evidence for building up historical reconstructions, but as testimony to God's revelatory dispensations with their culmination in Christ. This kind of reading discerns the work of the Spirit and enables the church to draw "fresh strength from God for mission and holiness. This, rather than a quasi–legal process of "appeal," is the primary and dynamic context within which the shorthand phrase "authority of scripture" finds its deepest meaning" (56).

Part of what the Report means by insisting upon scripture as the church's book concerns the importance of listening to scripture together. Two common approaches are insufficient. "We can no longer be content to drop random texts into arguments ... or indeed to sweep away sections of the New Testament as irrelevant to today's world" (61). The ghost of the underlying controversy may be hovering behind this sentence in the Report. Is the implication that those opposed to the gay issues appeal to proof texts alone, while those who favor them cross out passages in scripture on the grounds that they are historically conditioned? In any case, the Report's judgment does make sense. Both the proof texts and the historical considerations must be placed in larger theological constructions of the biblical message. If I am correct in discerning the implication of what the Report says, neither side in the controversy has an easy task. The "liberals" cannot simply remove the proof texts, nor can the "conservatives" deny that historical considerations have played a role in the church's interpretation of scripture. No one any longer would suppose that slaves must obey their masters (Ephesians 6:5–8, Colossians 3:22–25, 1 Peter 2:18). Moreover, Christ's words about divorce in the gospels are obviously no longer binding upon Christians in their strict sense. Despite the Report's appeal to study scripture together, it is by no means clear that this will resolve religious controversies.

Indeed, it is possible to suggest that the Report at certain places recognizes that the primary function of scripture is not to resolve controversies. In the passage, I have cited above, the Report takes a dim view of "a quasi–legal process of 'appeal'" (56), and in the preceding section it insists that "the purpose of scripture is not simply to supply true information, nor merely to act as a court of appeal" (55). In this regard, I should like to call attention to an essay by Anthony Harvey, included in the Church of England Doctrine Commission Report of 1981 (*Believing in the Church*) and entitled "Attending to Scripture." Harvey's argument depends in part upon the idea of faith as a journey requiring points of reference and upon the Christian story found in scripture as the chief of those points, on the grounds that assent to scripture is what gives the church its identity. My summary does not do justice to Harvey's essay, but it is one of his conclusions that interests me. If my reading is at all correct, he feels obliged to recognize that while the basic function of scripture is to create a story–formed community, it inevitably takes on the role of an arbiter of religious controversy. The two examples Harvey gives are "the ethics of homosexual behaviour" and "the alleged 'politicizing' of the gospel."

But his conclusion is that the quest for some doctrinal standard by which to resolve a dispute "will prove elusive." Different "parties to the discussion, though they all recognize the authority of Scripture and (often to a lesser extent) the tradition of the Church, nevertheless each regard a different passage of Scripture or aspect of the tradition as carrying decisive weight with regard to the question at issue."[9] What

---

9 Anthony Harvey, "Attending to Scripture," Essay 2 in *Believing in the Church: The Corporate Nature of Faith*, A Report by the Doctrine Commission of the Church of England (Wilton, Conn.: Morehouse–Barlow, 1982; first published by London: SPCK, 1981), pp. 38–9.

matters, however, is not the resolution of controversy, but the corporate wrestling with the meaning of the Christian story. In terms of the basic thesis of *Believing in the Church*, the church needs both the "boundary–marking" people who call attention to the past and the "sign–post" people who are concerned with moving towards the future.

Let me try to sum up what I have been trying to say about the Report's assessment of scripture and its authority. First, it seems to me that more emphasis needs to be placed upon what I take to be the scriptural recognition that perfected unity belongs firmly in the age to come, and that the present unity of Christians will always be flawed. Second, I do not think it possible to speak of *the* Anglican view of scriptural authority, whether we are to think of that historically or with reference to contemporary attitudes. Third, I am attracted by the Report's insistence upon the Bible as testimony to revelation and as the church's book; and I agree with what I take to be its implication that scripture is not primarily an arbiter of religious controversy. Nevertheless, it is difficult not to draw the conclusion that the Report takes this secondary function quite seriously and is looking for an easy path and a way of resolving controversy.

The three points I want to make all drive in the direction of the more difficult path. I remain convinced that the repudiation of infallibility is characteristic of Anglicanism and that this carries with it the conclusion that all human authority is fallible. To argue that the Report seeks an easy path, then, is to argue that it puts the Anglican Communion on a slippery slope that would give it a novel character. This argument can be made more clearly by turning to what the Report says about polity and to what it proposes as an Anglican covenant.

Polity and the Anglican Communion
While each of the 38 churches in the Anglican Communion has its own canons and judicial procedures, what binds them together is at present purely consensual in character, despite the attempts described in the Report to discern "an unwritten *jus commune* of the worldwide Anglican

Communion" (113–15). The Report appeals to the description of "Anglican life in communion" given by the Anglican Congress of 1963 as "mutual interdependence and responsibility in the Body of Christ" (8). [Is there any significance in the fact that the Report reverses the order of the two nouns?] Interdependence means "mutual love and care for one another," and it can involve "standing together" and acting "in solidarity" in Christian mission (9). The Report calls attention to "Ten Principles of Partnership," a document based on the Report of the Anglican Congress (Appendix 3.5). The ten principles clearly articulate the consensual character of partnership in mission. They include reference to "respect for the authority of the local church" (1), "common commitment, mutual trust, confession and forgiveness" (2), "willingness to learn from one another" (5), and raising "creative and loving challenges that could lead to positive re-evaluation of long held traditions and assumptions" (6). The Report elsewhere speaks of "the communion we enjoy as Anglicans" as a "covenantal affection" and "a fellowship of churches" (48). This fellowship includes "a proper and welcome diversity," but one limited "by truth and charity" (85–86). What all this means is that the Anglican Communion is, at least in principle, "*a relationship of trust*" (40).

The consensual character of what unites the member churches in communion with one another does imply certain obligations. The decisions of a particular church are not necessarily purely local ones, but can have an impact on the Communion as a whole (24, 28). Needless to say, the decision of the American church to consecrate a gay bishop and that of the Canadian Diocese of New Westminster to allow rites for same sex unions illustrate the point. Initially, however, the Report insists only upon the necessity of consultation with the wider Communion. It argues that this is what happened during the long debate concerning the ordination of women (12–21), but has failed to happen up till now concerning the issues surrounding homosexuality. It may be that the Report has overstated its case. It does point out that the 1978 Lambeth Conference merely responded to the fact that four of the member churches had already ordained women to the priesthood and eight others had accepted the ordination of women in principle (16). In any case, no argument about what has, or has not, been done needs to call into question the importance of consultation and dialogue if there is to be an Anglican Communion at all. This consideration obviously qualifies and puts limits on diversity and autonomy (71–86). While autonomy is "fundamental to Anglican polity" (72), it is "not the same thing as sovereignty and independence" (75), but must be understood as "autonomy–in–communion" (76) or as "freedom–in–relation" (80), in other words as interdependence.

The Report construes the institutional aspects of the Anglican Communion, specifically the "Instruments of Unity," as designed to foster interdependence; and it recognizes that none of them at present have canonical or juridical powers. Their authority is purely persuasive and advisory, but this does not mean they have no authority. We might distinguish *potestas* from *auctoritas*, and argue that authority must be persuasive and is effective because of the voluntary assent of those who accept it. Bishops represent "the focus of unity" for the Communion; they "represent the universal Church to the local and *vice versa*" (63–64, cf. 124). Up to a point, then, the Report endorses Cyprian's understanding of the episcopate as a unified entity shared equally by all the bishops. Such a view finds clearest expression in the "Presiding" bishop of the American church and the "Primus" of the Scottish Episcopal Church. But the Report at one point recognizes that even the Archbishop of Canterbury is merely *primus inter pares* (99, note 55). For Cyprian in the third century the unity of the church depended upon the *consensual* concord of bishops, all of whom were equal. And at present the Instruments of Unity honor this principle. The first Lambeth Conference in 1867 took place only with the proviso that it would have no "legislative power," but would be merely advisory (102). This has remained true to the present, however much Lambeth has taken on an increasing moral authority. The same sort of judgment applies to the Anglican Consultative Council, established in 1968, and to the

Primates' meeting, recommended by the 1978 Lambeth Conference. Thus, we can speak only of a "consultative and advisory authority" (104).

The obvious difficulty is that these consensual arrangements have never worked very well at an institutional level either within the member churches or in the Communion as a whole. One example is worth mentioning because it involves what I should regard as the real birth of the Anglican Communion at the first Lambeth Conference in 1867.[10] In 1853 Robert Gray, who had become the first Bishop of Capetown in 1847, established new bishoprics at Grahamstown and Natal. He temporarily resigned his see, but the letters patent that restored him to it also recognized him as the Metropolitan of Africa. Also, in 1853, John William Colenso became the first Bishop of Natal. Some eight years later Colenso began publishing his doubts about the inerrancy of scripture, and in 1863, Bishop Gray deposed him. Colenso appealed to the judicial committee of the Privy Council, which ruled in his favor in 1865, on the grounds that his appointment antedated the letters patent granting Bishop Gray Metropolitan authority. Nonetheless, the next year Bishop Gray excommunicated Colenso. There were various attempts to resolve the controversy, including an appeal to the Lambeth Conference of 1867. The result of all this was a schism not healed till the appointment of a new bishop for Natal and Colenso's death.

The Colenso case was not the chief reason for the first Lambeth Conference, but it illustrates the way in which the Anglican Communion gradually developed like a city expanding too rapidly and ahead of its infrastructure. To be sure, the Scottish Episcopal Church (1689), and the American Episcopal Church (1789), existed before the nineteenth century as independent Anglican churches, but they were historical accidents. By 1840 there were only ten colonial bishops, and in 1867 only 144, including those in Scotland and the United States. In

---

10 See Alan M. G. Stephenson, *Anglicanism and the Lambeth Conferences* (London: SPCK, 1978), pp. 38–43.

general, it is possible to conclude that the Anglican Communion is not only a fairly recent development, but also one that has evolved gradually in ways not easily foreseen. For this reason the Windsor Report's recommendations for further development of the consensual structures of the Anglican Communion make perfect sense to me. I say "consensual" advisedly, because I want to end by dissenting from one crucial aspect of its proposals.

The Report, however, does at one level seek merely to strengthen the consensual arrangements that have up till now characterized our Communion. "We do not favour the accumulation of formal power by the Instruments of Unity, or the establishment of any kind of central 'curia' for the Communion" (105). And in another place, even though it is in a dependent clause, the Report recognizes that "the paramount model must remain that of the voluntary association of churches bound together in their love of the Lord of the Church, in their discipleship and in their common inheritance" (120). Appealing to the evolving character of the Anglican Communion and to the recent Lambeth Conferences' recommendation for "enhanced responsibility" on the part of the Primates (65–66, 104), the Report urges that ecclesiastical procedures for consultation be clarified (cf. 34) and makes specific suggestions designed to clarify the relationship of the four Instruments of Unity to one another, as well as the proposal of a Council of Advice for the Archbishop of Canterbury (97–112, Appendix One). Up to this point, the Report appears to retain the present consensual arrangements and to argue merely for their clarification. We should still, of course, have no easy path.

It is at this point I should wish to register my strong dissent from the Report. My conclusion is that both in the Report, and in the proposed covenant, there are ideas and recommendations that seek for an easy path, that represent a contradiction of the Report's disavowal of "formal power" (105), and that would at the least put us on the slippery slope towards a canonical and juridical solution of our problems. With respect to the member churches, surely it is one thing to require consultation and dialogue, but quite another to prohibit unilateral action (74–78). This prohibition seems to me to hover in the background of much of what the Report says about autonomy and interdependence. Moreover, in its discussion of "reception" (68–69), the Report outlines a process of theological debate and discussion, formal action (by the member churches?), and increased consultation. This might imply that consultation need not require the member churches to refrain from controversial decisions. But the discussion continues by arguing that reception "only makes sense if the proposals concern matters on which the Church has not so far made up its mind" (69). Does this mean that the Church cannot change its mind? And has it not done so regarding matters like slavery, contraception, and the remarriage of divorced persons? My difficulty becomes still greater in considering the Report's recommendations regarding the Instruments of Unity. Granted that the text of the Report puts the words in the form of a question, it clearly envisages the possibility of granting the Lambeth Conference a "magisterium" and some authority "approaching" the capacity to make "binding decisions" (106). The role proposed for the Archbishop of Canterbury as "*the* significant focus of unity" looks a little like a contradiction of the Cyprianic view of the parity of bishops (109).

All my difficulties, and the basis for my dissent, come to a head with Appendix Two, the proposed Anglican covenant. It may be true that insofar as it "is largely descriptive of existing principles" the covenant would be "relatively uncontroversial" (118), and the Report rightly insists that it is no more than a proposal offered for discussion and debate. Indeed, the implicit references in the Covenant to the Lambeth Quadrilateral (Articles 1–3, 10–12), its advocacy of "listening" (Article 4) and "fostering ... a common mind" (Article 7), and other portions of the document would seem to endorse the consensual character of the Communion. Nevertheless, what I find astonishing is that "essential matters of common concern" (Articles 9, 16, 23, 26; cf. Report 82, 93–94) appear to have replaced matters essential to the church's faith and practice or matters necessary to salvation. The mechanism proposed for dealing with such matters is still more alarming to me. The Instruments of Unity would have power to designate "a Communion issue" (Article 23, even though in Article 24 they are said to "exercise no jurisdiction over autonomous member churches save to the limited extent provided in this Covenant and the laws of the member churches"). But the provisions of the covenant are scarcely "limited." The process described in Articles 26–27 ends by giving the Archbishop of Canterbury the power to "decide all questions of interpretation of this Covenant," and "the decision of the Archbishop shall be regarded as authoritative in the Communion until altered in like manner."

It is impossible for me to understand these provisions as anything other than canonical and juridical proposals. Presumably for the covenant to be effective, it would have to be endorsed canonically by the member churches. At best, it would be possible to conclude that the Report regards the consensual aspect of the Anglican Communion as necessary, but insufficient, for addressing controversy, and that it supposes the way out of this difficult path would be to take the easy road of juridical and canonical remedies. But it seems to me that such a road would undermine the consensual aspect of Anglicanism, and mark a radical departure from a tradition that has usually prized freedom sufficiently to be content with ambiguity and controversy. If trust lies at the heart of what binds us together, I fail to see how trust can be compelled. I end by siding with Trollope, and by remaining convinced that we have been given no easy paths.

9

"THY GRACE SHALL ALWAYS PREVENT ..."

Gareth Jones

Introduction

One tries to write objectively about the present state of the Anglican Communion. It has genuine vitality, spiritual depth, too, of the kind that inspires and nurtures. One should not despair entirely, whatever the present situation, when the Communion embraces so many people in very different places who are working to hold together something that has been meaningful for over one hundred years.

At the same time, however, there are such stories of hypocrisy and cowardice, so many of them involving parts of the Communion's leadership, that objectivity risks doing an injustice to the present crisis. Many writers trace the situation that has lead to the publication of Windsor back to the notorious debate on homosexuality at the 1998 Lambeth Conference in Canterbury. Accounts of that day remain disturbing: the manipulation, the emotional blackmail, the desperate bargains struck the nights before, the apparatchiks and their cell phones, pacing the halls. Some have described the atmosphere as akin to a political rally.

I suppose I was one of the apparatchiks, though not present on that particular day. As theological consultant to the House of Bishops of the Church of England, I had been down to Canterbury several times, and was part of the team back in London supporting the Conference.

We were all aware, however dimly on the specifics, of the threats and challenges occurring down in Kent, how close events were to breakdown and how desperately the Archbishop of Canterbury was having to struggle to avoid a fracture in the Communion. There have been discussions of those days that have heavily criticized the Archbishop, too many of them unpublished, but nevertheless circulated by his opponents, but mine would not be one of them. If it was clear that the debate and its circumstances were ultimately about authority, then it was also clear to me that George Carey was acting with courage and integrity on behalf of a moral understanding of that debate.

Courage is too often undervalued in today's Communion, particularly moral courage, and particularly on the question of homosexuality and orders. Looking back on the events surrounding 1998, and looking around today at the circumstances of the publication of Windsor, the underlying tension does not seem to be authority, but rather hatred. Questions about biblical fundamentalism obviously have a place in the present crisis, but that is not where I would place the emphasis. The problem is that some Anglicans hate other Anglicans because they are homosexual. That hatred is real, visceral, and abiding. It cannot be overcome by education, and explaining the Gospel to people in inclusive language will not soften it. It must be defeated, and the only way to defeat hatred is to stand up, tell people that it will not be tolerated and, if necessary, fight it. Such is the real context in which one must discuss Windsor, its arguments about episcope and authority, and the impact it seeks to have upon contemporary Anglican reception of the question of homosexuality in the Communion.

I am not convinced that the roots of the present crisis go back solely to the 1998 Lambeth Conference, however. In the annals of the Church of England's recent moral cowardice, the House of Bishops' Statement *Issues in Human Sexuality* is genuinely heartbreaking.[1] The

---

1 *Issues in Human Sexuality* (London: Church House Publishing, 1991).

question of homosexuality in modern times, and more significantly how people in modern communities behave towards gays and lesbians, is one of the great fault lines of the recent development of civil society. Since the 1950s and 1960s the western democracies have addressed the complex moral, legal, economic, and political issues surrounding human sexuality, not always successfully and not always completely, but always in ways that were ultimately responsible towards their populations. No one would suggest that civil society has reached the end of this particular road, but enormous progress has been made by addressing the circumstances that provoke hatred of gays and lesbians. *Issues in Human Sexuality*, by contrast, fails entirely to consider this most fundamental issue, which is why it has been at best a piece of ecclesial expediency, and at worst an abdication of the church's voice in this fundamental debate.

Issues in Human Sexuality is an example of moral cowardice because here was an opportunity to say unequivocally that judging people on their sexuality was wrong and immoral, and that being part of the body of Christ was not determined by the gender of one's partner. There was an opportunity to tell people who hated others for being gay that they were not Christian, and never would be Christians as long as such hatred was in their hearts. There was an opportunity to say once and for all that the bishops of the church taught a Gospel that transcended the bigotry that is evident in every town in England, and that they stood for God's passionate and inclusive embrace of everyone, irrespective of their sexuality. There was an opportunity, in short, to speak of the Gospel as truth rather than church expediency: to affirm love and reject hatred, once and for all.[2]

That opportunity was lost and, fourteen years later, the present Archbishop of Canterbury must deal with the now worldwide consequences. Windsor is a key feature of Archbishop Rowan's strategy

---

2 It is quite possible that the House of Bishops *intended* to take such an opportunity in *Issues*; they simply failed to do so effectively and decisively.

for doing just that. The question I want to consider is what kind of argument Windsor turns on, and what that argument looks like in a wider theological perspective. My overriding concern is not to decide whether Windsor constitutes an Anglican argument. Rather, I want to think about whether it will help the Communion deal with Christians who hate other Christians solely because they are gay or lesbian. Such a concern was clearly *not* a part of the mandate to the Lambeth Commission; but it should have been, and it will be the battlefield on which the success or failure of the Archbishop's strategy is ultimately judged.

Windsor

The Report does not speak of Anglicans hating fellow Anglicans, but the Chairman of the Lambeth Commission, Archbishop Robin Eames, does observe in his Foreword that: "The depth of conviction and feeling on all sides of the current issues has on occasions introduced a degree of harshness and a lack of charity which is new to Anglicanism" (5). The Chairman contrasts such harshness and lack of charity with the "bonds of affection" (5), language that pervades the present crisis and which grants the best possible impression of relations between the diverse provinces of the Communion. Interpreted most positively, these same bonds of affection lie behind the mandate to the Lambeth Commission on Communion; for any discussion of inter–provincial communion and the Archbishop of Canterbury's role in reconciling inter– and intra–provincial tensions is based on that same sense of abiding love, established in Christ.

Others in this volume have considered the wisdom of such a starting point for the mandate, and the honesty of the rhetoric of bonds of affection. My own concerns are more limited, and stem from the mandate's charge to the Commission to examine the "legal and theological implications" arising from the decisions made by ECUSA and the Diocese of New Westminster in Canada, and "specifically … the canonical understandings of communion" (8). It seems to me that the point of Windsor, beyond obtaining breathing space in 2003–4, was to identify the canonical basis upon which provinces might be bound, gently but firmly, to positions they would not wish to hold if left entirely free to choose. In other words, I am interested in the paradoxical sense of the bonds of affection: to what extent provinces will be *compelled* to maintain communion via Canterbury, where they might not otherwise *elect* so to do.

The key section of the Report on this question is *Canon Law and Covenant* (47–50, paras 113–20), which begins with two descriptive paragraphs before citing a key text from the Primates Meeting in Kanuga, 2001:

> The principles about communion, autonomy, discernment in communion and inter–Anglican relations, enunciated at global level by the Instruments of Unity, have persuasive moral authority for individual churches; they do not have enforceable juridical authority unless incorporated in their legal systems (and generally they are not incorporated) (47, para 115).

That same Kanuga accord goes on to recognize that: "This may be contrasted with the juridical experience of the particular church, in which enforceable canon law, the servant of the church, seeks to facilitate and order communion amongst its faithful" (47, para 115); and Windsor itself notes that: "No church has a systematic body of 'communion law' dealing with its relationship of communion with other member churches" (47, para 115). The inferences here are clear enough: as recently as Kanuga 2001 the Primates have confirmed a self–evident legal reality, namely that no province has any basis to interfere in the affairs of another. Setting aside theology at this stage, the canonical position appears straightforward: as of 2001, each province exists independently of every other, there being no mechanism to bring them into legal cohesion or identity.

This situation undoubtedly has historical origins that, while important, are not immediately significant at this stage of the argument. That the provinces have originated and grown up in diverse and contingent circumstances, therefore, is less important to Windsor (which barely mentions the history of the Anglican Communion) at this juncture than is the absence of what it will soon refer to as "communion law" (48, para 117). The Report never quite argues that this situation is an impediment to the survival of the Communion, but the inference is nevertheless clear: if the Communion is to survive the crisis over human sexuality and the actions of certain provinces, then *all* provinces need to pay attention as never before to the legal basis of their mutual interrelatedness. This proposal effectively makes up an entire, and lengthy, paragraph:

> This Commission recommends ... consideration as to how to make the principles of inter–Anglican relations more effective at the local ecclesial level. This has been a persistent problem in Anglicanism contributing directly to the current crisis, and could be remedied by the adoption by each church of its own simple and short domestic 'communion law', to enable and implement the covenant proposal below, strengthening the bonds of unity and articulating what has to–date been assumed (48, para 117).

The point is not elaborated here, but what seems to be suggested is something akin to the first stage of an Anglican Communion canon law: not binding *per se*, as canon law would generally be interpreted, but binding *per accidens* in that Primates would elect into a network of communion laws which would then "enable and implement" the level of unity urged by the Archbishop of Canterbury. Once Primates elect into such a network, however – as envisaged by the proposed Covenant (see below) – there would be an element of compulsion: "unity with teeth not smiles", one might say.

Three points arise from such a proposal. First, Windsor acknowledges the non–canonical status of such proposed communion law: "The Commission considers that a brief law would be preferable to and far more feasible than incorporation by each church of an elaborate and all–embracing canon defining inter–Anglican relations ..." (48, para 117). While one's blood runs cold at the thought of 44 provinces attempting to devise and legislate for such canons (as Windsor itself acknowledges), the proposal here is really political: better by far to have Primates sign up to a covenant that then binds their own behavior in ways that are not possible within their own churches, than have those same churches debate the pros and cons of Anglican membership. (It is also a pragmatic decision, of course: such a covenant at least has an outside chance of success, whereas 44 canonical processes are doomed to failure simply by the odds.) The proposal in paragraph 117 therefore reveals the world Windsor really inhabits: ecclesial expediency born of desperation. If the only way to hold together African and North American churches other than financially is to devise a non–canonical "Anglican canon", then that is what Windsor proposes.

In case such a reading seems unduly skeptical, however, one should acknowledge, second, that Windsor elaborates a fairly predictable yet extensive litany of the principles, purposes, and benefits of membership in the Anglican Communion. I will go into some of this material in more depth in the following section, but here I want to recognize that such a discussion in Windsor comes close to establishing a kind of ontology of the Communion, or at least, an ontology of being the kind of Christian (and Primate) that finds him/herself an Anglican. What I mean by this suggestion is that Sections A and B of Windsor are concerned to set out an argument about *being* an Anglican, where the emphasis is very much upon being *in communion*. Such an argument again has a practical purpose in that it draws the reader (and the Primates) into a shared narrative, one that reminds them of what makes them Anglicans in the first place. That reminder is deliberate and, as I have noted, clearly political: its intention is to be gently but, if necessary, firmly coercive.

At the same time, however, that shared narrative is also established in Word and Sacrament (see 24–5, paras 45–7), which means ultimately established in the body of Christ and thereby the revealed will of God.[3] Any sense of a shared Anglican narrative is necessarily part of the shared apostolic narrative that defines the true Catholic Church, Anglican diversity thereby evoking Catholic unity as it always does in any properly Anglican ecclesiology. Just as there is always an unbreakable relationship between canon law and theology for Rome, therefore, so in Windsor there is always an implicit but pivotal link between the proposed communion law and the apostolic unity that all Anglicans share, particularly the Primates as successors to the Apostles. Stated bluntly, communion law will be established in an Anglican understanding of apostolic ecclesiology, and an Anglican understanding of apostolic ecclesiology will be established in an historic and catholic understanding of Word and Sacrament.

This understanding of the relationship between the juridic and the sacramental, third, must then be established in practical ecclesial politics, that being the point of the proposed covenant. Turning to that text, therefore, one reads in paragraph 13:

> Each minister, especially a bishop, shall be a visible sign of unity and shall maintain communion within each church and between it, the See of Canterbury and all other Communion churches. (2) No minister, especially a bishop, shall: (a) act without due regard to or jeopardize the unity of the Communion; (b) neglect to cooperate with ministers, especially bishops, of member churches for the good of the Communion and Church universal; (c) unreasonably be the cause or focus of division and strife in their church or elsewhere in the Communion; (d) if in episcopal office, unreasonably

---

3 See Archbishop Robin Eames' opening question in his Foreword to *Windsor* (p. 4): "What do we believe is the will of God for the Anglican Communion?"

refuse any invitation to attend meetings of the Instruments of Unity (67, appendix 2, article 13).

The bonds of affection are now also bonds of discipline, embracing the full conduct of ministers and particularly bishops in their relations with the See of Canterbury. Why? Because the new communion law requires a level of obedience that affects an understanding of a trans–Communion ecclesiology, one in which "the good of the Communion and Church universal" is now made an explicit focus of Anglican unity. Thus, Windsor spells out the practical implications of building a new covenant on the basis of a shared understanding of apostolic ecclesiology, implications that are born of the Church of England's original and originating (for the Communion) claims to be catholic and reformed. It is, in short, an argument with real purchase on the theological questions.

On the Ecclesial Vocation of an Archbishop

Windsor's section on "Canon Law and Covenant" is very carefully worded, paragraph 113 speaking guardedly of the identified "communion law" as "an unwritten *ius commune*" (46, para 113). The cautious inference here is that, somewhat mysteriously and tentatively, a common sense of obligation somehow emerges out of the varied ecclesial and theological bonds of affection that the Primates and churches of the Anglican Communion share. That caution is sensible, since the ideology of Windsor is very much that the communion law being suggested is something that the Communion has always had and always observed, and that consequently what is now being proposed is simply the teasing out explicitly of what hitherto has been implicit.[4] If that teasing out can be accomplished to everyone's satisfaction then Windsor, with its enhanced understanding of the Instruments of Unity, becomes viable.

---

4 The trick, of course, is to persuade the Primates to accept this argument, which means offering enough to make it worthwhile; hence, the specific price to be paid by ECUSA and the Diocese of New Westminster.

Two questions arise at this juncture. First, what price will have to be paid for everyone to subscribe to such an understanding of an unwritten *ius commune*? That will be examined in the next section on establishment and authority. Before that, however, second, what sort of argument have we got here in Windsor? How does it really work? To answer these questions I want to compare the argument in Windsor to an earlier Catholic text, the Congregation for the Doctrine of the Faith's *Instruction on the Ecclesial Vocation of the Theologian* (henceforth *Instruction*).[5]

Instruction is notorious because of the heavy–handed way in which it has been used to silence certain theologians, among them Tissa Balasuriya in 1997. Such heavy–handedness is underpinned by the nature of the collaboration between the theologian and the magisterium when, as *Instruction* makes clear: "… such collaboration becomes a participation in the work of the Magisterium, linked, as it then is, by a juridic bond".[6] The juridic bond is the perceived problem, because while it is entirely logical in terms of the contractual obligations placed upon a Catholic theologian when he or she receives the canonical mission or the mandate to teach, still such a bond is believed to cut across religious, moral, and intellectual freedom.

If *Instruction* were solely about a big stick it would not be very interesting, no matter how effective it proved. As the text makes clear, however, there is a subtle, powerful and convincing theological argument at work here, one that goes back to Vatican II's *Lumen Gentium* and in particular *De Ecclesia*.[7] In a signal passage of that text on "The Universality of the People of God", one reads:

> The universal body made up of the faithful, whom the Holy One has anointed … is incapable of being at fault in belief. This is a property which belongs to the people as a

---

5 *Instruction on the Ecclesial Vocation of the Theologian* (London: Catholic Truth Society, 1990).
6 *Instruction*, p. 15.
7 *De Ecclesia* (London: Catholic Truth Society, 1965).

whole; a supernatural discernment of faith is the means by which they make this property manifest, when, 'from Bishops to the last layman', they show universal agreement in matters of faith and morals. This discernment of faith, which is roused and maintained by the Spirit of truth, is the cause of the unfailing adherence of the People of God to the faith that was once for all delivered to the saints ...[8]

I want to make two points about this passage and its importance for the argument in *Instruction*, particularly as it appears to an Anglican theologian. First, one finds it startling because one recognizes behind it a specifically Catholic theory of obedience and the potential for conflict over "universal agreement in matters of faith and morals". Not for nothing does *De Ecclesia* add at this point: "This all takes place under the guidance of the sacred magisterium, when the People of God, in loyal submission to it, accepts not the word of men but what is really the word of God".[9] On this matter, *Instruction* adds: "It is the mission of the Magisterium to affirm the definitive character of the Covenant established by God through Christ with His People in a way which is consistent with the 'eschatological' nature of the event of Jesus Christ",[10] developing this theme through a series of reflections upon the hierarchy of the church, namely, the pontiff, the episcopal college, and the presbyterate. This power and authority resides in these bodies, argues *Instruction*, because they are successors of the apostles and as such, again quoting *De Ecclesia*, "receive from the Lord ... the mission of teaching all peoples, and of preaching the Gospel to every creature, so that all men may attain salvation ...".[11] The apostolicity of the Church of Rome means that its hierarchical character is established in a theory of power and authority that centers upon historical

8 *De Ecclesia*, pp. 19–20.
9 *De Ecclesia*, p. 20.
10 *Instruction*, p.11.
11 *De Ecclesia*, p. 24.

succession as the revelation of the will of God, and which regards the magisterium as being responsible for giving definitive voice to the eternal truth of the faith.

The juridic bond between the theologian and the magisterium takes on a fresh complexion when one understands it in these terms, therefore. That is not the full extent of *Instruction's* argument, however, as one sees with the second point I want to make here. The argument in *De Ecclesia* is an argument about *being*: although there are a variety of epistemological questions in this part of *Instruction*, the citation of *De Ecclesia* as authority at this point reduces these questions to the level of ontology. Just as a universal agreement in matters of faith and morals is governed by that supernatural discernment of faith that is itself established in baptism into mystery, so questions of knowledge in theology are, for *Instruction*, governed by questions of being. The channel for this government is the magisterium, as *Instruction* makes clear:

> Among the vocations awakened ... by the Spirit in the Church is that of the theologian. His role is to pursue in a particular way an even deeper understanding of the Word of God found in the inspired Scriptures and handed on by the living Tradition of the Church. He does this in communion with the Magisterium that has been charged with the responsibility of preserving the deposit of faith.[12]

The conviction here is rich yet stark: being "in communion" with the magisterium is the source of teaching authority for catholicism, not solely because the juridic bond is the functional expression of a legal contract, but because the juridic bond is underpinned by the deeper, eschatological nature of the faith as entrusted to the church. Or, stated

---

12 *Instruction*, p. 7.

in another (albeit equivalent) kind of language: it is the church's apostolicity that makes its teaching true, which means that its teaching – its exposition and understanding and communication – must be both juridically and eschatologically bonded to the authoritative source of that teaching; i.e., the church itself. Only God, certainly, can make that bonding true; but God has shared that power with the church, in the Holy Spirit and as articulated in its historic teaching office, the episcopate.

In this respect, one can see that *Instruction* is not really about theologians at all, but rather bishops, in the sense that their authority derives from God, and the theologians' authority derives from bishops. The question of a bishop's teaching, therefore, is really a question about that bishop's relationship to the body of Christ, so that questions of *continuity* in that same teaching are really questions of origin: tracing back a bishop's authority to teach means tracing back his or her origin to God's will – hence Archbishop Eames' opening question in his Foreword about discerning the will of God for the Anglican Communion. Anglicanism has always answered that question in general terms, however, preferring to understand the business of tracing back episcopal authority as a general though historic principle, rather than a specific questioning of any particular bishop's authenticity. The treatment of Bishop Gene Robinson, consequently, whatever the rights and wrongs of the issues involved, is a new development for the Anglican Communion. If addressing Bishop Gene's consecration also involves an attempt to identify specific and limiting mandates for episcopal authority that then become trans–Communion, then the Primates will have gone far beyond their own historic origins in worldwide Anglicanism.

These issues are fundamental to how one reads Windsor in the light of its similarities and dissimilarities with other catholic texts. Windsor is not the same sort of document as *Instruction*, and I do not believe that most Anglican Primates want to impose a magisterium of sorts upon the Communion. Yet, the real difficulty with Windsor is that it does not appear to understand that such is the logic of its central argument. The *ius commune* is not the same thing as a juridic bond, therefore, at least not in appearance or intention. In so far as both are established in an understanding of the universal church's apostolicity, however, and in so far as that apostolicity is true because it originates in the revealed will of God, then both the *ius commune* and the juridic bond *must* be authentic because God, somehow, reveals them to be authentic. For *Instruction* that revelation is witnessed to by the work of the magisterium in upholding universal agreement in matters of faith and morals. For Windsor that revelation is witnessed to by the work of the Primates in upholding the Instruments of Unity. Both arguments, however, and both witnesses, have authority because the bishops who articulate them are *true* bishops, that is, they are apostolic.

The great strength of *Instruction*, whatever one thinks about the church politics involved, is that it recognizes that the bond between episcopal agreement on the one hand, and teaching the faith on the other, must be *necessary* and therefore established in something that transcends contingency. That bond is necessary because it originates in the will of God, and is therefore determined by eternal truth. The only logical alternative to this argument – given that there cannot be alternate eternal truths – is for the bond between church and teaching to be contingent rather than necessary; an accident of history, one might say. But historical accidents, whatever their attractions, have no binding authority. Jesus of Nazareth was not Son of God because he was a perfectly good man in word and action. Jesus of Nazareth was a perfectly good man because he was the Son of God. The distinction is absolute, and *Instruction* knows it.

Windsor contains a much more conservative argument than might first appear, consequently. It is possible that the Report, when it relates its tentative arguments about the *ius commune* to the fundamental principles of the Anglican Communion, is writing about something contingent, something that arose through the accidents of British colonial history; but if it is then it is very poor theology, and the people involved are not poor theologians. The stronger likelihood must be that Windsor has a similar understanding of the church and its bishops as one finds in a Catholic text like *Instruction*, and that consequently the origin and authority of the *ius commune* must have the same kind of theological underpinnings. The choice is marked: either the *ius commune* just happens accidentally, or it is the necessary expression of a deeper coherence of which the Instruments of Unity are the clearest expression the Communion has. If it is the former then the Communion is an historical federation that may have outlived its usefulness because it is no longer able to deal with contentious issues. If it is the latter, then, the Primates cannot undermine the Communion without also thereby undermining their own participation in the body of Christ. Whichever it is, though, Windsor is clear that there is not a way around the present question: provinces must now identify their good reasons for being Anglican, in engagement with the Instruments of Unity.

That is Windsor's implicit argument. The question now is partly whether it is a good argument *per se*, and partly whether it is a good argument for the Anglican Communion *per accidens*. Much more importantly, however, one must consider whether it can address and deal with Anglican hatred of other Anglicans on the grounds of their sexuality.

Establishment and authority

First things first: the argument in *Instruction* is a good one, *if* one holds that the right of speaking about the truth involves an obedience to those who have a responsibility for receiving and upholding the same truth. Notwithstanding *Instruction*'s comments about the theologian's epistemological duties, therefore,[13] speaking about the truth necessitates going beyond such social considerations to where, for the Catholic Church, one enters into episcopal jurisdiction, an insight going all the

---

13 *Instruction*, p. 8.

way back to Matthew 16. *Instruction* makes the point very clearly: "The commitment to theology requires a spiritual effort to grow in virtue and holiness".[14] That growth occurs by direction from priests and bishops and under their care, which pastoral gift illuminates the more fundamental reality underpinning this argument, that speaking of the truth means speaking of God, and only God makes that possible. An obedient relationship with one's bishop, consequently, is a fundamental part of the theologian's vocation: it only ceases to be relevant if the theologian no longer wishes to speak of the truth, in which case bracketing out the truth implies bracketing out discipline and authority, too. At that point – admittedly reached by some contemporary theologians – one understands theology as the study of socially–conditioned linguistic models, rather than the articulation and interpretation of orthodox Christian doctrine. Both may have a role in today's world (and church), but only one is theology, as the church understands it.

It is possible that Windsor understands theology as just such a socially–conditioned linguistic model, but very unlikely given its stated views on the communion of the body of Christ (see 24, para 45). It is far more likely that Windsor shares *Instruction*'s fundamental commitment to the truth of Christian doctrine in general, whilst acknowledging the historically conditioned nature of the Anglican Communion in particular. It is what Windsor refers to as "double 'bonds of affection'" (14, para 45): Anglicans are bound to one another sacramentally as part of the body of Christ, and historically as something that has grown into the worldwide Communion. It is the classic Anglican both/and rather than either/or: in the terms posed above, the contingent circumstances of Anglicanism are themselves established absolutely in the Trinity and incarnation. The Communion might allow a certain amount of pragmatism about the way member

---

14 *Instruction*, p. 8.

churches interpret ecclesial and moral jurisdiction, therefore – as Archbishop Eames observes, it is almost *de rigueur* – but that pragmatic understanding of the truth never overwhelms the revealed truth. Windsor is very clear that what churches might want to do can never be a substitute for witnessing to the truth, which is the basis for the compulsion placed upon ECUSA and the Diocese of New Westminster.[15] The logic of the theological problem at Windsor's heart, consequently, militates in favor of a resolution that looks a lot like the one found in Rome's *Instruction*. And let me be clear: the kind of *ius commune* that Windsor speaks of *should* be nothing more than the elaboration of the founding principles of Anglicanism's orthodox beliefs. "Signing up" for the Communion, then, must involve accepting the binding confessions of the apostolic church and the binding beliefs of trinitarian incarnationalism. Considered thus, it seems almost inconceivable that 44 Anglican Primates cannot come together and agree on the confession of their churches' faith. What are archbishops *for*, after all, if it is not to articulate their churches' confessed faith? At its simplest – and Windsor is straightforward on this question – the *ius commune* really is nothing more than the working out of some very elementary obligations that are then placed on member churches because they elect into the Communion. Which is what, of course, the proposed covenant is banking on: Anglican churches will buy into the covenant because theologically they cannot avoid doing so without denying the sacramental implications of their ecclesiology.

Windsor's proposed covenant *should* work, therefore, because the *ius commune* has been correctly identified as the key point at which one can tease out of an Anglican archbishop what it is to be an Anglican *and* a catholic Christian. Windsor will *not* work, however, because its arguments' consistency and sincerity will not be matched by the

---

15 It is interesting yet also dispiriting that, publicly at least, no authority has ever attempted to compel the Province of Nigeria to be *charitable* towards its fellow Anglicans in Canada and the USA, given that charity is a more significant – and New Testament – Christian principle than a particular understanding of human sexuality.

consistency and sincerity of the Primates. There are two reasons why Windsor will fail, one bad one good, and it is as well to have the bad one out of the way as soon as possible. The sticking point with too many of the Primates is that they do not appear to understand or value the theological foundations of the discipline that underpins Windsor. There is no point in speaking of the "Ministerial Obligations of Unity" if the only archbishops who uphold that position are men like the Presiding Bishop of ECUSA, whilst others feel free to take liberties not solely with their bonds of affection with the See of Canterbury, but also the confession of faith that establishes those bonds of affection. Whether one views such latter behavior as ignorant, hypocritical, misguided, or simply idiotic, any notion that the *ius commune* might flourish in the Communion is naïve so long as such individuals continue to pay nothing more than lip service to some of the central beliefs of the apostolic faith.

Before such people take great offence at this analysis let me acknowledge immediately that the good argument why Windsor will not succeed militates very much in favor of the position they appear to uphold. It is this: any one member church within the Communion has no jurisdiction over any other church in that Communion. It is the point Enoch Powell made about the Church of England, writing in 1986 of the Synod of Westminster:

> For the Church of England is territorial. It is of necessity the Church *in* England which the Crown governs. The preposition *in* is significant and fruitful. *Ecclesia anglicana* before the Reformation meant the Church in England, that is, the part of the Church which subsisted in England. It was over the Church in England that the Crown became Supreme Governor. Logically its governorship extended no farther than the outer limits of its territorial sovereignty … the counterpart of the inclusiveness of the Church of England is its geographical exclusiveness: only an Englishman – strictly

speaking, an inhabitant of England – can be Church of England – others may be Anglicans, if they see fit.[16]

What is true for York and Canterbury is true for every other province in the worldwide Communion: no Primate has the authority or jurisdiction to legislate about the affairs of another Primate's province. It is no good arguing that questions of jurisdiction should take a back seat to the ideas that are enshrined in the *ius commune* since the notion of the geographical specificity of a bishop's authority goes back at least as far as the Council of Nicaea in 325 CE, and arguably as far back as the Gospel of Matthew.[17] If the doctrine of the Son's consubstantiality with the Father is central to the ecclesial orthodoxy established at Nicaea, so is the territorial sovereignty of the bishop. In which respect some of Windsor's critics are right, no matter how much one might condemn their actions: on this question of jurisdiction the proposed covenant is just as confused as the position it is attempting to remedy.

The heart of the matter, therefore, goes something like this: for some very good theological reasons, Windsor wants to persuade Primates to give up part of what they were granted at Nicaea, namely, territorial jurisdiction and sovereignty. In return, those same Primates will be able to say that they recognize the confessional foundations of an apostolic and catholic faith that transcends the historical accidents that lead to the establishment of the Anglican Communion. The *mechanism* whereby this compromise will be delivered looks a lot like a Catholic model of discipline and authority, diluted to suit the tastes of the province in question. That same mechanism *assumes* agreement wherever dispute does not arise, and challenges dissent in the name of unity wherever disagreement breaks out, as in the question of human sexuality.

---

16 Enoch Powell, "The Church of England and Parliament", in P. Moore (ed), *The Synod of Westminster: Do We Need It?* (London: SPCK, 1986), pp. 117–31; 118–9.
17 On this question, see Norman P Tanner (ed), *Decrees of the Ecumenical Councils: Nicaea I to Vatican II* (Washington: Georgetown University Press, 1990).

It looks and feels, in short, like a version of the notorious "flying bishops" clause of the Church of England's Episcopal Ministry Act of Synod: wherever argument arises and whatever the cause, the Primates agree *prima facie* to defer their own authority to the Communion's *ius commune*, in the name of an enhanced sense of the Instruments of Unity. The final piece in the jigsaw is that there will in effect be just one "flying bishop" for the Communion: the Archbishop of Canterbury. The image is acute: one man (for now) circumnavigating the world and calling meetings of archbishops, some willing, some unwilling, all in the name of a unity that cannot be canonically defined, but is nevertheless theologically asserted as the deep structure of Anglicanism. Such is the price to be paid for the sake of today's Communion.

Conclusion: dealing with hatred

Like most essays, this one took some months to research and write, the months following publication of the Report. As with this essay so with Windsor, there is an argument and a series of critical points. There are strengths and inevitably weaknesses, as there are too with Windsor. Ultimately, one can be persuaded or not by the argument but, again as with Windsor, one treats the issues seriously. Everyone who has written for this volume, I am certain, shares the same commitment evidenced by Windsor, namely that faith and reason must come together in order to discern God's will for the Anglican Communion.

The depressing reality, however, is that the people who would most benefit from reading such a series of arguments are precisely the same people who will not read them. The politics of Windsor's reception, if one can speak of such a thing, are already clear: a sophisticated if partial acceptance by ECUSA, the Diocese of Westminster and their supporters; some acknowledgement, but mostly calculated insult, from their opponents. The spectacle of certain Primates, scheduling events to clash with the Archbishop of Canterbury's eucharistic celebration, or spuriously proclaiming the

Communion "dead" whilst others respond with humble obedience, is chilling. Such acts are not responses to Windsor: they are deliberate attempts to apply as much pressure as possible in an attempt to win yet further concessions.

Arguably, Windsor was always doomed to this particular fate. Whether one traces such a failure to the original mandate, as others have argued, or to too many years of moral cowardice, as I believe, the resulting situation is the same. The politics of Windsor's reception are the politics of ecclesial gesture, the politics of reinforcing and retrenching the undifferentiated positions that predominated before the Report was published. Under such visceral circumstances, there seems little, if any, hope that something as slight as an argument might persuade people to behave charitably. It is not, after all, a matter of love but rather hate, and there can only be one conclusion to such a matter: either hate will win, and the Communion will end; or else those who hate must face discipline, as outlined by Windsor's proposed covenant. At the time of writing, however, such discipline seems far away. Those who hate others because of their sexuality have the upper hand, so much so that every liberal confronts the real possibility of being made homeless by their own church.

We have been here before, of course: Hooker was harshly treated, too, and in the seventeenth century the Church of England was nearly destroyed before the dissenters were expelled and genuine apostolic and episcopal authority reasserted in the 1660s. As then, so now, the real issues were not about civil or political change and the role of the church in responding to social pressures, but rather an ordered and inclusive church, one in which everyone could find a home because everyone *belonged.* It was an ordered church because it was apostolic, and because it recognized the authority and oversight of those God had placed in authority. It was an inclusive church because it recognized the fundamental *breadth* of human spirituality, and affirmed the role of doctrine and canon in nurturing and giving life to that spirituality. For better or worse, that polity has survived for nearly 350 years in its reaffirmed state: a polity in which everyone finds a place near God because everyone believes everyone comes *from* God, and responds accordingly to their spiritual and, yes, physical needs.

There was a deeper theology at work here, one summed up in the words of the old collect from the *Book of Common Prayer*: "Thy grace shall always prevent and follow us." Of course, one can judge such arminianism from solely an historical perspective, seeing therein the doctrinal and ecclesial tensions of a lost era; but that would be to miss the real point. Anglicanism has survived thus far because it has instinctively recognized the truth of the old, accepted yet unarticulated truths of prevenient grace: that God comes before as well as after us; that God prepares our humanity as much as he redeems it and reconciles us to him. At their best, Anglican doctrines of humanity and creation, the seedbed of our christologies and theologies, are always arminian: we seek to include because we believe God *has* included. We seek to receive Christ because Christ has already received us, not solely in the sense of willingly shedding his blood for our sake, but also in creating us each as we are.

All this glory – the glory of being the one church that was based upon genuine inclusivity – is now in danger of being lost. Not because an Anglican magisterium has finally declared arminianism heretical, or because a state has outlawed a church's attitude towards minorities, or arguments about the true meaning of the Bible have been lost. This glory stands to be lost now because some Primates in the Anglican Communion cannot agree to embrace the world as God has created it, and as God has created some men and women. It is a self–inflicted tragedy, but one that, even at this late hour, allows of resolution if people can but find the courage to speak and act against hatred and wanton destructiveness. If Windsor makes it possible to resist such behavior, albeit some way down the road, then it should find a home in the Anglican Communion. If it does not then it must be rejected now, before it can do irreparable damage.

10

The Rhetoric of Unity

George Pattison

I preface the following comments with an important admission. I am not someone who has ever been involved in the governance of the church beyond the kind of participation in deanery events obligatory for parish clergy in the Church of England. Like most clergy, I have avoided getting involved in synodical or "macro–level" church affairs, recognizing my own lack of competence in the political and administrative skills needed to make a significant contribution at that level. As a working clergyman, I have chosen to remain close to the simple daily forms of church life manifest in the conduct of worship, pastoral care, and teaching. In deciding to write critically about a major issue in church governance, I am therefore well aware that I do so in a very amateur capacity and that I have a very limited existential sense of the demands placed upon those who bear these burdens as a normal part of their ministry. I do not wish to belittle the anguish, prayers and sincere reflection of those whose ecclesiastical work bears such fruits as the Windsor Report. As always, it is so much easier to criticize from the sidelines than to stand in the crossfire of opinions and take responsibility for policy.

Nevertheless, the image of the church that is being projected by such documents as the Windsor Report (and, as another example, the recent proposals regarding doctrinal discipline in the Church of England) cannot but influence the way in which all our ministry and witness is perceived and received. Especially in our media–dominated time, the way in which the church represents itself in such widely publicized documents comes, in practice, to define what our contemporaries see the church as being. When the underlying ecclesiology of such documents is disputable (as I believe the ecclesiology of Windsor to be), the potential for damage at every level of church life is enormous. Therefore, even the amateurs both may and, perhaps, should speak.

What, then, is the issue?

Perhaps the simplest way to focus this is to recall a question which a parishioner asked me back in the 1980s: "What's all this in the papers about 'Anglicans', Rector – I thought we were Church of England?" Set alongside this the reference, now common in the media, to "the worldwide Anglican Communion" or, simply, "the worldwide church". These seemingly slight differences mark an epochal shift – or, at least, a tendency that could result in an epochal shift. The current exposure and usage of the term "Anglican" reflects and furthers a deep question about the identity of the Church of England itself. Is our Christian identity, that is, the identity of Christians making their Christian journey in the context of the Church of England, to be decided primarily in terms of our relations to the "worldwide Anglican Communion"? If we assume that we are indeed a worldwide church (like but, perhaps, "fudgier" than the Roman Catholic Church), then it would seem hard to disagree. Yet this assumption itself flies in the face of history. The Church of England did not come into being in an attempt to establish a counter worldwide church to that of Rome: it came into being as an answer – an obviously imperfect answer – to the challenge of being Christian in a particular set of social and political circumstances of which the national designation "England" played a central part. That we have subsequently become a part of a "worldwide" church has had as much to do with the accidents of history and empire as with any collective expansionist strategy. There was no intrinsic motive for the ecclesiastical polity articulated and defended by Jewel and Hooker to become anything more than an English phenomenon.

Times change – of course, and we no longer inhabit that social or political space. The British Isles have been through four centuries of massive upheaval and transformation, and neither the Henrician nor the Elizabethan settlements, nor yet the Restoration, nor the Glorious Revolution, need predetermine our contemporary response to contemporary issues. Probably the Church of England itself will undergo some kind of disestablishment over the next couple of generations, although it is likely to be a splendidly British process of half–measure, compromise and inconsistencies, with all the strengths and weaknesses of our traditional "muddling–through" way of doing things. What being a member of the Church of England will then mean will necessarily be something very different from what it meant fifty years ago or means today. We cannot simply preserve the past nor can we replicate it. Often, we shouldn't want to – for all the famed "tolerance" and breadth of the Church of England, it frequently resorted to force, torture and execution in its early centuries in order to ensure uniformity. Such things have been left behind, hopefully forever. Yet, however tangled the historical tale, our history serves a lesson common to the churches of the Reformation: that the forms of church organization, as of worship, apologetics and evangelism, must relate to the reality of the society in and, in an important sense, *for* which the church exists.

This could be heard in a "little England" way, and perhaps the anxiety not to be too parochial and insular has itself contributed to the popularity of the idea of the worldwide Anglican Church as a primary locus of contemporary ecclesiastical identity. But this could also be seen another way: that the difficulty of facing up to the actuality of contemporary Christian life and witness in Britain has itself been a major factor in making it so attractive to imagine ourselves as members of a worldwide church. Even if there are only half–a–dozen other people in our village church on a cold Sunday morning, we have the consolation that millions more throng Anglican churches worldwide, from LA to Brisbane to Lagos. And, in the heroic witness of Anglicans in such contexts as that of the anti–apartheid struggle in South Africa, we have a contemporary source of hagiography for which our own church life in its preoccupation with the daily round and common task provides little opportunity. I can certainly recognize some such motive in my own attempts as a newly fledged priest in the early 80s to enthuse parishioners with a more global vision of Anglicanism. Perhaps they did need to be shaken out of certain parochialism, but perhaps their instinctive resistance to such a global vision had its reasons too. Haven't the defining moments of Christianity always been in real engagement with what is actual in our lives, rather than administrative solutions to administrative problems? *Lex orandi* – not only *lex credendi* but *lex gubernandi* as well!

I am not proposing that we make the parish pump the measure of our church life. The social revolution of the most recent times means that very few of us today have lives defined by the boundaries of an isolated rural community. We are a people always on the move: very few live from birth to death in the same house, nor even in the same community. We follow education, work and retirement from place to place, and, in our working lives as in our vacations, we are constantly on the move. Our business partners in Hamburg or our friends in Rome are often as much a part of our workaday reality as people in the same street. To work out the form of Christianity most appropriate to our life and mission in this situation means reckoning with that situation. The term "contextualization", so widely used in modern missiology, is no less applicable to our situation as it is to others. The kind of church we need will therefore be very different from that of those in other contexts. In this regard, it is probably more urgent for us to be pursuing the kinds of bonds being forged through ecumenical contacts with other north European churches (as witnessed in such agreements as those at Meissen and Porvoo) than to slant our agenda to that of churches in very different situations. This does not mean to say that we can simply slip all obligations to other Anglican churches: it is simply to raise the question as to whether it is self–evident that they are really our "natural" partners in framing a church structure, a theology and an evangelistic strategy for our place and time. My fear is that the rhetoric of the "worldwide Anglican Communion" in fact obfuscates the very realities that we most need to be facing and that to be seduced by this rhetoric is to succumb to a myth that will make us even more incapable of effective Christian living in our present reality.

This fear is confirmed by the way in which Windsor treats the whole theme of unity. The Report begins with the stirring words:

> God has unveiled, in Jesus Christ, his glorious plan for the rescue of the whole created order from all that defaces, corrupts and destroys it. The excitement and drama of that initial achievement and that final purpose pervade the whole New Testament, and set the context for understanding why God has called out a people by the gospel, and how that people is to understand its identity and order its life. (1)

The implications for church life are then spelled out in the following paragraph:

> Those who, despite their own sinfulness, are saved by grace through their faith in God's gospel (Eph 2:1–10) are to live as a united family across traditional ethnic and other boundaries (Eph 2:11–22), and so are to reveal the many–splendored wisdom of the one true God to the hostile and divisive powers of the world (Eph 3:9–10) as they explore and celebrate the astonishing breadth of God's love made known through Christ's dwelling in their hearts (Eph 3:14–21). The redeemed unity which is God's will for the whole creation is to be lived out within the life of the church as, through its various God–given ministries, it is built up as the Body of Christ and

grows to maturity not least through speaking the truth in love (Eph 1:10, 22–3; 4:1–16). The church, sharing in God's mission to the world through the fact of its corporate life, must live out that holiness which anticipates God's final rescue of the world from the powers and corruptions of evil (Eph 4:17–6.20). (1)

With these biblical foundations in place the report continues to give an essentially triumphalist version of church history in which this mystical and eschatological unity is manifested in the church's life in time – and, as this life is described in page after page, there is not a whiff of irony, not a hint that when we are talking about the Anglican Church we are not talking about the one, unified church of the apostolic age (if, as historians suggest is extremely unlikely, there ever was such a thing) but about a fragment of a fragment. Perhaps this rhetoric might have a degree of plausibility in a Roman Catholic context and still more in the context of Orthodoxy, but it is, frankly, incredible in relation to our own history. This abstract triumphalism is given flesh when, in some of the few concrete historical comments, the (Anglican) church's resistance to slavery and to acts of genocide, and its solidarity with indigenous peoples, and its work in disaster relief are flagged as springing "from the organic reality that is life in communion". This is, of course, an extremely selective reading of Anglican history. Undoubtedly there are splendid episodes to recall and celebrate. There are many fruits of our common life. But it can only be wilful ignorance when university–educated theologians suggest that this is representative of the whole picture. Many Anglicans supported slavery and were slave owners. The Church of England bishops in the House of Lords repeatedly resisted the limiting of the death penalty. Many gave chauvinistic support to the imperial war effort of 1914. And so on. We are not worse than others, but we are not better. We share – necessarily – in the fragmentation, the ambiguity and the imperfection of all historical institutions and, in our individuality, in the darkness of all individual life.

We may all be inspired by the kind of transcendent vision of unity depicted in Ephesians; we may, in some sense, already be participant in the inner communion of the divine life to which our adoption as children of God calls us: but to treat these transcendent determinations as if they are empirical attributes that can simply be assigned to the church with straightforward indicative forms of speech is surely a disastrous categorical error. When the Report affirms that "Life in the Anglican Communion, as a communion of churches, is indeed nourished by the presence and work of the Holy Spirit, building up the body in love", I suspect that the little word "indeed" is a symptom that the authors are protesting too much and at one level know it – for the Anglican Communion, like all ecclesiastical life, is marked by the fragmentation, ambiguity and imperfection of which I have spoken. Like the supernaturalism of many newer liturgies, Windsor enunciates counter–factual truths with a tone of such self–evidence that all resistance is, momentarily, disabled – that is, until we start to think about what is being said. Then we realize that the maximum we can say is little more that that "We pray and hope that life in the Anglican Communion ... will, despite our individual and collective shortcoming, be nourished by the presence and work of the Holy Spirit ..."

To treat as a fact what is an aspiration, a matter of faith and hope, is not simply to make a category–mistake. It is to place the discussion on a completely wrong footing. We are not an institution endowed with a plenitude of truth that such foes as liberals and fundamentalists threaten to steal from us. We are an assemblage of deeply fallible, morally compromised, intellectually limited individuals who believe ourselves to be claimed by God in Christ for a better life. This better life is one that, under the conditions of history, can only be known in a glass darkly. In working out what it means and what it demands of us, we can only ever match the certainty of divine truth with the uncertainty of our interpretation of it. This uncertainty drives us back once more to the exigencies of the actual situation in which we live. Only here, in the engagement with pressing, claimful reality (see Buber!) can we discover what God's word for us really is.

Only where we have ground under our feet can the ground under our feet become holy. In this perspective, we need to affirm the providential significance not just of the church's triumphs (such as they are), but also of the very fragmentation, ambiguity and imperfection of our historical experience. Is it our voluntary entry into this experience that, as it were, sows the seeds of the future possibility of redemption or, to speak more precisely, that allows the seed sown in Christ to take root and grasp the whole of our collective historical life. On this view, to claim an eschatological unity for any form of life, including ecclesial life, that falls short of the total ingathering of all that is lost and broken – the reunification of *all things* – would already be to falsify that vision of unity itself. It would be to claim for a part what can only be predicated of the real whole. This is not to relish brokenness for brokenness's sake: it is merely to humble ourselves under the logic of incarnation, to let ourselves be made sin to complete the sufferings of him who was made sin for us.

In identifying our immediate, pressing, claimful reality as the sphere of our primary Christian concern, we do, of course, stumble upon a real problem. There is a stratum of church life for which international episcopal and other institutions have become the pressing, claimful reality of those who participate in them. Their existential problem has become how to be at peace with brother bishops or partner churches. It is impossible to deny all legitimacy to such claims. One cannot simply claim "reality" for local or personal life and deny it to administrative or superstructural social elements. "Reality" is, in effect, a dynamic composite of multiple "realities" in which personal, local, national and international elements are all represented.

But there are important questions about prioritization, and I suggest that it is a greater priority for the leadership of the Church of England to be attending to the dynamics of Christian life and mission in England than to be attempting to co–ordinate that life and mission with the practice of churches operating in very different social and cultural situations. In this regard, the experience of the other churches of Britain and of north–west Europe generally, catholic and protestant, is likely to be the most fertile and fruitful ground for finding a larger and better understanding of divisive issues. This is not to indulge in a neo–colonialist belittling of the African or other churches' experience: they have their context, they have the freedom to frame their life in relation to it, and we can no longer impose our Eurocentric views on them (even were we to wish to). But the equation works both ways. We cannot afford to skew our church life to the agenda of other churches. Our situation is already far too precarious to allow for such diversions. If leadership is needed, it is needed specifically for those struggling with the question as to how to be Christian in, with and under the conditions sometimes described as late modernity or the aftermath of Christendom. That is already a more than sufficient task for any individual or collective Christian leadership.

Clearly, the above remarks have been written with half an eye on the specific issue that provoked the Windsor Report, even if it was not itself addressed directly in that report. This issue is, of course, that of homosexuality. I do not intend to say much about this, generally sharing the view expressed by Stephen Pattison in an article some years' since, that the less the church says about sex the better, since it nearly always gets it wrong. However, the issue cannot at this point be entirely evaded. In the specific context of my comments on Windsor, it is clear that a massive cultural shift in relation to homosexuality has taken place in the last forty years. It is salutary for those referred to as "liberals" in this context to recall that many of the strongest advocates of the sexual revolution of the 1960s still regarded homosexuality as a form of perversion. Yet, change has taken place and seems, at many points, to be irreversible. Today, under–40s are less likely to make moral judgements about homosexual behavior and more likely to condemn as immoral those perceived as being prejudiced against others on the grounds of sexual orientation. If the church is sometimes accused of having a long way to go, society itself has, in historical terms, only very recently made an epochal shift. And where scripture and tradition are honored as sources of theological thinking there are real problems for the church to address in determining its own response to this shift, since it is clear that both scripture and tradition are more easily used by the so–called "conservative" side of the argument. To get good news for gays out of scripture involves making controversial hermeneutic moves and being entirely clear about what we are doing.

Possibilities for placing the argument on a wrong footing abound. Here is just one. In a recent radio interview I heard a comment that Gene Robinson had put himself forward as a "decent and honest" human being and been accepted as such. Bishop Robinson himself, it should be said, has always laid a theologically appropriate emphasis on his own brokenness and sinfulness, but his supporter, in this context, exhibited a worryingly naïve approach to Christian leadership. Recall Tillich's phrase that we are only ever accepted "in spite of being unacceptable". The secular liberal view that sexuality is an entirely innocent dimension of unfallen naturalness in the midst of human existence is not a Christian view.

Sexuality, like politics or, for that matter sport, is inseparable from the power plays and distortions of fallen existence. Vanity, pride, cruelty, complacency, cowardice and every other expression of our not being what we ought to be is as manifest in our sexual lives as elsewhere. And, of course, this applies not only to minority sexual orientations, but also to those whose sexual orientation finds an easy expression in the "normality" of marriage and family life. There is entire parity. The homosexual is unacceptable. The heterosexual is unacceptable. The homosexual is accepted in spite of being unacceptable. The heterosexual is accepted in spite of being unacceptable. This applies to every Christian – and to every Christian leader. The understanding of our solidarity in sin as the constant counterpoint of our solidarity with regard to the promise of redemption should never slip from view. We do not commend ourselves on the basis of what we judge to be our virtues,

11

ON UNIMPORTANCE

Christopher Lewis

Anglicanism is a way of being Christian which eludes easy definition. Its origins go back to an Elizabethan Settlement that attempted to steer a course between the excesses of both Rome and Geneva and resulted in the Church of England. The aim was to be as inclusive as possible, but without compromising the essentials of the faith. Confessional statements of belief have been deliberately avoided. It follows that in order to discover what the originator of Anglicanism, the Church of England, has believed involves a subtle and comprehensive search of the liturgy, the ordinal, the 39 Articles of Religion and the writings of leading "divines". Theological reflection has been conducted through the study of scripture, then of the tradition of the church, both judged by reason. As with all things religious, there has been ample room for controversy in the Church of England, but a manner of living as a church has been found and there is a strong family resemblance down the years, with those who emphasize the more "catholic" aspects, and those who major on the heritage of the Reformation pulling first one way then the other. There are, however, identifiable contributions to the whole from the various parties and groups; catholics have brought good liturgy, protestants serious biblical study, broad churchmen insights from disciplines other than theology, charismatics an emphasis on personal religious experience. What has emerged owes much not only to theology but also to what works; there has been pragmatism.

Anglicanism spread gradually, forming communities of those in communion with the Archbishop of Canterbury: in the United States, then in Canada, then India, and so on. In the second half of the nineteenth century, a number of provinces were created and the bishops first gathered at a Lambeth Conference in 1867 in response to controversy, and with some opposition to the meeting from those who feared a decision–making body. They met to consult rather than to legislate, but they eventually saw the need for a statement of what they believed to be essential for a Christian church and that wish led to the Chicago– Lambeth Quadrilateral, approved at the 1888 Conference. It is worth rehearsing the text in full both for what it does and for what it does not say:

> A. The Holy Scriptures of the Old and New Testaments, as "containing all things necessary to salvation", and as being the rule and ultimate standard of faith.
> B. The Apostles' Creed, as the Baptismal Symbol; and the Nicene Creed, as the sufficient statement of the Christian Faith.
> C. The two Sacraments ordained by Christ Himself – Baptism and the Supper of the Lord – ministered with unfailing use of Christ's Words of Institution, and of the elements ordained by Him.
> D. The Historic Episcopate, locally adapted in the methods of its administration to the varying needs of the nations and peoples called of God into the Unity of His Church.

Those are the basics for the Communion and for its relations with other churches. Although numerous subjects have been covered at the Conferences: unity, the scheme for the Church of South India, the doctrine of man, contraception, racism, the authority of the Bible, the Quadrilateral has not been added to. Throughout, it has been clear that resolutions passed are not binding on churches, but merely express the view of those who have agreed to meet.

The Anglican Communion has not seen itself as a church, but rather as a family, federation or commonwealth of churches, related through their origins and their relationship with the Archbishop of Canterbury. The distinction is crucial, for a church is something with defined authority, methods of (often democratic) decision–making, and a capacity for organization. So far, the Anglican Communion has had the Lambeth Conferences, an Anglican Consultative Council dating from 1969, and meetings of the Primates of the various provinces from 1979. Those methods of consultation have been sufficient, for each province is autonomous and too much self–definition would divert attention from essential tasks. William Wolf makes the point succinctly: "The spirit of Anglicanism combines tentativeness of statement about itself with finality of commitment to Christ."[1] Richard Hooker puts it more eloquently: "God alone excepted, who actually and everlastingly is whatsoever he may be, and which cannot hereafter be that which now he is not; all other things besides are somewhat in possibility, which as yet they are not in act."[2]

The Windsor Report

The origins of the report are in response to a perceived crisis in the Anglican Communion. The reaction is far from the measured reasonableness of Hooker where all but God is "somewhat in possibility", for the Report vigorously defends the unity of the Communion by strengthening the ties and "instruments" that bind it.

The central error is to give the Anglican Communion more ecclesiological significance than it in fact possesses. The degree of unity in the Communion has varied over the years, but with the advent of disagreements over homosexuality, it would have been appropriate to loosen the ties and enable sharply different provinces to develop in their

---

1 W. J. Wolf (ed), *The Spirit of Anglicanism* (Edinburgh: T & T Clark, 1979), p. 187.
2 Richard Hooker, *Of the Laws of Ecclesiastical Polity* (Cambridge: Cambridge University Press, 1989), p. 66.

own way. That would have been sociologically and theologically realistic, for it is unreasonable to expect African and North American (and indeed other) Christians to agree over a contemporary emotive moral issue, the interpretation of which is influenced by vastly dissimilar social contexts. It was Pascal who commented that what is truth on one side of the Pyrenees is error on the other, and it would be appropriate for the Anglican Communion to recognize at least some of the force of that aphorism.

Instead of lightening the links between the churches of the Communion, the firm aim of the Windsor report is to make them stronger and more legalistic, thus adding a new strand to the Lambeth Quadrilateral, namely an ecclesiological one, defining the legal interdependence of the provinces. The Communion is on the move towards mutual regulation. What has been a family with its full range of rows and reconciliations is becoming a cage in which sustained fighting is all but inevitable.

The means (or "instruments" to use the Report's chosen term) for this transition are spelled out: the existing institutions are to be strengthened and new ones added with the consequence that authority becomes less dispersed and more centralized. It is suggested that the Archbishop of Canterbury, as the focus of unity, articulate the mind of the Communion, especially in areas of controversy, and that he be given a new Council of Advice to support him in this role. The Anglican Consultative Council (ACC) should be made "more effective and more accountable, by being drawn from those persons who have a voice within the highest executive body of each province" (77), together with a more organized pattern of meeting for the Primates' standing committee and that of the ACC. The question is asked whether the ACC might be "the body which can take something approaching binding decisions for the Communion" (58). There is a proposal that the Lambeth Conference itself be given more clarity in relation to the "corporate episcopacy" and "worldwide leadership" of the bishops. More extreme still, in the light of the experience of the conference resolutions in 1998, there is the suggestion that there be a new and more exalted kind of resolution which could be stated to "touch upon the definition of Anglicanism" or upon "the authentic proclamations of the Gospel" (78); such resolutions would constitute definitive teaching.

The same theme is pursued with the proposal of an enhanced responsibility for the Primates' meeting, which in addition to being an opportunity for consultation, would become a gathering of enforcers of Lambeth resolutions, for it "should monitor developments in furtherance of resolutions of the Lambeth Conference in addition to the process of reception" (79). In order to perform this role, it should meet more frequently and have more formal and businesslike sessions. The proposals continue with a Secretary General in closer touch with the Archbishop of Canterbury and the ACC Chair, and a larger secretariat with the added role of monitoring developments in all the provinces.

Perhaps the most significant of all the proposals is one stemming from a meeting of the Primates in 2002, namely that canon law be yet another instrument of unity (61). The recommendation is that each church sign up to its own "communion law" which would commit the church in question to a common Anglican Covenant, a preliminary draft of which is given in an appendix to the report (81ff). The aim of such a covenant would be to express the common identity of the members, their relationship to each other, and their method not only of avoiding disputes, but also of managing them when they happen. The covenant is seen as preventing unilateral action: both of the kind engaged upon by the Episcopal Church in ordaining a bishop involved in a same gender union, and of the kind where a bishop from elsewhere has been asked by dissenting groups to provide pastoral and sacramental oversight in a particular diocese. In the preliminary draft, the obligation is spelled out that ministers and especially bishops shall not "act without due regard to or jeopardize the unity of the Communion" (84). In the last four articles, legal procedures are proposed for managing issues over which there is dispute.

From the above, it can be seen that the tendency is towards making the Anglican Communion into a church which can regulate its parts. There have been some developments in this direction over the years, speeded up at the 1998 Lambeth Conference when, contrary to wish of many of the bishops, a long resolution on sexuality was passed. There was applause at the conference when the Archbishop of Canterbury endorsed the final version of the resolution before the vote was taken.

Unity

The central problem of the Windsor Report is that it assumes that unity must necessarily increase, especially in the face of a "crisis". Unity is a truth of the Christian faith, but it is one that needs to be balanced with other truths. It follows that new mechanisms for ensuring unity are not in themselves good. They may be oppressive and result in the curbing of initiative. Thus the ordination of women to the priesthood and to the episcopate might well have foundered if the new "instruments" had been in place. At the moment the "problem" is perceived as that of same–gender unions and the ordination of people involved in such unions, but we have no way of predicting what will come next as a challenge and opportunity for the Anglican Communion. Then the Communion will be saddled with a structure which makes prophetic risk hard. With the wide range of different cultures represented within the Communion, it will lack the looseness of structure that would enable individual churches to develop in different ways. To present the alternatives in such situations as the glory of greater unity on the one hand, and the sad slide towards disintegration on the other, is logically and ecclesiologically false. The Communion could rediscover its roots as a consultative family of churches.

At first, there was the United Church of England and Ireland and the churches of the "different colonies and dependencies of the British Empire."[3] They saw no need to meet until there was

---

3   R. T. Davidson (ed), *The Lambeth Conferences of 1867, 1878 and 1888* (London: SPCK, 1896), p.10.

disagreement, so in a sense the Anglican Communion owes its origins to Bishop Colenso whose liberal views led to opposition. To quote one commentary on the movement: at a time when the streams "were showing signs of dribbling off into independent channels and perhaps individually losing themselves into parched cracks in a dry earth, Colenso stands out as a watershed which brought them all together."[4] Yet, they were careful about the manner of their meeting. Some bishops came for "brotherly counsel and encouragement" to the 1867 Conference. Others, including the Archbishop of York, stayed away. On that occasion and later, the resolutions were of a formal kind and the autonomy of the provinces was frequently referred to. There were many stipulations designed to preserve that autonomy and the 1888 Conference drew up guidelines to avoid interference and to prevent rogue priests from wandering into dioceses where they lacked the permission to function. The 1897 Conference similarly expressed its disapproval of two bishops exercising jurisdiction in the same place.[5]

Later conferences were occasionally more prescriptive, but they kept, on the whole, to their chosen role of encouragement and consultation for, as the 1930 Conference said: Anglicanism has "a dispersed rather than a centralized authority having many elements which combine, interact with, and check each other."[6]

It is a new and more corporate shape for the Communion that is now being proposed. The chosen image of the church in the Windsor Report is the body of Christ (19–21, 82). While that is a helpful image for some purposes, it has become so widely used in Anglican liturgy and popular theology that it is reached for without due thought in church reports. It speaks of the binding together of parts under the head and its implications are corporal, hierarchical and static. Although the head in the original image is Christ, it is inevitable that his headship carries over to other leaders, and is therefore a means of strengthening the authority

---

4 Dewi Morgan, *The Bishops Come to Lambeth* (London: Mowbray, 1967), p. 56.
5 *The Lambeth Conferences, 1867–1948* (London: SPCK, 1948), p. 288.
6 *The Lambeth Conferences*, Part 2, p. 85. See also Stephen Sykes (ed), *Authority in the Anglican Communion* (Toronto: Anglican Book Centre, 1987), pp. 11–22.

of particular people and structures in a church. If some part of the body does not function as the rest of the body expects or wishes, the whole is seen as sick or ill; that is how the current situation in the Anglican Communion is described in the Windsor Report (25–33). There is no explanation of why this corporate image of the church is preferred over others when attempting a theology of the Anglican Communion. Paul Minear found 96 images of the church in the New Testament, and many of these might be more suitable and indeed creative: the bride of Christ, the people of God, the vine, the new creation.[7] The Anglican Communion needs imaginative and outward–looking biblical images to encourage it to develop appropriately.

Homosexuality

During the 1998 Lambeth Conference, the Archbishop of Canterbury said "If this conference is known by what we have said about homosexuality, then we will have failed."[8] In that case, success eluded them. The subject attracts attention because sexuality is a currently emotive issue into which the bishops, the media, and many others are caught up.

Is it a vital issue? The answer to that question must be affirmative if we are asking whether it is important to people at a personal level, for it is part of their experience. The question, however, must also be asked of the church in general: Is homosexuality near the top of the hierarchy of subjects to which the church should attend? That there is an argument in train is not in doubt, but who exactly defines it as an important argument and why?

There is a hierarchy of truths in Christianity, which is not set by the ways of the world, but by the beliefs of the faith. There are essentials which center round the life, death and resurrection of Jesus and around the love of God and neighbor. Then there are matters of lesser significance, such as precise details of liturgy, attitudes to usury, the exact layout of (and length of stay in) hell, what to wear in church, and whether to select people by lot. In spite of the fact that some of

---

7 Paul Minear, *Images of the Church in the New Testament* (London: Lutterworth, 1961).
8 Anglican Communion News Service, 7 August 1998.

these minor matters receive attention in scripture and in the tradition of the church, they have been demoted (as "adiaphora") for a variety of reasons.

In the latter part of the nineteenth century, eternal punishment in hell was a subject of major debate. Indeed the 1867 Lambeth Conference was called in part because of agitation (ironically by the Canadian bishops) about John Colenso, Bishop of Natal, who, as well as doubting whether polygamists should divorce all but one wife prior to baptism (he was concerned about the fate of the other wives), was bold enough as to deny eternal punishment in hell. It is worth reflecting on why eternal punishment was not a major subject at, say, the 1988 Lambeth Conference. The Bible was the same, as was much of the tradition of the church; what had changed was their interpretation in the light of reason and experience. Not only did views on eternal punishment fail to provoke controversy among the theologically learned, but also preachers would be laughed at or disregarded if they majored on such views in the pulpit.

Crises come and go. At the 1888 Lambeth Conference, the dispute over polygamy continued, and the vote suggesting that polygamists be baptized only once they had reduced their wives to one, was passed by 83 votes to 21. What then about the wives of polygamists? The vote proposing that they should be admitted to baptism in some cases was passed: 54 to 34.

The 1930 Lambeth Conference gave qualified acceptance to contraception, reversing earlier resolutions. More interesting, however, is this comment on the 1930 Conference: "The Anglican ship is laboring in heavy weather, and not a few hands seem to be ready to help the wind and the waves to rock the boat."[9] The media were blamed for stirring up panic. What was the issue? It was the rejection by Parliament of the Church of England's 1928 revision of the Prayer Book. That snub was seen as a major Communion–threatening issue at the time because the Prayer Book (and its revisions) were perceived as essential to the Communion's unity.

---

9 N. S. Talbot, *Before We Meet* (London: Longmans, 1930), p. 4.

We elevate issues because they happen to be of concern to our particular age and place, but the church should be a check on such emphases. In the case of homosexuality, a subject, which gets scant attention in the Bible and in the tradition, is raised above others by the more protestant part of the church because it is seen as a test case in the battle against liberalism. So they want to heighten the temperature in order to obtain legislation on an issue, which has been, is, and will be best handled pastorally by bishops and others, as are similar secondary matters within the life of the church. The result is that God's mission in a needy world receives less attention. How does the church respond to a post–Christian and also post–atheist society in a creative and outward looking manner? The priority should be to attend to God.

For its part, the other side in the contest elevates the issue because of a supposed situation of persecution which makes homosexuality the test case of the church's moral attitudes: does the church show real love to the neighbor in its midst? In a western culture which is changing rapidly on this and other issues, there is no doubt that homosexuality is becoming more accepted, and that there are issues of far greater importance in the contemporary world to which the church should attend. Helping Christians who are persecuted in Muslim countries, reflection on the debates about abortion and cloning, the kinds of issues tackled by Amnesty International, the ecological future of the earth: all these subjects are of greater moral urgency than attitudes to homosexuality.

Other churches and other cultures have been much more relaxed about sexuality, seeing it as of being of importance to the people concerned but of no great significance to institutions.

Neither the Anglican Communion nor the issue of homosexuality merit the time and energy which are currently being put into them. The Anglican Communion should look to its origins and revert to being a family which meets to listen and consult. Homosexuality is a second order matter, which should be handled pastorally and locally; the church has more important tasks to which it should attend.

PART III

THE VALUE OF DIVERSITY

12

IN DEFENSE OF DIVERSITY

Andrew Linzey

The "problem" and the mandate

Archbishop Robin Eames in his Foreword to Windsor claims that "if realistic and visionary ways cannot be agreed to meet the levels of disagreement at present or to reach consensus on structures for encouraging greater understanding and communion in future it is doubtful if the Anglican Communion can continue in its present form" (6). But what precisely is the "problem" to which Windsor's recommendations purport to respond? It is explained in the mandate given to the Commission by the Archbishop of Canterbury to, *inter alia*, consider "the legal and theological implications flowing from the decisions of the Episcopal Church (USA) to appoint a priest in a committed same–sex relationship as one of its bishops, and of the Diocese of New Westminster to authorise services for use in connection with same sex unions ... and the ways in which provinces of the Anglican Communion may relate to one another in situations where the ecclesiastical authorities of one province feel unable to maintain the fullness of communion with another part of the Anglican Communion" (8). The Commission is asked to provide practical recommendations "for maintaining the highest degree of communion", and also to consider "the exceptional circumstances and conditions under which, and the means by which, it would be appropriate for the Archbishop of Canterbury to exercise an extraordinary episcopé" (8).

It is important to consider this mandate at the outset because the way the "problem" is framed inevitably influences the result. This can be grasped by considering alternative mandates that could have been presented to the Commission. The mandate could have asked the Commission to reflect upon the lively disagreements, sometimes creative, sometimes less so, that have characterized Anglican attitudes to sexuality, and to discern God's will in them. The Report could have been asked to lay out a plan for study and discussion throughout the Anglican Communion on theological issues relating to sexuality, including discussion with sexual minorities, who sometimes feel alienated from the church. It could have asked what specifically Christian ways there might be of living with differences, especially since some differences over sexuality have always, to some degree, been evident within the Christian community. The mandate could even have seen the "problem" as lying with those who oppose homosexual practice, or who cannot accept the valid deliberations of other autonomous provinces of the Communion. It could have seen a difficulty in the widespread persecution of homosexual persons[1] still present in countries where the Anglican Communion has a strong presence. Rather, by locating the difficulty in the canonically legitimate actions by autonomous provinces, and by highlighting the vocal opposition they have created among some Anglican churches, the issue is selectively presented at the outset. Moreover, by (prematurely) giving an indication of how the "problem" could be resolved, namely through the exercise of archiepiscopal power, the result is, to some extent, anticipated.

The point to be grasped is that the Report's work and recommendations flow from its mandate. Whether that mandate was the best, or only, or most adequate way of characterising the "problem" (if a problem it is) for the Anglican Communion is not self–evident. It is not at all clear, given Anglican history, that disagreement, even sharp

---

1 I use the words "homosexual" and "gay" throughout to denote same–sex behavior by homosexuals, lesbians, and bisexuals.

disagreement, should be avoided; neither is it self–evident that complex issues of sexuality should not legitimately lend themselves to the evolution of differing approaches, sometimes markedly so. Most of all, it is not obvious that those who – in the Commission's words – "yearn for expressions of communion which will provide stability and encouragement" (5) are articulating aspirations that could, or should, be met under all circumstances, or that the meeting of such aspirations, even if legitimate, should issue in the bold changes to Anglican self–governing as the Report proposes. The assumption seems to be that "unity" means principally "uniformity" in belief and practice, but whether that is attainable or desirable on the issue of sexuality is question begging.

Perhaps it is unfair, or unrealistic, to have expected the Commission to have considered the actual terms of its mandate. It had a job to do and, according to its own lights, it did it. But it should be for others to consider whether the mandate given at this juncture in Anglican history was the most theologically desirable or profitable. All Christians, including Anglicans, live under the judgement of God, and also the judgement of history. It has yet to be seen whether the mandate, and the Report which flowed from it, will serve the long–term interests of the Anglican Communion by articulating 'the problem' in the wa it has.

The putative "illness"

The foregoing has relevance to the precise way in which Windsor subsequently articulates the "problem". A "healthy" Communion, we are told, is rooted in the unity of God and should issue in the "radical holiness" of its members (11, para 3). The "problem", we are told, is actually an "illness". No definition is given of this word, and no evidence is supplied to warrant use of it. It is simply given as though its use is unexceptional. The "surface symptoms" of the "illness" are constituted by the apparent deviation of ECUSA and the Canadian provinces from what is termed "the standard of Anglican teaching" on the subject of sexuality as detailed in the statement by the Primates in 2003 (17, para 25). And, secondly, the "overwhelming" concern by Anglicans and others that these developments are "departures from genuine, apostolic faith" (18, para 28).

Then we are provided with an account of the "deeper symptoms" of the "illness". These include the apparent failure by ECUSA and the Diocese of New Westminster: (i) to "offer an explanation to, or consult meaningfully with, the Communion as a whole about the significant development of theology which alone could justify the recent moves by a diocese or a province" (20, para 33); (ii) to go through "procedures which might have made it possible for the church to hold together" (21, para 35); (iii) in believing that "they were deciding … things upon which Christians might have legitimate difference, while large numbers of other Anglicans round the world did not regard them in that way" (21, para 37); (iv) in thinking that they were "free to take decisions which many in the rest of the Communion believe can and should be decided at the Communion–wide level" (22, para 39); (v) in breaching "trust" within the Communion (22, para 40), and finally (vi) in failing to recognize authority, specifically the "supreme authority of scripture" (23, para 42). The section concludes: "It is because we have not always fully articulated how authority works within Anglicanism, and because recent decisions have not taken into account, and/or worked through and explained, such authority *as we all in theory acknowledge,* that we have reached the point where fresh thought and action have become necessary" (23, para 42; my emphases).

The problem with this account is that it assumes precisely what cannot be assumed, namely *"such authority as we all in theory acknowledge"*. There is no universal jurisdiction within Anglicanism, that is, there is no central, overriding authority, which has the power to oblige conformity among autonomous provinces. Indeed, it is the long–standing *characteristic* of Anglicanism that provinces are autonomous bodies tied together only by "bonds of affection and loyalty", and even that historical phrase has not been defined, and is therefore capable of differing interpretations. Appealing to an authority which "we all in theory acknowledge" is a beguiling, but vacuous claim. There is no authoritative or mutually agreed procedure, set of principles, canonical law, instruction, fiat, or command that ECUSA and the Diocese of New Westminster have failed to acknowledge in pursuing the actions they did. On the contrary, their own internal provincial procedures have been followed throughout.

All the "symptoms" of "deeper illness" turn out, on reflection, to be question begging or unreal. On (i), there is no formal obligation on autonomous provinces to explain or consult meaningfully on matters that come within their own jurisdiction. On (ii), it may or may not have helped church unity for ECUSA and the Canadian Diocese to go through (unspecified) "procedures", but there is no requirement on them to do so. On (iii), again, ECUSA and the Canadian Diocese violated no code or authority in deciding matters for themselves which, self–evidently, were, and are, matters of difference between Anglicans. On (iv), once again, there is no obligation, judicial or otherwise, for such matters to be decided by reference to the Communion as a whole; neither is it wholly clear whether such a consensus could be achieved, or what precise authority it would have. On (v), it is claimed that ECUSA's actions and those of the Canadian Diocese were a violation of a relationship of "trust", but since neither has willingly or knowingly entered into such a contractual relationship, none, by definition, can exist. Finally, on (vi), it is spurious to suppose that ECUSA and the Canadian Diocese have spurned "authority" since no central executive or juridical authority exists. The issue of scriptural authority will be considered later.

Now, of course, questions may be legitimately asked about how prudent, wise or mindful such actions were. Actions that arouse controversy are always capable of differing interpretations. But the implied claim that such bodies have acted in bad faith, or contrary to some agreed authority, or contrary to some doctrinal standard, is groundless. The notion that these actions *per se* are "departures from genuine, apostolic faith" is hard to fathom unless everything that the apostle Paul said is to be regarded as absolutely binding and, in any case, there is no authoritative Anglican statement to that effect. There is no creedal statement within Anglicanism about same–sex relations. Moreover, the assertion that other provinces have acted in a manner that "many in the rest of the Communion believe can and should be decided only at the Communion–wide level" (apart from being question begging because there is no central executive authority), sets up a standard that should equally apply to other Communion–wide disputed questions, such as the marriage of divorcées and the ordination of women as priests and bishops.

Interdependence means not giving offence

Having maintained that there is a central authority within Anglicanism, Windsor now turns to offering an interpretation of it that justifies limits to the freedom that all Anglican provinces have traditional enjoyed, and which has become the hallmark of Anglicanism itself. The first appeal is to "the communion we share". Communion, we are told, involves *inter alia* mutual relationships, a mutually recognized common ministry, and agreement on essentials. The upshot is that "the divine foundation of communion should oblige each church to avoid unilateral action on contentious issues which may result in broken communion" (26, para 51). Turning to the "bonds of communion", emphasis is placed on the authority of scripture, and on bishops, especially as teachers of scripture. The role of the Archbishop of Canterbury is described as the "chief pastor of the entire Communion" (31, para 65). There are, we are told, "acceptable and unacceptable forms of diversity" (para 71), but these are left largely unspecified. The notion of autonomy as applied to Anglican provinces is, apparently, "a far more limited form of independent government than is popularly understood by many today" (35, para 75). A province is autonomous "*only in relation to others:* autonomy exists in a relation with a wider community or system of which the autonomous entity forms part" (para 76). Autonomy is thus defined as: "the right of a church to make decisions in those of its affairs which also touch the wider external community of which it forms part, which are also the affairs of others, *provided those internal decisions are fully compatible with the interests, standards, unity and good order of the wider community of which the autonomous body forms part*". A restriction that includes "potentially contentious initiatives, *prior to* implementation …" (paras 79 and 82; my emphases).

Then follows a discussion of "adiaphora" (things which do not make a difference) based on an interpretation of St Paul's theology. The Report claims that St Paul insists that "in such matters as food and drink … are matters of private conviction over which Christians who take differing positions ought not to judge one another" (38, para 87).[2] But the Report argues that "not all differences can be tolerated":

> … Paul is quite clear that there are several matters – obvious matters being incest (1 Corinthians 5) and lawsuits between Christians before non–Christian courts (1 Corinthians 6) – in which there is no question of saying "some Christians think this, other Christians think that, and you must learn to live with the difference". On the contrary, Paul insists that some kinds of behaviour are incompatible with inheriting God's coming kingdom, and must not therefore be tolerated within the Church (39, para 89).

Not surprisingly, the Report goes on to consider *how* one can tell and *who* is to decide these all–important matters, and accepts that the "Church in each culture, and each generation, must hammer out the equivalent in complex and demanding judgements" (39, para 91). But it says that two questions must be asked:

---

2 Ironic actually because, as Acts 15.19–20 shows, the issue of food and drink were of major concern to the early church. Also, previous Lambeth conferences were themselves concerned with the issue of temperance and alcohol misuse, and there is now much debate among ethicists about vegetarianism. All this goes to show that what constitutes "adiaphora" is a more complex issue than the Report allows.

First, is this in fact the kind of matter which can count as 'inessential', or does it touch on something vital? Second, if it is indeed 'adiaphora', is it something that, nevertheless, a sufficient number of other Christians will find scandalous and offensive or that they will be forced, for conscience's sake to break fellowship with those who go ahead? *If the answer to the latter question is 'yes', the biblical guidelines insist that those who have no scruples about the proposed action should nevertheless refrain from going ahead* (40, para 93; my emphases).

The sharp limitations proposed here not only on provinces, but also on the decision–making of all Christian communities, need to be pondered. The first principle that provinces may only act "*provided [their] internal decisions are fully compatible with the interests, standards, unity and good order of the wider community of which the autonomous body forms part*" would, if adopted, have precluded both the re–marriage of divorcees and the ordination of women within the Anglican Communion. As the Report acknowledges, the decision by the Anglican Consultative Council to support the ordination of two women priests in 1970, by a narrow margin of 24 votes to 22, was highly contentious, and subsequent decisions by provinces either to ordain or not ordain women were similarly so. And action was taken *before* the matter was considered by the Lambeth Conference, as John Macquarrie, and others, noted subsequently.[3] Lambeth simply validated the changes *de facto*.

Hence, there was, as the Report understates, "a measure of impairment" (15, para 21). In fact, this "impairment" in the Church of England alone has involved heated, acrimonious controversy, and necessitated the appointment of alternative episcopal oversight.

---

3 John Macquarrie [untitled speech during the Conference], *The Report of the Lambeth Conference* 1978 (London: CIO Publishing, 178), Appendix, p. 118. Although Macquarrie thought the issue should have come before a Lambeth Conference, he was equally insistent that the ordination of women was a secondary issue, and that Anglicanism had always allowed for diversity in practice. See also his defense of diversity in *Christian Unity and Christian Diversity* (London: SCM Press, 1975).

Whatever the rightness or wrongness of ordaining women, no one could plausibly claim that such ordinations have always been "*fully compatible with the interests, standards, unity and good order of the wider community of which the autonomous body forms part*". As also acknowledged, different provinces exercise differing standards in the matter of allowing the remarriage of divorcées in church – and this, it must be admitted, in spite of the less than apparently unambiguous teaching of Jesus. If matters relating to our "common ministry" and the nature of Christian marriage are issues that can be decided by provinces, even though they clearly relate to Communion–wide "standards, unity and good order", why should not others, such as the consecration of an openly gay bishop? What over–riding grounds have we for this particular exclusion?

If the 1978 Lambeth Conference was right in respecting the "autonomy of each of its member churches, acknowledging that the legal right of each church to make its own decision about the appropriateness of admitting women to Holy Orders", while recognizing that such provincial action "has consequences of the utmost significance for the Anglican Communion as a whole" (14–15, para 16) in a matter so fundamental as our shared catholic ministry, on what possible grounds could, say, the purely local, diocesan provision of blessings for same–sex couples require prior "Communion–wide" endorsement?

The problem is compounded when consideration is given to the second proposed principle that, even if something is deemed inessential by some, but nevertheless causes a sufficient number of other Christians to be scandalised or offended, then "*the biblical guidelines insist that those who have no scruples about the proposed action should nevertheless refrain from going ahead*" (my emphasis). Such a principle would, by itself, have certainly ruled out the ordination of women (not to mention women bishops) and the remarriage of divorcées in church – both issues on which there is continuing controversy. Windsor has simply overlooked how large sections of the Anglican Communion, in

Britain and overseas, have been repeatedly offended or scandalized by innovations and developments whether they be ministerial, moral or liturgical.

And what are we to make of those other supposedly "obvious" issues of which St Paul speaks, including, most revealingly, lawsuits between Christians before non–Christian courts? No matter how admirable St Paul's sentiments may have been in one time and place, it is difficult, here as elsewhere, to believe that they have, without question and argument, continuing force and validity. And yet these assertions are made with the apparent full force of being "biblical guidelines" relevant for today. The Report's short excursus into biblical exegesis only shows how highly problematic it is to enumerate simple "biblical guidelines" for moral behavior – without the benefit of the accompanying Anglican notions of "reason" and "tradition". Windsor emphasizes the "supremacy of scripture", but Anglicanism has never committed itself to the inerrancy of every line of the Bible. Scripture needs to be critically interpreted, and, in fairness to St Paul, he never made the mistake of thinking he was infallible. It is disturbing to think that a handful of paragraphs offering uncritical commentary on Paul should be regarded as the scriptural "last word", even the main one. The partiality of the analysis is revealed when one considers why the deeply felt offence by gay people at their exclusion from ministerial and episcopal ordination is not even taken into account. Why should only the offended feelings of heterosexuals count in the church?

Instruments of uniformity

The Report now turns to how authority should be exercised in the Anglican Communion. Four "Instruments of Unity" are considered: the Archbishop of Canterbury, the Lambeth Conference, the Anglican Consultative Council, and the Primates Meeting. It argues that their "moral authority" should be more clearly articulated. Specifically, the Archbishop is proposed as "the focus of unity"; and the others as "Instruments of Communion" (44, para 105). The Archbishop's role should be enhanced with the establishment of a Council of Advice (46, paras 111–112). The Archbishop's right to invite to the Lambeth Conference should be on "restricted terms at his sole discretion if circumstances exist where full voting membership of the Conference is perceived to be an undesirable status, or would militate against the greater unity of the Communion" (45–46, para 110).

Most notably, Windsor urges the Primates to consider "the adoption by the churches of the Communion of a common covenant which would make *explicit and forceful* the loyalty and bonds of affection which govern the relationships between the churches of the Communion" (48, para 118; my emphases). This covenant would cover, *inter alia*, the management of communion affairs "including disputes". It would be signed by each of the Primates and, in due course, become "Communion law" in each of the member churches. The Report contends that the "Anglican Communion cannot again afford, in every sense, the crippling prospect of repeated worldwide inter–Anglican conflict such as that engendered by the current crisis' (49, para 119). The proposed "mechanism" would constitute an "international obligation" so that "in the event of a church changing its mind about the covenantal commitments, that church *could not proceed internally and unilaterally*" (49, para 119; my emphases).

This section bristles with difficulties at every turn. In the first place, the use of the term "Instruments of Unity" is nowhere defined, and is question begging. The word "instrument", by definition, implies a means to an end, i.e. a tool or thing used to perform a particular action. But it is by no means clear that any of the agencies should be properly defined in that way. For example, the purpose of the Lambeth Conference is not to effect or contrive unity. As was made clear by Archbishop Longley who called together the first Conference in 1867, it was to be a meeting solely for "brotherly counsel and encouragement". Even more: "In case any risk of divergency to the point even of disruption should arise, it is clear that the Lambeth Conference as such could not take any disciplinary action." "Formal action" would continue to reside where it belonged in "individual [member] churches", though the advice of Lambeth should "carry very great moral weight".[4] This view has been variously reaffirmed by subsequent Conferences. The Report earlier refers to a Lambeth resolution as representing the "standard of Anglican teaching", but Lambeth is not an authorized teaching body, it has no juridical authority, its resolutions have, at best, only advisory or "moral" weight, and not even attendance is formally required of diocesan bishops. Lambeth may, at best, be an *expression* of unity, even a *cementing* of it through inter–personal counsel and encouragement, but it is misleading to describe it as an "instrument" of unity. Similar observations apply to the other putative "instruments of unity".

Windsor says that it does "not favour the accumulation of formal power by the Instruments of Unity, or the establishment of any kind of central 'curia' for the Communion" (44, para 105), but then goes on to describe a form of "management" that will enable something very similar, if not identical. The Archbishop will have "enhanced" power, supported by a non–elected "Council of Advice", even to the point of "restricting" the nature of Lambeth invitations. He becomes effectively a patriarch in all but name – "a central focus of unity and mission within the Communion" (45, para 109). It must follow of course that such an exalted position will have increased power – exercised either by personal right or in conjunction with others. And that is exactly what is proposed, since the "covenant" makes member churches liable to a new wide–ranging system of authority that expressly excludes "internal or unilateral action" on any disputed matter.

The Report makes its reasoning clear: "Our opinion is that, as some matters in each church are serious enough for each church currently to have a law on those matters – too serious to let the matter

---

4 Archbishop Longley cited in Dewi Morgan, *The Bishops Come to Lambeth* (London: Mowbray, 1957), p. 58. The first Lambeth Conference was only set up with the explicit archiepiscopal assurance that these conferences were to be for "brotherly counsel and encouragement", but "no more", p. 60. And this, it should be noted, was at a time when there was widespread concern about the apparently unorthodox writings of Bishop Colenso.

be the subject of an informal agreement or mere unenforceable guidance – so too with global communion affairs" (48, para 117). But the practical result must be a harmonization of *all* church "law" throughout the Communion, and its real, effective enforcement, even against the wishes of individual member churches. And the exercise of this enforceable discipline, however advised, will be centred on the Archbishop of Canterbury. What is this but the "accumulation of formal power", the establishment of a "central curia", and the adoption of a quasi–papal role for the Archbishop himself? Those Primates who sign the covenant document will, ineluctably, be locking themselves into a new system of discipline and authority from which they will be unable to escape.

To grasp how far we have moved from the *modus operandi* of historic Anglicanism, one needs only to recall the words of Archbishop Donald Coggan at the Lambeth Conference of 1978: "There are those who would say perhaps that authority ought to be centred in the person of the Archbishop of Canterbury himself, but down the years the feeling against that has, I think rightly, been strong. It is not, I believe, of the genius of Anglicanism to have at its head someone who is papal or patriarchal, though that has been discussed many a time".[5]

Moreover, when we consider what areas will be covered by the new "Communion law", it becomes clear that since the express purpose is to exclude "world–wide inter–Anglican conflict, *such as that engendered by the current crisis*" (49, para 119; my emphases), the issue of ordaining homosexual persons as priests and bishops, as well as the authorization of same–sex blessing ceremonies, will ineluctably be included among them. In other words, the traditional autonomy of provinces to exercise their own judgements in these matters – as well as others – will be eclipsed. For the sake of unity – understood as not much more than the uniformity of belief and practice – traditional freedoms will be sacrificed. The result will be a more centralized Anglican Communion than ever before.

---

5 Archbishop Donald Coggan [untitled speech at the Conference] in *The Report of the Lambeth Conference 1978*, ibid, p. 122.

Conformity or excommunication

The final section now turns to how the "crisis" apparently generated by ECUSA and the Diocese of New Westminster can be immediately resolved. It concludes that "all [presumably both those for and against] have acted in ways incompatible with the Communion principle of interdependence, and our fellowship together has suffered immensely as a result of these developments" (50, para 122). The Commission "regrets" the consecration of Gene Robinson; the 74th General Convention resolution of ECUSA which welcomed same–sex liturgies; the Diocese of New Westminster's approval for the use of public rites for the blessing of same–sex unions; the General Synod of the Anglican Church of Canada's statement affirming the "integrity and sanctity of same–sex relationships", and finally that a number of Primates and other bishops have intervened in the affairs of other provinces (50–51, para 123).

The rationale in relation to ECUSA is unambiguous: "By electing and confirming such a candidate in the face of concerns expressed by the wider Communion, the Episcopal Church (USA) has caused deep offence to many faithful Anglicans both in its own church and in other parts of the Communion" (52, para 127). ECUSA is asked to express "regret", bishops who took part in the consecration are asked to reconsider their positions, and ECUSA is asked to affect a moratorium on the consecration of persons in same gender unions (53, para 134). In relation to the Diocese of New Westminster, the Report observes that "there is not an unqualified freedom on the part of any bishop or diocese to authorise liturgical texts if they are likely to be inconsistent with the norms of liturgical and doctrinal usage extant in the province's *Book of Common Prayer* or other provincially authorised texts" (55, para 138). The authorization of any such texts "in the face of opposition … constitutes a denial of the bonds of Communion" (56, para 141). Because they go "against the formally expressed opinions of the Instruments of Unity they constitute action in breach of the legitimate application of the Christian faith as the churches of the

Anglican Communion have received it, and the bonds of affection in the life of the Communion, especially the principle of interdependence" (56, para 143). An expression of "regret" is called for together with a moratorium on future authorization of such texts.

Windsor concludes with a warning that it "would rather not speculate on actions that might need to be taken if, after acceptance by the Primates, our recommendations are not implemented. However, we note that there are, in any human dispute, courses that may be followed: processes of mediation and arbitration; non–invitation to relevant representative bodies and meetings; invitation, but to observer status only; and, as an absolute last resort, withdrawal from membership" (60, para 157).

Flawed ecclesiology: no room for the Spirit

There are a number of deeply troubling aspects to the Report which concern not just the treatment of homosexuals, but also the future of the Anglican Communion.

We need to look again at the opening pages. "God's people are to be, through the work of the Spirit, an anticipatory sign of God's healing and restorative future for the world" (11, para 2). The Communion among Christians "is the specific practical embodiment and fruit of the Gospel itself … and to inaugurate a new creation". Again: "The unity (specifically celebrating the diversity within that unity) to which Christ's body is called" is enabled by the work of the Spirit specifically through "the apostolic, prophetic, evangelistic, pastoral and teaching ministries which the Spirit enables' (11, para 3).

The Report says that, "Over the centuries Anglicans have lived out the gift of communion in mutual love and care for one another. We have at times embraced costly grace in standing together in opposition to racial enslavement and genocide" (13, para 9). But what Windsor nowhere acknowledges is that ECUSA and the Canadian Diocese see their actions *as responses to the Spirit* – as prophetic signs that witness to the care that Anglicans ought to have for *all* its members, including gays. It shows no understanding of the "costly grace" (including vilification, public misrepresentation, and threats of violence) that our American and Canadian brothers and sisters have been prepared to bear. It doesn't seem to occur to the Commission that their witness is precisely an attempt to be "an anticipatory sign" of God's healing and restorative future. Our "mutual love and care" ought at least to begin with understanding why our fellow Christians have acted in the way they have. Instead, the account given only sees *their* actions as a threat to the rest of *us*. The divine "gift of communion" should at least have involved the Commission in demonstrating that they have actually attended, without prejudice, to the voices they are so willing to publicly oppose. If communion, as we are told, is an obligation on us all, then this should apply to the work of commissions as well as provinces.

Secondly, there is no attempt to situate or contextualize the actions of American or Canadian Anglicans. Throughout the Report, the impression given is that they are wayward, obscurantist or willful, unmindful of the concerns of the wider Communion. But the analysis is lacking context, and that context is the deeply held belief that the Christian tradition has been unjust and discriminatory towards homosexual people. Even worse, that it has participated in, if not fuelled, their worldwide vilification and still active persecution. Only one paragraph of the Report is devoted to homophobia and the demonization of homosexual people. It cites in support the Lambeth resolution of 1988 that provinces should "reassess, in the light of … study and because of our concern for human rights, its care and attitude toward persons of homosexual orientation" (57, para 146). But it doesn't consider that the actions of fellow American and Canadian Anglicans might actually be responding to this, and similar, calls. It wants to take as read Anglican commitment to the rights of homosexuals, whereas in fact the violence of the anti–gay language deployed by some Anglican agencies belies this. The Commission seems unaware of the terrible forces of hatred and prejudice under which gay people are forced to live throughout the world.   Moreover, the

Commission utterly lacks any kind of appropriate self–analysis about the discriminatory nature of Anglican practices towards homosexuals, including the Church of England's recently sought dispensation to dismiss employees specifically on grounds of sexual orientation.[6]

The same paragraph accepts that "it has to be recognised that debate on this issue cannot be closed whilst sincerely but radically different positions continue to be held across the Communion". But since the result of adopting the Report's recommendations will be to outlaw any provincial action deemed controversial by another, it will put an effective stop on all further action until there is a consensus among all Anglican provinces. There can be debate it seems, but no action until a majority of provinces agree.

Unity in diversity

Thirdly, there is an insufficient grasp of the nature of Anglican diversity on moral issues.[7] Like many church reports, it likes to think that there is greater uniformity than actually exists. It scolds ECUSA and the Diocese of New Westminster for failing to observe the "standard" of Anglican teaching, but omits to mention that it is, like all such "teaching" based on Lambeth resolutions, wholly advisory at best. Nowhere is this clearer than on the issue of war and violence. Successive Lambeth Conferences of 1930, 1948, 1968, and 1978 declared that "war as a method of settling international disputes is incompatible with the teaching and example of Our Lord Jesus". But that hasn't stopped individual churches authorizing priests to serve in the armed forces as chaplains, even though they are required to wear military uniform and are subject to service discipline. And neither has it stopped individual Christians and ordained ministers making up their own minds about

---

6 See my critique of discriminatory Anglican practices, Andrew Linzey, "Time for the church to take the beam out of its own eye", *The Independent*, 15 May, 2004, p. 45.
7 I have made the same case for moral diversity, and in similar words, in my "On Theology" in P. A. B. Clarke and Andrew Linzey (eds), *Theology, the University and the Modern World* (London: LCAP, 1988), pp. 58–59.

the rights and wrongs of particular wars, and participating in the ones they believe to be just. Among the ranks of the Church of England can be found the widest possible range of positions from CND campaigners, dedicated pacifists, NATO generals to ex–Greenham Common protesters. I should add that, even though I believe that the possession of nuclear weapons, as part of a "defense" strategy, is intrinsically evil, I am still in communion with my diocesan bishop who believes that the possession, threatened use, and even actual use of such weapons is morally permissible.[8]

But if such diversity of opinion is not only possible, but also legitimate, within the Anglican community on such a fundamental and basic question as to whether we may justifiably kill, injure, terrorize, not only individual human beings, but most of the earth and its inhabitants, then the same freedom must also be legitimate on each and every moral issue. If there can be diversity here, there must be diversity everywhere. It really will not do for some Christians to speak as though there is a legitimate diversity of view on questions such as the use of nuclear weapons, but a "line" that must be followed on such issues as divorce, abortion, and homosexuality. The fact is that there is diversity of opinion on every moral issue of any importance confronting the church today.

And yet, this fact is often disguised, subject to particular interpretations, or indeed a cause of embarrassment. But why? It is frequently accepted as axiomatic within Christian churches that uniformity of opinion on moral issues is desirable. But why? The strongest argument is that the church should possess the "mind of Christ" and therefore be of one opinion.[9] But the mistake here is to suppose that the "mind of Christ" is monochromatic and that correspondingly there is one view of every moral issue that our Lord wishes for each individual Christian, or for the whole church. Such an

---

8 "Not every conceivable use of nuclear weapons would violate the principle of discrimination and proportion", Richard Harries, *Christianity and War in a Nuclear Age* (London: Mowbray, 1986), p. 140.
9 See Harry Blamires, *The Christian Mind* (London: SPCK, 1963), pp. 3f. for a classic statement of this position.

understanding presupposes what was not even true of the historical Jesus. In the not wholly unjustified words of Archbishop John Habgood, there is a "popular misconception, especially apparent among people who write angry letters to bishops that the teaching of Jesus was simple. In fact he rarely gave a simple answer to a simple question".[10]

It is important that my argument here should not be misunderstood. It is not that any Anglican should adopt any moral view that he or she wishes. Neither is it that it does not matter what moral views Christians hold. Nor yet, is it that some views are not better, that is rationally and theologically preferable, than others. As I have indicated, I regard the possession of nuclear weapons as beyond the pale. But I cannot deny, and neither can the church as a whole deny, that there exist thoughtful, sensitive and prayerful Christians who have explored this, and other matters, with all due seriousness, and have come to opposite views. We must give up as infantile the notion that all Christians have to morally agree on every issue.

In my view, then, the Archbishop and the Primates would have been better advised at the outset of the controversy to have simply affirmed the fact of moral diversity among Anglicans and the freedom of diocesan bishops and provinces to act according to their consciences. Unity and communion would have been better served by a frank and honest recognition that disagreement is not in itself a sign of infidelity to Christ, or the demands of truth, or the fellowship that Anglicans can, at best, have within the church. Sometimes one may be forgiven for thinking that there is a half–neurotic fear of difference that pervades Christian moralizing in some sections of the church today.

Fourthly, if what is meant by the "fullness of communion" is in reality "uniformity of belief" then it seems inevitable that the Anglican Communion has set itself on the road to perpetual conflict as one section of the Church vies for intellectual or numerical supremacy over

---

10 Archbishop John Habgood, *Church and Nation in a Secular Age* (London: Darton, Longman and Todd, 1983), p. 75.

the rest. As we receive it today, Anglicanism has been shaped by three distinct factions each with their own particular emphases: "liberal", "catholic" and "evangelical". These are of course only labels, and many of us (myself included) are able to identify with more than one of these emphases from time to time. Currently, Anglicans with an "evangelical" emphasis are numerically strongest in some parts of the church and within certain provinces. It is only understandable, therefore, that they should seek to influence church polity in the direction of those convictions that they hold dearest. But if there is not to be perpetual conflict, it is vital that each faction does not seek during the period of its (almost certainly transitory) ascendancy to push the Communion too far in adopting principles or practices that permanently exclude other emphases and integrities.

Fifthly, the consecration of Gene Robinson does not, by itself, exclude anyone. On the contrary, it was intended as a symbolic statement of the need for greater inclusion of homosexual people within the Anglican Communion. The so-called "crisis" that has followed is not occasioned by any infringement of that province's canonical procedures, but chiefly by the reaction of some provinces who cannot, apparently, live in communion with that particular bishop or province, and who have, in some well-publicized cases, decided to intervene in the autonomous affairs of that province.

Historic Anglicanism will become untenable if provinces do not respect not only the geographical integrity, but also the moral and theological integrity, of other provinces who, after due deliberation in accordance with canonical procedures, decide that, in all conscience, they need to pioneer and embody in their own church life their own deepest convictions. Conversely, pioneering provinces must also respect that others will not always agree with them, and have the right to move as slowly as they wish or, indeed, in an opposite direction. Unity-in-communion requires that we hold on to each other, even, and especially, when we believe that the other is deeply mistaken. But what one part of the church cannot be allowed to do is to rule out for all time the embodiment of theological and moral sensibilities that others, in all good conscience, feel compelled to realise. Such would be the way of stagnation as well as conflict.

Sixthly, Windsor would have better served the Anglican Communion if it had utilized the necessary expertise to provide a historical perspective on the current "controversy". For if one looks at the previous issues, vigorously, and sometimes acrimoniously, debated at Lambeth Conferences, one cannot be but struck by their now – to us – limited significance for the future well–being of the church. That roster includes debates about artificial contraception, the indissolubility of marriage, temperance, and the place of biblical criticism. Invariably, each generation thinks that it has discovered the core "Gospel" issue that will make or break the church. Our maturity as Anglicans should consist, not only in a serious engagement with the apparently pressing issues of our time, but also in a realization that, by God's providence, the passage of time frequently relativizes even our deepest convictions. Future generations of Anglicans (if Anglicanism has a future) may be astonished that abjuring same–sex relationships was once seriously considered as a criterion for full communion. Living with diversity is a practical embodiment of the Anglican conviction that truth will win out – given time.

Seventhly, the Archbishop is urged by the Report to refuse or to restrict an invitation to the next Lambeth Conference to Bishop Robinson. Such invitations are of course within the personal discretion of the Archbishop, but it must be hoped that he will think long and hard before acceding to such a request. Not since Bishop Colenso in 1867, has the archbishop exercised his power to non–invite any fellow diocesan bishop, and it would be without precedent for the Archbishop to do so to any diocesan bishop who has not been found guilty of an ecclesial offence. Such a step would constitute a form of ex–communication, without parallel and precedent within the Communion. More importantly, the symbolic – and historical – significance of any such move should not be underestimated or the nature of the controversy it would engender. It would symbolize, *inter alia*, the Communion's corporate rejection of the first openly gay bishop in Anglican history, and would – and should – be interpreted as a public rejection of the cause of justice for gay people.

Diversity or centralization?

Eighthly, it may be argued that the degree of moral diversity currently accepted within the Communion makes for an untidy, sometimes confusing, even disparate church. But what is the alternative? It is a more centralized church, with a clearer set of rules, and the power to enforce them. Such a church would become less free and necessarily more coercive. It would achieve a kind of uniformity, but at the expense of conviction and conscience. Is this what God is really willing for the Anglican Church? Is this, then, the vocation of Anglicanism to become a mirror image of other centralized churches where church law is obeyed, even though obedience is sometimes only nominal and half–hearted? Is this compliance really the "fullness" of communion, to which the Spirit is calling us? Windsor offers its remedy, namely more centralized control, without any appreciation of how problematic the exercise of such centralizing mechanisms has been (and still are) in other churches.

It is wrong, of course, to suppose that living with diversity is easy. On the contrary, it requires a preparedness to be confronted and challenged, both personally and intellectually, and to consider that even in matters close to our hearts, we may be mistaken. I have already given the example of nuclear weapons and indicated how painful it is for me to be part of a church that does not share my basic moral conviction. But living in communion is not meant to be a pain–free experience – indeed, it cannot be if we are interested in a kind of belonging that allows room for learning and growth. Each church within Christendom has its own particular gifts, traditions and heritage, and perhaps it is the vocation of Anglicanism, within the wider body, to be an experiment in a kind of unity that includes a wider range of diversity than hitherto imagined.

But the question to be pondered is whether any church can be responsive to the Spirit without controversy, without heated debate, without sometimes at least infringing what some regard as the best interests of the church including "standards of unity and good order"? The history of the church is littered with examples of how the Spirit chose individuals and movements to provoke and disturb. Only last year, during the centenary of John Wesley, Anglican leaders expressed their repentance at the action of their forebears that drove the movement called "Methodism" out of the Anglican fold, quietly forgetting that, in its day, charismatic preachers and the supposedly wild excesses of Methodists were regarded by the Anglican establishment as threatening as the gay liberation movement is today. Anglicans need to remember that in addition to being heirs to the Catholic tradition, they are also heirs of the Reformation – a movement, which, whatever its excesses, was surely also a response to the movement of the Spirit. Those who have the difficult task of "managing" the church often forget that movements that disturb and upset the faithful can also be the work of the Spirit.

Most glaringly, the picture of the Spirit is one that really never disturbs, frightens, or challenges believers. But, if by the same Spirit, we are called to a genuinely prophetic ministry then we shall want to be involved in a much deeper kind of discernment of movements and sensibilities that appear to challenge or jeopardize current orthodoxy. It is one of the weaknesses of the Report that it does not even ask the question whether the movement for the dignity and rights of homosexual people is not, in part, the result of a kind of prompting by the Spirit that wishes to remind us of the full humanity of every person.

It is revealing that the Report congratulates Anglicanism on resisting racial discrimination, and what is called (quite erroneously) "the heresy" of apartheid. As someone who was involved in that struggle, it may come as a surprise to some to learn that many churchpeople at the time were quite indifferent to that issue (including not a few bishops), and the Anglican record, while thankfully impressive overall, is not, to say the least, wholly unblemished. And neither, it must be said, is the Anglican record on colonialism, slavery, and even the introduction of race relations legislation other than chequered. It will not do to "back shadow" (to use the contemporary idiom) previous Anglican opposition to progressive movements simply because, unlike the cause of justice for gays, they have finally triumphed.

Non–offense as the basis of communion

Ninthly, "offence" is an inadequate (and only tenuously biblical) basis for censoring the actions of fellow Anglicans. If all must be unoffended, then reform (in its widest sense) must proceed at the slowest possible rate, if at all. This is a recipe for a moribund church. And, without doubt, it would be a church without women as priests and bishops, since this development, bold and audacious as it is, does not continue without offense, and even the daily possibility of schism. And yet, is not the Anglican Communion stronger, truer to itself, now that it has allowed this development, whilst also respecting the consciences of those who differ? Offence should be an occasion for heart–searching and discernment, but it should never be a biblical stop–all to the possibility of reform. The traditional freedom of provinces is perceived as threatening and troublesome rather than as the gift of one part of the church to another. The idea that we might have something to learn from the prophetic action of fellow churches is nowhere articulated. Interdependence comes to mean not learning from one another, but rather "not giving offense". Given the existing structure of Anglicanism, the Commission's call for ECUSA bishops, who have committed no canonical offence, to reconsider their position is both *ultra vires* and impertinent.

But, of course, Windsor doesn't remotely understand the offense, which its recommendations cause both to the gay community and to those who believe in justice for gays. The "understanding" and "sensitivity" required is all in one direction; gays are just meant to be quiet and submissive. Their voice really isn't heard; their offended feelings not even noticed; nowhere is there the slightest appreciation of why Bishop Robinson's consecration meant so much to many thousands of Anglicans, who felt alienated or vilified.

The logic of exclusion

Tenthly, the Report says that addressing the gay issue specifically was not part of its mandate, and that is true, but the issue permeates its discussion and should be addressed directly. There are some "evangelicals" who believe that practicing gay behavior is wrong and contrary to scripture. That is a coherent position in its own terms, and it must be said that it has been the position held by many Anglicans throughout the centuries. But some "evangelicals" want to go further, and say that gay behaviour is incompatible with *any* form of Christian discipleship. And that view is evident from the rather limited biblical exegesis in the Report where it refers, uncritically, to the view of St Paul that certain kinds of behavior disqualify individuals from eternal life. Now, the logic of that position is clear: all gays, including those who conscientiously differ, should leave the church. They should be debarred from all the sacraments, including baptism, and confirmation, as well as ordination. "Evangelicals" seldom present their case in such strong terms, but that is the logic of it. It won't do (if we are to follow Windsor's own biblical exegesis) to say that only *representative* Christians should go, such as priests and bishops, since what is wrong behavior is wrong behavior – and is not made right because one is a layperson or *vice versa*. Indeed, what is shown clearly by the recent controversy over the proposed consecration of Jeffrey John is that some oppose not only wrong behavior as they see it, but also what they call "false teaching", that is anyone who takes a different view.

But we must be clear about the implications of all this. If that is to be the position, then gays – *and* those who believe in justice for gays – will have to leave the church. And where will this leave the Church of England in particular? Well, many gay people serve, and have served, the church with great distinction. Their ranks include many laypeople and priests – and I'm told some bishops. It means that the church will exclude a good section of its existing membership as well as dishonoring the memories of those who have, according to their own lights, faithfully served the Communion over the years. That may well be the way the Anglican Communion is heading – and it seems clear that that is at least the intention of those who now propose a new "Communion law". Well, so be it. But let it be stated frankly and in a spirit of Christian candor. Don't let's hide it or dissemble it. Let it come out into the open, and let's face the implications of it with as much generosity of spirit as we are able as Christians. But let us be quite clear: those who are gay *and* those who conscientiously believe that the tradition has got it wrong will either have to align themselves with another part of the Communion that will not succumb to the new Communion law, or leave; integrity will require no less.

Let us also be clear about the far-reaching nature of this decision. For it will affect many more people than its proposers suppose. The Archbishop of Canterbury for one. He has said publicly that he has ordained an openly gay person when Bishop of Monmouth, and his other than wholly traditional views of gay relationships are a matter of public record, and he has not, honest as he is, recanted them. Other bishops and priests are in similar situations. There is therefore something unreal about the Report supposing that current loyalty to the Archbishop should be the test of Anglican fealty since it is already known (and was known prior to his election) that he holds views, and has performed ministerial actions, that some find unacceptable. The Report sees no irony in wanting the Archbishop to become a visible focus of unity, and an "Instrument" of discipline, despite the fact that he is already regarded, by those who want that view to prevail, as a "false teacher" himself. It will be doubly ironic if some Anglicans find themselves separated from the see of Canterbury because they support the ministerial actions and public writings of the current Archbishop of Canterbury.

Insistence that gay behavior, and "false teaching" on this subject, cannot be allowed will effectively mean that this one issue becomes the cornerstone of contemporary Anglican orthodoxy. It may (probably will) be commanded by a majority and made into law. But let us also think about what this says about our understanding of what Christian discipleship means in our time. Currently, priests are allowed to do a range of things that some Christians may (certainly would in some cases) find unacceptable or unbecoming a Christian minister (and, not a few would add, Christian laypeople too). These include: hunting foxes, accumulating wealth, smoking, smacking children, attending bullfights, investing in arms production, participating in the armed forces, and drinking alcohol. I hold strong views myself about some of these matters. But to isolate sexual behavior, and specifically one form of it, as in need of absolute censure – so that ordination or membership is totally excluded betokens, it must be said, a deeply disproportionate understanding of Christian morality. While certain verses (uncritically utilized) of St Paul can be garnered in support of it, even in context it is balanced by reference to other activities – many of which we do not legislate on and some (such as Christians bringing cases before a secular court) – which we currently find unexceptional.

Moreover, when viewed from the perspective of the teaching of Jesus, we find other matters, notably, violence and revenge, lack of forgiveness, acquisitiveness, hardness of heart, and spiritual hubris, highlighted and uncovered as the primary stumbling blocks to Christian discipleship. Indeed, Jesus' actions indicate a special regard for the outcast, the diseased, the friendless, and the socially alienated that makes one wonder whether specific action against gays as a persecuted community is really compatible with a Christ–like life at all. To select homosexuality – among all the range of possible prescriptions, obligations and admonitions that might legitimately emanate from the Christian moral tradition – is itself a sign of a contemporary obsession with physical sexual behavior that should be regarded as unhealthy.

Now, some "evangelicals" might reply that, for consistency's sake, the line *ought* to be more tightly draw and exclude most, or all, of the unacceptable behaviors I have mentioned. Well, that could certainly be done, and doubtless there are some who would like it to be done. But what would be the result? It would be a church in which fewer were eligible for ordination, indeed only after rigorous scrutiny could anyone be admitted at all. Such would be a purist church, which legislated in detail for its members and its representatives – and some churches of that kind have existed and do exist today. But, in the process, such a church would cease to be a church as we have understood it, and would, in fact, become a sect. Now, there may be a case for the establishing of such sects, but we should be quite clear that they would no longer be recognizably "Anglican", at least as we have come, historically, to understand that word. Such a body might conceivably exclude "sin" or, rather, overt expressions of it, but might it not also exclude the Spirit, who promises a deeper understanding of Christ, even to the point of revealing new things to us?

We cannot exclude the possibility that the Spirit is speaking to us through the current "crisis", but in ways in which we do not yet fully apprehend. One of the regrettable features of the Report is that it grasps only the apparent damage to the "bonds of unity" in the current dispute, but nothing of the possibility of spiritual renewal. And yet no one has a handle on the Spirit – and the strident notes of condemnation, which are so evident from the other side, do not obviously lend themselves to a sense that they are Spirit–led voices revealing more of the mind of Christ. The Spirit blows where she wills, and it may be that we are being disturbed and challenged to re–think our traditional categories of what constitutes sexual sin and Godly sexual behavior in a way that many of us find deeply uncomfortable and unsettling, but which, in the fullness of God's time, may lead to a richer understanding of the Gospel and a more humanly compassionate church.

13

COMMUNION AS DISAGREEMENT

Thomas E. Breidenthal

The Windsor Report asserts that "unity, communion, and holiness all belong together" (1). This assertion is correct, in my view. With regard to *unity*, Christianity teaches that the human race is one: whether we like it or not, we are all connected to one another. No matter how much we may attempt to evade or delimit this connection, the sheer fact of it is inescapable. The stranger is always revealed as my neighbor, as someone who is near to me, for good or ill, whether in claiming my help, as the homeless person on my doorstep, or in offering help, as the stranger who offers me the extra change to pay my subway fare. Given this inescapable nearness, Christianity teaches that connection is something to be embraced, not escaped. God does not offer us salvation apart from, or as an escape from, our common membership in the human race.

For all the danger that we pose to one another (and this danger is a feature of our nearness to each other), we were created for community and in community, and cannot exist apart from community. Jesus has opened the way to a radical and universal embrace of connection to one another, both by his example as a human being, and by his power as the incarnate word of God. Jesus has shown that our connection to one another is a thing to be redeemed. The redemption of the unity of the human race is a key tenet of the

Christian hope, and the unity of Christians is a station on the way to the realization of that goal.

This understanding of unity is central to our discernment of our present situation as Anglicans. And so we come to *communion* and *holiness*. Communion names our willingness to embrace unity within the household of faith. The church comprises the fellowship of those followers of Christ who have committed themselves to the discipline of communion – that is, the embrace of union – first with one another, and then ultimately with the human race as a whole, in order to be schooled in holiness. Thus communion is not so much a formal relationship as it is a moral practice – that is, it is not so much something we are in as something that we do. As followers of Jesus, seeking fellowship with all human beings, we practice being in communion with one another, so that we might be sanctified.

Here the church as the household of faith mirrors every Christian household as a laboratory where the embrace of the neighbor is learned and practiced.[1] But the crucial difference between individual Christian households and the household of faith is this: in individual households we learn to love the neighbor under the condition of familiarity. In the household of faith, the challenge is to stand around the table with those who are unfamiliar to us, and further, with those whose understanding of discipleship may, in all good faith, be fundamentally at odds with ours. This is a hard and exacting discipline, enjoined by Jesus on his friends for the world's sake. In large part, the church has failed this test, as is shown in our history of schism after schism.

In light of this perennial failure, the Windsor Report rightly draws our attention to the preciousness of the worldwide communion we enjoy as Anglicans. The Report is also right to point out that such communion requires self–discipline on the part of its members, and

---

1 See Thomas Breidenthal, *Christian Households: The Sanctification of Nearness* (Eugene, Oregon: Wipf and Stock, 2004), pp. 159–60.

care for each member by all the other members. The Episcopal Church failed in this regard, perhaps, when it confirmed the election of Gene Robinson as the Bishop of New Hampshire. But in pressing this point, the Report makes an assumption, which is fundamentally problematic. It identifies communion with agreement on all matters regarded as essential – or, at least, with agreement on procedures for the adjudication and resolution of disagreements. In so doing, the Report mirrors the mistaken assumption of most ecumenical dialogue, namely, that unity is to be achieved by narrowing the disagreement gap.

I challenge this assumption. With the best of motives, the ecumenical movement has sought to achieve table–fellowship by recognizing areas of agreement, and then to inch from these recognitions toward the distant goal of table–fellowship. But this is to proceed by going backwards. If communion is a moral practice whereby in the name of Christ we maximize unity in the face of disagreement, then communion cannot be about agreement. In the name of Christ, the procedure should be reversed. Assuming that ecumenical dialogue presupposes common membership in the larger household of faith, such dialogue should begin with table–fellowship, not end with it. Any mutually recognizable commitment to the way of the cross should be sufficient grounds to establish communion, no matter how many disagreements remain to be worked through. This ensures that the hard work of communion – which includes the ongoing attempt to resolve disagreements – is not endlessly put off.

As Anglicans, we presently enjoy communion with one another. This communion, by the reasoning of the Report, stands in danger of being diminished by our disagreement over the consecration of an openly gay bishop in a committed relationship and over the blessing of same–sex unions. If, with the Report, we assume that communion is the result of agreement, it is true that our communion has already been impaired. But I think we ought to imagine our communion as the beginning of our life together in Christ – a life still rife with suspicion, mixed signals, cultural misunderstandings, and economic inequities, yet always ripe with the fruit of word and sacrament. (This is, after all, the reality that sustains ecumenical dialogue.) If we saw communion as the beginning of life together, and not as a sign of agreement with one another, then deep rifts would not threaten our communion, but would bring communion to the fore as the constant beginning–point to which we return as the people of God. Marriage may provide a helpful analogy here. A couple need not be in full agreement to marry, nor can even deep disagreements in themselves break the marriage bond.

It is true to say that Anglicanism has been marked by its inclination to regard communion both as a moral practice and as a precious fruit of that practice. This disposition to discern and maintain fellowship in the face of disagreement is often called *comprehension*, after F. D. Maurice's famous use of this term to summarize the genius of the Church of England. Because I am swimming very close to Maurice here, and because Maurice's notion of comprehension is often misunderstood, I want to be very clear here what I take Maurice to be saying. Comprehension is often associated with a broad inclusivity: everyone is welcome under the tent.

But if we return to what Maurice himself taught, the movement that governs both the individual believer and the church as a whole is an outward movement: not a welcome into the fold, but a risky turn away from "system" to the neighbor, who always stands outside system. In this view, we would not assume an inclusiveness in which every opinion and every lifestyle finds a place. Rather, we would assume the abandonment of a controlled ecclesiastical environment in favor of an openness to a broad range of Christian and non–Christian witness, in the name of Jesus, the incarnate word, who gave himself over to membership in the human race without any limiting clauses. On this model, communion leads to exposure: we find ourselves witnessing to truth on the broadest possible field. What makes such exposure feasible for Maurice is the assumption that Christ is always to be found when the neighbor is turned to in this way. Christ precipitates everywhere, because the turn to the other is the turn to Christ, and the turn with Christ.

Inherent in Maurice's turn to the neighbor is the idea of exodus. Israel exits Egypt in order to enter into communion with God on the holy mountain. Israel needs to redefine herself so that the story of the people of Israel becomes more than their shared history as slaves and wanderers: they need to become a people identified on the basis of communion with God so that they might become a people open to the stranger. Thus it is, for example, that the Israelites are instructed to include the stranger in their Passover meal. To be sure, Israel remains a people set apart. But this separation serves ultimate unity: Abraham is called to a special vocation in order that all peoples may find a blessing in him.

Here we must be very careful, however, since the Christian tradition has assumed time and again that this prophetic vision has been realized in the establishment of the gentile church. This claim is made at the expense of the Jews, who rightly insist that the unity of the human race has not yet been achieved. The gentile claim forecloses on the ongoing salvific role of the children of Israel. In so doing, it sets the church up as a destination rather than a point of departure. As a point of departure, the church is a community in which all ethnicities are given the opportunity to enter into the painful, but revelatory, exposure of Israel's children. That is to say, they are empowered to follow Jesus to the cross, where, in the midst of alienation and hatred, the neighbor is embraced with open arms.[2] As a destination, the church can be nothing

---

2 See Miroslav Volf, *Exclusion and Embrace: A Theological Exploration of Identity, Otherness, and Reconciliation* (Nashville: Abingdon Press, 1996), pp. 125–131.

more than another community of self-proclaimed privilege. When we Christians talk of our exodus, let us be clear that we mean expulsion from all communities and identities that offer us ultimate separation from or mastery over any conceivable neighbor.

It might seem that such an exodus leads us away from communion, not toward it, since, under the condition of human sin, the fellowship we enjoy with one another is generally collusive and exclusive. We are usually drawn to one another because of shared interests, and these interests lead to the formation of mutually advantageous covenants ensuring the exclusion of unwelcome outsiders. So exodus entails a certain rejection of communion, especially when – as is usually the case – that communion is maintained at the expense of the stranger. But of course exodus is not simply a movement from bad communion into no communion. Its first goal is fellowship with Jesus himself, who leads us out of our closed communities into a communion with him that excludes no one. Communion with Jesus requires openness to the neighbor, as when Jesus rebukes James and John for offering to bring fire down on the Samaritans who will not let Jesus take his rest among them (Luke 9:54–5). Communion with Jesus thus issues most immediately in the individual disciple's communion with the stranger (as is illustrated over and over again in Acts – consider Philip and the Eunuch, Peter and Cornelius, Paul and Lydia).

Thus, communion with Jesus entails communion with any neighbor whosoever, including many who are not themselves followers of Jesus. But since Christian discipleship also brings us into contact with other followers of Jesus, it is inevitable that exodus will also issue in the formation of that peculiar fellowship we call the church. How do we become the church without allowing our communion as followers of Jesus to lead us straight back into the world of exclusion and privilege? How do we prevent our fellowship with one another from collapsing

---

3 Dietrich Bonhoeffer, *Life Together* (New York: Harper and Row, 1954), pp. 35–6.

into the false embrace of collusion? Dietrich Bonhoeffer suggested that we can do this if we maintain sufficient distance between ourselves to allow Christ a space among us.[3] But this risks devaluing the unmediated interactions of Jesus' followers with one another. The question remains: how can we give ourselves to one another without holding back, while at the same time maintaining the outward thrust of the Gospel toward the stranger?

One way to do this is to welcome disagreement as an occasion to explore and practice the kind of communion that can tolerate a high degree of conflict, precisely because it is not grounded in mutual self–interest. In the world, communion and agreement necessarily go hand in hand, because communion is all about banding together to achieve common goals. As soon as there ceases to be a critical mass of common goals – that is, as soon as difference outweighs agreement – the fellowship disintegrates. But under the aegis of the coming reign of God, widely divergent views and agendas can be entertained and fiercely debated without communion being impaired. This is because the communion we have in Christ exists for the purpose of turning with Christ to the neighbor – any neighbor. No amount of disagreement can turn my neighbor into anything less than the proper object of my love. And no amount of disagreement can turn my fellow Christian into someone I am not in communion with, if only her conviction and mine, however much they may be at odds, are each grounded in witness to the Gospel and loyalty to Christ.

As I suggested earlier, this kind of communion is an exacting discipline. The Anglican Communion is uniquely equipped for such a discipline. By divine providence a family of churches has emerged out of the evil of empire and colonialism. We share much that is good (the Prayer Book tradition) and much that is not so good (our victimization by and/or complicity in empire). The point is that we are already bound together not only by our love of Jesus, but also by ties of historical connection and mutual affection, developed over almost a century and a half of conversation and cooperation. This tie has helped us weather a number of issues in the past. As I have already suggested, communion in the face of disagreement and difference is the hallmark of Anglicanism.

This hallmark is nothing new. We think of difference as a modern problem, but it was a hot topic in the sixteenth century, with the emergence of the nation state in the West, and the rapid discovery and colonization of new worlds by European powers. In these new circumstances an old theological idea gained new currency: the *ius gentium*, or law of the nations. This law referred to those generally recognized rules that governed the relations between different peoples, even when there wasn't a universal political authority to enforce them. These rules included the right to pass freely from one land to another, and to engage in the free exchange of ideas. Francisco de Vitoria, one of the greatest minds of the Counter–Reformation, invoked the *ius gentium* in his defense of the Mexican people against their occupation and enslavement by the *conquistadores*, arguing that the law of nations presupposed the humanity and dignity of all human beings (no matter how different from us they might be). He also argued that the law of nations mandated as much free interchange among human beings as possible.[4] In other words, at the political level, disagreement and fellowship were not incompatible. Unfortunately, Vitoria could not apply this insight to the life of the church, because he had to remain loyal to a vision of the church predicated on the identification of communion with agreement.

But Richard Hooker *did* make this move. Since Hooker was the greatest defender of the Elizabethan settlement, we tend to assume

4 Francisco de Vitoria, *Political Writings,* (eds) Anthony Pagden and Jeremy Lawrance (Cambridge: Cambridge University Press, 1991), pp. 278–84.
5 Richard Hooker, *Of the Laws of Ecclesiastical Polity,* (ed) Arthur S. McGrade (Cambridge: Cambridge University Press, 1989) Book 1, Chapter 10:14, p. 98.

that his theological agenda went no further than the creation of a viable national church within the British realm. But his larger vision embraces an international federation of churches united by the free interchange of ideas and differences. Hooker explicitly invoked the *ius gentium* in this regard: "Now as there is great cause for communion, and consequently of laws for the maintenance of communion, amongst nations: So amongst nations Christians the like in regard even of Christianity hath been always judged needful. And in this kind of correspondence amongst nations the force of general councils doth stand."[5] Hooker goes on to consider how general councils might adjudicate disagreements among the churches, but this should not blind us to the fact that, for Hooker, such councils presuppose communion – they do not create it. The whole point is that the churches come together voluntarily and on an equal footing. There is no emperor acting as convener, and this is why Hooker associates the kind of general council he envisions with the *ius gentium*: it is itself an example of free interchange, motivated by the sheer desire to be and to remain in contact. It could be argued then, that Hooker is not so much interested in agreement as he is interested in keeping the lines of communication open. In this regard it is instructive to hear what Hooker has to say about the law of nations:

> Civil society doth more content the nature of man than any private kind of solitary living, because in society this good of mutual participation is so much larger than otherwise. Herewith notwithstanding, we are not satisfied, but we covet (if it might be) to have a kind of society and fellowship even with all mankind. And an effect of that very natural desire in us (a manifest token that we wish after a sort an universal fellowship with all men) appeareth by the wonderful delight men have, some to visit foreign countries, some to discover

6 Hooker, *Laws*, p. 97.

nations not heard of in former ages, we all to know the affairs and dealings of other people, ye to be in league of amity with them: and this not only for traffic's sake, or to the end that when many are confederated each may make other the more strong, but for such cause also as moved the Queen of Sheba to visit Solomon".[6]

If the churches are to be understood on the model of the various peoples seeking contact and interaction with one another, presumably because of the humanity the nations share in common, then the overriding motivation for church councils is not the enforcement of agreement, but the removal of obstacles to the free interchange of ideas. Where disagreement stands in the way of communion, it must be addressed – but voluntarily, with all sides open to change. And even then, I would suggest, the discussion must itself be informed by a kind of mutual fascination with one another: the more we disagree out of our common faith, the more we should regard one another as Sheba regarded Solomon – curious, and ready to be humbled.

I am well aware that there are some disagreements that cannot be squared with communion of any kind. There should be no satisfaction in the Episcopal Church USA that it was the only denomination (beside the Roman Catholics) not to split between North and South over the issue of slavery. Likewise, there is clear New Testament witness to the appropriateness of separation when fundamental matters of faith and practice cannot be resolved (e.g., Matthew 18: 15–17; 1 Corinthians 5:5; Revelation 2:20). Clearly, the consecration of an openly gay bishop in a committed relationship and the blessing of same–sex unions are matters of sufficient moral gravity to suggest for some a warrant for the breaking of communion. Nevertheless, the power of communion as a moral discipline is directly related to our ability to entertain the maximum amount of moral and doctrinal disagreement with the minimum amount of mutual disrespect as fellow believers in, and disciples of, Jesus Christ. This discipline must be exercised among us, for the sake of our sanctification.

I am proposing that we welcome genuine disagreements that arise out of the matrix of Christian faith, on the grounds that they provide an opportunity for a deeper communion and a more powerful witness to our commitment to Jesus Christ. There can be no more powerful witness to Christ than our willingness to stay at the table, in humility, with those who disagree most with us. It is not the temptation to disagree, but to exclude that weakens our witness. May the "instruments of unity" which enable our communion – however they end up being construed – render us more able to disagree, not less.

14

"OUR REAL WITNESS": WINDSOR, PUBLIC OPINION AND SEXUALITY

Elaine Graham

I want to begin with two anecdotes and a couple of lines from Windsor.

1. Speaking to a congregation of 4,000 in Durham New Hampshire shortly after his consecration in October 2003, Gene Robinson, Bishop–Adjunct of the Episcopal Diocese of New Hampshire, commented to rapturous applause: "We [the Episcopal Church] couldn't buy publicity like this! Let's use every inch of it." He was of course referring to the intensive coverage that his election as an openly gay man had received in the world's media.

2. "Perhaps the greatest tragedy of our current difficulties is the negative consequence it could have on the mission of the Church to a suffering and bewildered world. Even as the Commission prepared for its final meeting the cries of children in a school in southern Russia reminded us of our *real witness and ministry* in a world already confronted by poverty, violence, HIV/AIDS, famine and injustice." (Robin Eames, Foreword to Windsor, 6, my emphasis).

3. On a visit I made to San Francisco in 1990 to research churches' responses to AIDS/HIV, the minister of one congregation told me that it had made the decision to abandon the practice of administering communion via a shared chalice, and to revert to individual cups. It was explained that this was due "to fear of infection." My reaction – of horror and consternation – must have registered on

my face, for my informant hastily rushed to reassure me. The change had occurred in order to protect those who were HIV+ (for whom, due to their fragile immune systems, even the most minor ailment could prove dangerous) from the risk of other people's germs.

These three form the basis of my reflections on the topic of the churches, public opinion and sexuality. I want to think about the kind of public image the churches – especially the Anglican Communion – has developed as a result of its debates and decisions over sexuality, especially the fraught issue of the public ministry of gays and lesbians; and I want to reflect on the priorities of the churches as a result. It would appear as if the churches are irrevocably at war with one another over sexuality, and it is unlikely that these disputes will be resolved easily. But how come attitudes to sexuality and to homosexuality in particular have become effectively a test of Christian orthodoxy? What are the ways forward? My chief argument will be that "dialogue" is at the heart of the process: that historically, the development of Christian theology has always emerged out of negotiations between the perennial sources of experience, reason, tradition and scripture; that dialogue between the principles and practices of faith and cultural context is also fundamental; and that the very identity of the Anglican Communion, in its commitment to unity in diversity, is premised on the same understanding of the need to embrace plurality of perspectives in a common search for truth. Yet, at the same time, there is an inbuilt "bias to inclusivity", an imperative to listen to the margins and embrace the risk of change, that must inform our processes of discernment.

Nearly eighteen months after his consecration in an ice hockey rink in New Hampshire, V. Gene Robinson still continues to attract media attention. The intensity of the coverage fails to abate, mainly due to the fault–lines within the Anglican Communion that his election revealed. This action by the Episcopal Church of the USA, and the adoption of rites for same–sex partnership blessings by the Canadian Diocese of New Westminster, have been the catalyst to soul–searching within the Communion, to virulent objections elsewhere in the world to what have been seen as unilateral action from North America, and triggered the process which lead to the publication of the Windsor Report in October 2004.

So the last thing you might expect Robinson to do would be to welcome that media furore. But at the time, and subsequently, he has continued to regard his own appointment as a kind of *kairos* moment: not only in terms of what it says about the ministry of gay, lesbian and transgendered (GLBT) priests, but also in the way it has acted to draw new people, attracted by the church's attempts to become inclusive. He spoke at his consecration, and continues to speak, about reaching out to people on the margins of society and to see this as a crucial aspect of the church's calling.

It is good that Robinson is so positive about the role of the media when it must have engendered enormous personal cost. Although supportive messages outweigh the negative correspondence in his postbag, the media are in part responsible for stoking up his notoriety, so it is surprising to hear him put it in such a positive light. I interpret this as his attempt to turn the tide of the media's insistent theme, which they push relentlessly, that the churches in general (and the Anglican Communion in particular) are preoccupied with sex and heading inexorably toward schism and self–destruction. The overall public image, therefore, is that the church condemns acts of making love (for some people, anyway), but relishes the prospect of making war within its own ranks about matters of personal morality.

Coverage of incidents of sexual abuse by priests, ministers and church officials in churches around the world add to this impression: the church is obsessed with sex, but its repressive attitudes only result in pathological and abusive behavior. There is evidence to show that the Roman Catholic Church in North America and Ireland, where a number of scandals have received widespread coverage, has been badly hit in terms of membership and support. It would be facile to ascribe any simple cause and effect, but the decline in the public eye may be indicative of wider changes in attitudes to do with trust in public institutions. Nowadays, people demand greater accountability and transparency from politicians, scientists, public servants – so why should the church be any different? Western societies are altogether less deferential than before, and greater mobility and choice mean that religious observance is no longer taken for granted. The credibility of organized religion has to be earned, and so its public image is vital. So even if people have not stopped attending church as a direct result of the scandals, it has contributed indirectly to an erosion of trust in the church as an institution *worthy* of trust.

Part of the public perception is that this is an instance of hypocrisy – the church is seen as condemning sex, and yet unable to police transgressive or immoral behavior within its own ranks. It is vulnerable to attack as out of touch, obsessed with its own internal affairs, maintaining outdated structures and attitudes, and failing to connect with ordinary people. And so I turn to the words from Dr Eames, the Chair of the Lambeth Commission, who makes a stark juxtaposition between the processes of the Windsor Report, and what he calls "our *real* witness and ministry." A tiny, but revealing comment, in my view, and one which unfortunately reinforces the image of a church preoccupied with its own concerns, dimly aware of "poverty, violence … famine and injustice" outside its own walls, but seemingly incapable of breaking off from its own internal debates in order to respond. It is a grim parable about the lack of communication between church and world, a graphic insight into the way that particular kinds of preoccupation about (particular kinds of) sexuality have hijacked and narrowed the social witness of the Anglican Communion.

But let's pause at this point, and give some consideration to the relationship between the churches' confusion and division over sexuality and put that in context in relation to recent data concerning public opinion on sexuality. How accurate is it to presume that the churches are pursuing anachronistic moral values, and are out of step with public opinion on sexuality?

Evidence from surveys, such as British Social Attitudes, an annual digest of statistics and opinion polls, makes for fascinating reading. Two sociologists, Alasdair Crocket and David Voas, have recently collated statistics on attitudes to sexuality and in particular on homosexuality, and compared data for church–goers with all ages with non–church–goers.[1] Overall, evidence suggests that there has been a rapid liberalization of attitudes.[2] According to Crockett and Voas, the British Social Attitudes report for 1983 recorded just over half of the respondents (50.3%) saying that homosexual relations were "always wrong". If you compound into that the proportions of those stating same–sex relationships are "mostly" (12%) or "sometimes" (8%) wrong, it works out at around 72%, with and only just over a quarter saying they were "rarely" (4%) or "never" (25%) wrong. By 2000, however, these proportions had shifted to 55% declaring disapproval, and those labelling same–sex relationships as "never wrong" as rising to over 38%.

Mind you, that means that even today, the British public is still divided – even those statistics return a slight majority disapproving. And it varies according to gender, class and generation too: but all the evidence points to younger people being more accepting of same–sex relationships. When similar statistics are analyzed for those who identify themselves as "religious", however, the picture changes. As a whole, Christians have a higher disapproval rating – but interestingly, the polarization between those accepting and those disapproving is much greater than in society as a whole. Those who said they were "not religious" had a 40% disapproval rating, as opposed to 55% amongst religious people in 1983 – quite close to wider averages. By 2000, only 28% of non–religious people totally disapproved, as compared to just over 40% of religious people. So attitudes have changed amongst

---

1 Alasdair Crockett and David Voas, "A Divergence of Views: Attitude Change and the Religious Crisis over Homosexuality", *Sociological Research Online*, Vol. 8, No. 4, 2003, available at: http://www.socresonline.org.uk/8/4/crockett.html [accessed 06/02/05].
2 For data relating to sexual behavior across the population, see Anne M. Johnson, Catherine H. Mercer, Bob Erens, Andrew J. Copas, Sally McManus, Kaye Wellings, Kevin A. Fenton, Christos Korovessis, Wendy Macdowall, Kiran Nanchahal, Susan Purdon and Julia Field "Sexual behaviour in Britain: partnerships, practices, and HIV risk behaviours", *The Lancet*, No. 358, 2001, 1835–42.

religious people, but not as sharply as elsewhere. (The higher proportion of more elderly people in the church may account for some of it: views of younger Christians are closer to those of their general age cohort than their older co-religionists.)

So in that respect, the churches' hesitancy about homosexuality at least is increasingly out of step with wider society. But that is not in itself, of course, a reason for a liberalization of attitudes within the churches, as if Christianity should simply adjust to the prevailing *Zeitgeist* in order to appear relevant. But it does offer food for thought, I think, about the factors that insulate church people against the general liberalization process that has affected British (western) society over the past 40 years, and the extent to which something which is ceasing to be a problem for a large part of the population still continues to be a stumbling-block for the churches. Add to that, issues of women bishops in some traditions, or the ordination of women in the Roman Catholic Church and you begin to get a picture of a church that is by definition conservative, slow to change and out of step – an institution that is perceived to be leading an altogether too sheltered life to be recognizable or relevant to the population at large.

But what I want to say relates precisely to this process of how to relate the values of our surrounding culture, and how far to stick to "traditional" teachings. One of David Lodge's early novels was titled *How Far Can You Go?*[3] and concerned a group of young Roman Catholics in the 1960s during the turbulent times of Vatican II and the sexual revolution. So how far should the churches go in reformulating their position on human sexuality? How should it weigh the allegiances between "Christ" and "culture"?

The Jewish feminist theologian, Judith Plaskow, once published an article entitled, "The Right Question is Theological."[4] Against some of her "secular" Jewish feminist friends, she argued that

---

3 David Lodge, *How Far Can You Go?* (London: Secker and Warburg, 1980).
4 Judith Plaskow, "The Right Question is Theological" in S. Heschel (ed), *On Being A Jewish Feminist: A Reader* (New York: Schocken Books, 1983).

political and ethical campaigns were not simply "cultural" matters for Jews, but were rather theological. They had to be debated as such. Any specific matter of ethics, and any particular programme of social action or mission, must be rooted in first principles: namely the nature of God and human participation in the life of God. Issues of who we are, how we live and how we relate – and whether and to whom we make love or war – are at root theological and ecclesiological questions.

Now, at first glance, this may appear to be retreating into the very introversion and self–absorption alluded to in the lines of Eames' foreword to Windsor. But my point is that to argue that issues such as sexuality and sexual ethics call forth so many fundamental questions about what it means to be human that, without proper theological enquiry and discernment, our pastoral and ethical interventions will ring hollow. After all, the essence of *praxis* is both action and reflection in pursuit of God's will – value–directed and value–informed action. And the issue of human sexuality is a case in point. It challenges us at all sorts of levels to think and act decisively, because it is fundamentally about what it means to be *faithful* to our own experience as human beings in a given place and time, but also to one another in personal, ecclesial and social relationships. It calls forth questions of what it is to be faithful to God and to the faith traditions in which we stand, however reluctantly or marginally.

So when the church does speak and act in the world, it ought to have something meaningful and distinctive to say, something that proceeds from that context of covenanted and faithful lives – not only in conventional bonds of heterosexual marriage or gay partnerships, but in the broader Christian calling to discipleship. For that reason, we always have to ask questions about who we are, what it means to order our lives authentically and prophetically, and how people of faith can discern the word of God in their own situation. That involves a constant dialogue with the resources of faith and the world around us. Over the past twenty or thirty years, largely due to the influence of theologies of liberation from the two–thirds world, and indeed feminist and GLBT theologies, we have been encouraged to engage in what is often called "contextual theology": a realization that our thinking and talking about God is shaped by our situation, the questions we bring to that situation, and questions about what faith is calling us to undertake in that situation.

There is a tendency to think that this is a "new way of doing theology". In some ways, the liberation theologians from basic ecclesial communities were making bold claims about their "theology from below" against the prevailing dominance of scholastic, academic, western theology that claimed to be universal and neutral. Yet, all theology reflects its human situation, and the best we can hope for is that it also reaches beyond the limits of language and context to speak in some way of transcendence. Actually theology has always been contextual, it's always been orientated towards the human, concrete and immediate, and we can rightly reclaim that as something, which is close to the heart of all theology, rather than something that Christians have only done since 1968, or whenever.

It seems to me that a convincing account of the origins of Christian theology rests in such contextual, practical tasks: of adult nurture, of forming the corporate identity of the community, and communicating the faith to others. That's how theology as formal "talk about God" emerged: from the pastoral task. Because that's where the questions about "'what it means to be faithful" in relationships, society, to one's context, and to God have always emerged. Theology is directed towards the practical purposes of shaping a discourse of life by which faithful discipleship in the world could be conducted.[5]

Theologies that don't talk and don't listen are exceptional. But there are always some – and the danger is that they absorb cultural values uncritically – such as endorsements of what is assumed to be "Christian" values of heterosexual marriage or nuclear families which are, arguably, not even biblical and of quite recent origin. So we certainly

---

5. Ellen Charry, *By the Renewing of your Minds: The Pastoral Function of Christian Doctrine* (New York: Oxford University Press, 1997).

have to be self–critical about the values we defend and uphold, and be prepared to challenge assumptions about what is, or has always been, normatively "Christian".

So the relationship between the profession of faith and the exercise of distinctive identity is a perennial question for the church, and requires us to reflect on what is contingent, and what is essential, about the Christian ethos, what the relationship should be between particular expressions of faith and universal norms, what aspects of Christian practice can adapt to cultural change, and what is non–negotiable in the face of the "secular." In short, how to remain faithful to the specifics – our own locatedness in a particular point of history, in particular cultures that understand our reproduction, our embodiment, our desire, in certain ways, and the universals – the things of Christ that transcend all cultures, times and places. Neither simply going with the flow of our culture's tolerances and prejudices, nor sticking to what we perceive as the timeless truths of scripture or tradition, will do. But of course this is precisely where the fault–lines begin to open up, when it comes to discerning how far the church should accommodate itself to the prevailing culture and how far it should uphold the standards of its own inherited tradition.

These are not new questions for Christians, and they are not peculiar to debates about sexuality. They are fundamental to the theological task – of understanding and following God – that faces us all. Christian practice and doctrine has always emerged out of a process of dialogue between the church and world, a dialogue that is mutually critical and corrective – as in fact it always has been. Christian thought has always adapted to the culture in which it has found itself, because it is an incarnational faith. There is always some negotiation between the pillars of scripture, tradition, reason and experience. And rightly so: furthermore, a diversity of ways of reconciling these different authorities has also always characterized Christian practice and doctrine.[6] Indeed, as

---

6 H. Richard Niebuhr, *Christ and Culture* (San Francisco: Harper and Row, 1951).

the Windsor Report itself argues, that very tolerance of a plurality of voices is a fundamental tenet of the Anglican Communion itself. Critics of this position may wish to argue that the current situation is, in part, about marginalized churches from Africa seeking a more central position in the church's deliberations, and that this inclusion is more important than the role of so–called "sexual minorities". However, I would insist that dialogue and tolerance of plurality is paramount, because it is essential to the exercise of a proper theological imagination.

Yet, if we are thinking about dialogue, not only within the church, but also between church and world, then it is important to see that is not always one way. It is mutually adaptive and corrective. I have already indicated some of the ways in which there is much within the inherited tradition of the Church of which it needs to repent. The question here is whether we regard theology as a timeless given, sufficient unto itself, or whether we allow for it to engage critically and constructively with other voices. My own reading of the history of doctrine suggests that it has always proceeded dialogically, and that the tasks of preaching the Gospel to the world, in the world, necessarily involve listening as well as speaking.

But that is not the same as an empty liberal accommodation to a passing spirit of the age. We must be counter–cultural if need be. There is good reason to argue, for example, that Christians do need to question some aspects of contemporary western sexual mores, particularly those discourses which ostensibly promote sexual liberty and self–expression, but which are actually highly prescriptive. For whilst a climate of greater openness and tolerance towards sexuality – as indicated in the research I quoted earlier – has emerged, it has also been accompanied by the widespread sexualization of much (especially popular) culture. Sexuality has become commercialized, and there is immense pressure, particularly on younger people, to conform to norms of sexual hedonism. Yet, this superficial level of permissiveness is accompanied by an alarming level of ignorance around sexual health, particularly amongst young adolescents, with the result that the United

Kingdom has one of the highest teenage pregnancy rates in Europe. It is important that the churches can be capable of developing a critique of these trends – one which is not puritanical, but recognizes that there is a difference between an honest and mature openness in discussions of sexuality that enables us all to make informed moral choices (especially in relation to adequate information about one's own sexual health and welfare), and the relentless commodification of sex which reduces persons to objects.

Feminist theologians, such as Carter Heyward, have reminded us that making love is also about making justice, and that sexual expression is a form of human embodied love that, ideally, communicates something of the divine.[7] This principle operates at different levels, from the global dimensions of the sex industry which are often mapped on to other patterns of economic exploitation, to our own understandings of the values and commitments – physical, emotional and financial – we are acting out in our relationships – intimate, public – with others. Yet, questions of justice and inclusion are also present when the church thinks about whose experiences count as worthy to contribute to its own thinking about what it means to be faithful. Back to the question of what the "real" priorities of the church should be: whose cries of protest, anger, abandonment and suffering will count as worthy to contribute to our debates and criteria about what it means to be faithful?

My last anecdote is about overturning our preconceptions about who is a risk to us – and indeed, the terms on which we define who "we" and "they" might be. Who is perceived as the problem and the threat to whom in that story? Fear of those who are different, fear of the unfamiliar, seems to awaken quite visceral emotions, almost as if some primal taboo of purity and pollution had been transgressed. But stories like that – which have been prefigured, I believe, in so many other similar incidents in the Gospels, where the norms and boundaries of

---

7 Isabel Carter Heyward, *Our Passion for Justice: Images of Power, Sexuality and Liberation* (New York: The Pilgrim Press, 1984).

acceptability and security are challenged – serve as a kind of hermeneutical principle by which we might exercise discernment. And chiefly, such a principle confronts us with the terms on which we define community, and whether our definitions are made according to our own needs and norms, or whether we are prepared to put ourselves alongside those with different needs, different perspectives.

If such discernment is, in part, about what it means to be community together, then our theologies of sexuality also need to be done from the perspective of what it means to be church. Yet, my point is that other people, unexpected and "marginal" people, may be better placed to show us what true church really is. So being faithful in this context means being truthful to testimonies formerly excluded or pathologized; and the obvious example here would be the way in which the stories of GLBT people have too frequently been ruled out as "unfit" for Christian consumption.

So for Gene Robinson, the entire media furore was worth it, because the church was acting out a way of being faithful to itself that offered a message of hope and inclusion to those who had too often been told that the Gospel was not for them. As I've said, the theme of marginalization, and reaching out to the margins, is something to which he has returned with frequency since his consecration. In his most recent episcopal letter to the diocese, he has this to say:

> Is preaching a message of "release to the captives, binding up the brokenhearted, and preaching good news to the poor" an ignoring of those who are quite happy in the life of the Church? Does it mean that we ignore the needs of the faithful, church–going folks? Are those already in the ranks of the congregation to feel sidelined by the calls to reach out to the margins?

Let's be clear. Although there are those who are obviously at the margins – the homeless, the addicted, etc. – all of us go to the margins at some point: when we face divorce, life–threatening illness, incarceration, heartbreak with a child, the death of a family member who is not in good standing with the family, or whatever upsets out natural, "nice" way of being: all of us, at one time or another, will be at the margins. And so, first and foremost, the discussion about those at the margins – and whether or not they will be acceptable to the Christian community, and to God – is really not a question about them but a question about us, all of us.[8]

We might develop Robinson's train of thought and argue that one of the chief criteria by which the demands of "Christ" and "culture" are to be weighed up is what has been termed *the bias to inclusivity*. In other words, whilst the particulars of the situation may change, certain themes remain constant throughout the tradition: a movement of the Spirit towards a larger apprehension of the nature of God's mission and a willingness to see those signs of grace in unexpected, even scandalous places. Whether it is the scandal of women as witnesses to the Resurrection, the scandal of rich and poor sharing one eucharistic fellowship, or the scandal of Gentile piety accepted alongside the rigors of Jewish law, it seems to me that "biblical" Christianity is full of examples of the shocking, unbounded, graceful generosity of God's accepting love. So one criterion for discernment would be this: will the church's words and actions break down the barriers to inclusivity, or do they speak of a theology that fails to look beyond the horizon of its own certainties, and is really only concerned in engaging in conversation with itself?

Being at the margins, or alongside those driven to the margins, is an essential – and uncomfortable – part of our pastoral, ethical and theological deliberation. Yet, it seems to me that it is a necessary act of faith, to learn how the demands of the concrete and immediate return us once again with new challenges, to the resources of our collective

---

8 V. Gene Robinson, "Yes, All Are Included", 27 December, 2004, http://www.nhepiscopal.org/artman/publish/printer_91.shtml [accessed 31/01/05].

values and traditions. Once more, however, the conversational, dialogical nature of Christian understanding is revealed: sometimes we need others to interpret things afresh on our behalf, to offer correctives to a tendency we all have to fashion truth in our own image.

When the institutional church seems determined to quash, rather than promote, human liberation, it is tempting to *lose faith* with any kind of organized religion. Yet, my argument about doing our theology and sexual ethics from the vantage–point of thinking about what it means to be faithful persons and faithful church should not be seen as a retreat from the changing values of the world. We need the church – or at least we need our communities of faith – in spite of it often being a frustrating and uncongenial place, and one, which many of our progressive secular friends regard as irrelevant, even dangerous. Any church voice in public life will have to work hard to be heard, and be respectful of the autonomy of a world come of age. Yet, we need to be looking for new opportunities all the time, and refuse (like Gene Robinson) to be cowed by a voracious and trivializing media. But that's also about faith and faithfulness: Christian engagement with the world needs to be faithful to the complexities of the human condition, faithful to authentic signs of living as Christ's disciples, and faithful to witnesses who went before us. More difficult still may be the possibility that God remains faithful to us, whatever the future may bring and however depressed we may be. Yet, we must continue the journey of faith – and our sexuality, like all our humanity – is one of the best invitations we have to undertake that road together.

I5

On Being Stretched

Martyn Percy

One of the chief virtues of living within a Communion is learning to be patient. Churches, each with their distinctive own intra–denominational familial identity, have to learn how to negotiate the differences they find within themselves. For some churches in recent history, the discovery of such differences – perhaps on matters of authority, praxis or interpretation – has been too much to bear: lines have been drawn in the sand, with the sand itself serving only as a metaphor for the subsequent atomisation. Yet typically, most mainstream protestant denominations have sufficient breadth (of viewpoints and plurality) and depth (located in sources of authority and their interpretation, amongst other things) to be able to resist those assaults that threaten implosion. Where some new churches, faced with internal disagreement, have quickly experienced fragmentation, most historic denominations have been reflexive enough to experience little more than a process of elastication: they have been stretched, but they have not broken. This is perhaps inevitable, when one considers the global nature of most mainstream historic denominations. Their very expanse will have involved a process of stretching (missiological, moral, conversational, hermeneutical, etc), and this in turn has led directly to their (often inchoate) sense of accommodation.

This is, of course, not to say that "anything goes". Even the broadest and most accommodating ecclesial traditions have their boundaries and limits. But the development of their global identity has involved them in a process of patient listening and learning, and of evolution and devolution. Speaking as an Anglican, therefore (and one who would locate himself in the broad "center" of the tradition), I hesitate to begin this brief essay by confessing that I am continually surprised by the amount of passion and rhetoric that has been created by the issue of homosexuality. In three successive movements (in what must pass for, musicologically, as both a tragic and comic opera), the Anglican Communion has threatened to unravel itself over arrangements in Canada, the USA and England. The historical minutiae of those events the dioceses of New Westminster, New Hampshire and Oxford have no need of reprise now, for they have each, in their own way, been responsible for the production of yet another Commission that attempts to deal with the (apparently) self-inflicted wounds that are said to afflict the Communion. And now that Windsor has been published, it is interesting to note that one of its primary tasks has been to point towards the importance of listening to one another in that school of theology, which is the learning church.

But given that Windsor does not make judgments, but, rather, initiates a process, what precisely is the core issue at stake within the process? The question is not as simple as it first appears, for behind the obvious symptomatic issue of sexuality, there lurks a complex nexus of other concerns that need to be addressed. In what follows, I have attempted to outline these in the hope that by identifying the issues, a specifically Anglican form of conversation might be generated. Strictly for the purposes of brevity, two clusters of issues have been identified. The first looks at storytelling and Christian narrative, and the second at polity, passions and power.

Storytelling and Christian narrative

The Lambeth Conference of 1988 called upon the church to listen to the stories of gay and lesbian people within the church. It seems to me that this was an intuitively wise initiative, for there is something quite fundamental about storytelling that should never be underestimated. In the past, a great deal of theology has accepted the security and power offered by the dominant discourse of non–narrative reasoning. In so doing, the origins of Christianity – which essentially lie in story and drama – are inevitably concealed. This is a pity, because the Christian faith is rooted in the Christian story, which is itself, first and foremost, rooted in the story of humanity's fresh encounters with God and the resulting experiences. So there is a serious theological strategy at work in paying attention to the stories people *now* have to share about their faith, sexuality and encounters with God. This is not mere subjectivity. It is, rather, testimony to the truth that God is always at work beyond the margins of our dogmatic and confessional boundaries.

Of course, not every story is going to be a valid expression of a faithfully exercised Christian life: God loves us, but he does not love all that we do. Our personal experiences cannot be a sufficient guide to what the purposes of God are for each of us as individuals, or for humanity as a whole. But equally, the particularity of our stories cannot be easily dismissed simply because a number of them are atypical. Here we need to understand that the unity of the church is not a mere mass of individuals with few convictions in common, but that of a differentiated body where the distinctiveness of each is already in play. So for the church to be consciously itself, it needs people to see and show how diversity works together. Or, perhaps put more theologically, it is about helping believers to see Christ in one another. Here our work as priests, ministers and laypeople – actually, all who are baptised into the faith – has to look closely at how to uncover for one person or group the hidden gift in another – especially when the first impression might be one of bewilderment, alienation or threat.

Implicitly, at least, Windsor recognizes that we cannot lose sight of the fact that our context is one of profound cultural change. We clearly live in an age when understandings of sexual orientation have shifted. An era that once (mainly) regarded homosexuality as a sin is giving way to a new generation that does not seem to regard the orientation as anything more than that: simply one way of being a sexual being. Moreover, I am far from convinced that "tolerant" attitudes to homosexuality are a recent and modern innovation. There are enough good cultural historians working in the field of sexuality – Alan Bray, Jeffery Weekes and John Boswell especially come to mind – each of whom have shown that other ages have displayed open or implicit tolerance of same–sex relationships. Their work suggests that what we regarded as "sin" in the 1950's was perhaps regarded as merely "alternative" in other centuries.

That aside, the difficulty of arguing for homosexuality as a sin seems to me, to rest partly on demonstrating that it is inherently harmful or corrupting, rather than arguing that it is contrary to nature. For a start, it plainly isn't. As many who study zoology will confirm, homosexuality is a minority but naturally occurring phenomenon amongst mammals. The idea that homosexuality is "natural" within nature, so to speak, raises problems for those who wish to describe the orientation and behavior as deviant or sinful. If the best we can say is that such behavior is part of the condition of the fall, then the phenomenon itself would be no worse than the wearing of clothes. To argue for homosexuality being sinful, therefore, one would need to show that it was somehow explicitly harmful, and this is where I, along with many other Christians, struggle. What actually could be *wrong* with two people of the same sex, of age and maturity, expressing their love for one another in a sexually committed relationship that expresses fidelity, faithfulness and sanctity? I am unable to fault such a relationship.

At this juncture some will want to say that they have no complaints about these kinds of relationships either. Their concern is with casual relationships, sex without commitment, and with multiple partners. And I would agree here; but would want to argue that my concern here extends to all sexual relationships, whether homosexual or heterosexual. I fully acknowledge that marriage, in its many social and cultural forms, is in some sense a sacramental sign. But I am equally confident that faithful long–term same–sex relationships, which model fidelity and mutuality, can also be a sacramental sign. The important thing to guard against is that sex is not reduced to anything less than a valid expression of love within a faithfully conceived relationship. Sex must not be reduced to a level of a commodity, or to being a "thing" that merely serves an individual's pursuit of their own fulfilment. Sex is for love, and it belongs, in my view, within a Christian understanding of relationships that establishes such unions as being equitable and exclusive.

I now turn to the Bible – an important concern of the Report. Clearly, Christian tradition and the scriptures hold important keys to resolving the disputes that currently wrack the church. But I would expect the Anglican Church to take account of a number of things at this point. First, the Bible is a consequence of Christianity, not its cause. Whilst I am entirely committed to upholding the authority of the Bible, it has to be read with care and discretion, and, crucially, interpreted. Christians do not disagree about what the Bible says so much as what it means, and what kind of weight to attach to the different passages, and their many nuances.

Second, it is true that some Christians believe that scripture has come from heaven to earth in an unimpaired, totally unambiguous form. In such a view, there is no room for doubt; knowledge replaces faith. Scripture is utterly authoritative: to question the Bible is tantamount to questioning God. But to those who believe that scripture is a more complex nexus of writings, the authority of scripture lies in the totality of its testament. Thus, the Bible does indeed contain many things that God may want to say to humanity (and these are to be heeded and followed). But it also contains opinions about God (even one or two moans and complaints); it contains allegory, parables, humour, histories and debates. In other words, the very nature of the Bible invites us to contemplate the very many ways in which God speaks to us, which are open to a variety of interpretations. The Bible is not one message spoken by one voice. It is, rather, symphonic in character – a restless and inspiring chorus of testaments, whose authority rests upon its very plurality.

Third, the Bible is very far from clear on matters such as homosexuality (or, by the way, the grammar and rules for heterosexuality). True, we have translations that seem to suggest the very opposite of this, but such translations are themselves (in part) "culturally produced". We also have to bear in mind that there are many forms of observance that the New Testament urges upon us, to which we now pay little attention. Many Christians do not think twice about taking out a mortgage (collusion with usury). Despite the prohibition on eating meat products made from blood in the *Book of Acts*, I have yet to meet a Christian who likes black pudding, yet denies themselves as the early apostles once did.

For Anglicans, the key question in relation to the use of the Bible is this: is scripture, assuming it can be established that its meaning is plain and clear [two different things], always right about all things moral and cultural? If the answer to this is "yes", then there is very little scope for any debate to be had about same–sex relationships. But if that is really the case, we might not perhaps have to go further, and begin to meet out some of the more violent punishments on people who fall foul of other kinds of Levitical law? But working on the assumption that most agree that scripture is not obviously "plain" – that is to say, Anglicans need to focus less on what the Bible says, and more on what it *means* – we have an obligation (and indeed vocation) to look together for the common purposes of God as they are revealed in scripture, tradition and the world today. Which includes, I think, the lives and stories of gay people within the church.

So, I have two preliminary questions to raise here. First, what kind of things can interpret and aid the consideration of scripture (e.g., culture, tradition, reason, etc)? And second, how can two (or several) groups of Anglicans, who see this "problem" quite differently, work together through scripture to reach a peaceable settlement within a church that is restless for healing from its divisions?

Passion, polity and power

It was Jeremy Paxman who once quipped that the Church of England is the kind of body that believes that there was no issue that could not be eventually solved over a cup of tea in the vicar's study. This waspish compliment directed towards Anglican polity serves to remind us that many regard its ecclesial praxis as being quintessentially peaceable and polite, in which matters never really get to out of hand. For similar reasons, Robert Runcie once described Anglican polity as a matter of "passionate coolness". In the past, and in my own reflections on Anglican polity, these are sentiments with which I have tended to concur:

> In some of my conversations with Anglican theologians ... I have been struck by how much of the coherence of Anglicanism depends on good manners. This sounds, at face value, like an extraordinarily elitist statement. It is clearly not meant to be that. What I mean by manners is learning to speak well, behave well, and be able to conduct yourself with integrity in the midst of an argument...It is often the case that in Anglicans' disputes about doctrine, order or faith, it is actually the means that matter more than the ends...politeness, integrity, restraint, diplomacy, patience, a willingness to listen, and above all, not to be ill–mannered – these are the things that enable the Anglican Communion to cohere...[1]

There can be no question that enabling ecclesial polity depends, to some extent, on managing anger. In macro–theological disputes, such as those over the ordination of women, part of the strategy that enables unity can be centered on muzzling some of the more passionate voices in the debate. Extreme feelings, when voiced, can lead to extreme reactions. And extreme reactions, when allowed full–vent, can make

---

1 Martyn Percy, "On Sacrificing Purity?" in I. Markham and J. Jobling (eds), *Theological Liberalism* (London: SPCK, 2000).

situations unstable. Nations fall apart; communions fracture; families divide. Things said briefly in the heat of a moment can cause wounds that may take years to heal. What is uttered is not easily retracted.

Good manners, then, is not a bad analogy for "ideal" Anglican polity. In a church that sets out to accommodate many different peoples of every theological hue, there has to be a foundation – no matter how implicit – that enables the Communion to cohere across party lines, tribal borders and doctrinal differences. And just as this is true for macro–theological disputes, so is it also true for micro–ecclesial squabbles. Keeping the peace in a congregation that is at loggerheads over church fabric and fittings, or perhaps unable to agree on an appropriate resolution in a complex ethical debate, is a no less demanding task for a parish priest. Often, congregational unity in the midst of disputes can only be secured by finding a middle, open way, in which the voices of moderation and tolerance occupy the central ground and enable a church to move forwards. In such situations, the cultivation of "good manners" is essential; civility quietly blossoms where arguments once threatened to lay waste. This is something that Windsor understands, and it is interesting to note how much attention it gives to the virtues of patience and restraint, whilst also acknowledging the place of passions and emotions in the sexuality debate. Clearly, there is a tension between these polarities (the polite–passionate axis), which is partly why the cultivation of "mannered–ness" in ecclesial polity can be seen as being essential as it is beguiling.

However, there are several important theological issues that surround this type of narration for a congregation, diocese, church or communion, that tend to question its apparent wisdom. "Good manners", for example, can be a form of quasi–pastoral *suppression* that does not allow true or strong feelings to emerge in the center of an ecclesial community, and properly interrogate its "settled" identity. This may rob the church of the opportunity to truly feel the pain of those who may already perceive themselves to be on the margins of the church, perhaps even disqualified, or who already feel silenced. "Good manners" can also become a cipher for excluding the apparently undeserving, and perhaps labeling seemingly difficult insights as "extreme voices". The prophetic, the prescient, and those who protest, can all be ignored by a church that makes a virtue out of overly–valuing a peaceable grammar of exchange. Put another way, if the "coolness" always triumphs over the "passionate", then the church is effectively deaf in one ear.

Quite naturally therefore, there is the issue of anger itself, and of strong feelings – especially in relation to sexuality, on all sides of the debate – with which Windsor is perhaps unusually concerned. In the body of Christ, how are these feelings received, articulated and generated? Quite apart from appropriate "righteous anger" (for example, on matters of justice), how does a mature church receive and respond to aggression within itself, and to strong feelings such as anger, dismay, passion, rage or enthusiasm? Rather like a good marital or parent–child relationship, learning to articulate and channel anger can be as important as learning to control it. It is often the case that in relationships where the expression of anger is denied its place, resentment festers and breeds, and true love is ultimately distorted. Strong feelings need to be acknowledged for relationships to flourish. If strong feelings on one or both sides have to be suppressed for the sake of a relationship, then it is rarely proper to speak of the relationship being mature or healthy. Indeed, some relationships that apparently present as being idyllic and peaceable (for example, "we never argue") can turn out to be pathologically problematic. Both parties, afraid of conflict and its consequences, deny their full truth to one another and themselves.

So in terms of ecclesial polity and pastoral praxis, the difficulty is this: the church is too used to defining all aggression as negative. Correspondingly, the church often fails to see the value of aggression or anger in the pursuit of just relations. Of course in retrospect we can acknowledge that freedoms for the oppressed have been won by aggressive behavior, even when it has been militantly peaceful or pacifist: the civil rights movement in North America and the peaceful protests of Gandhi spring to mind. But all too often churches and society collude in a fiction, believing that an end to slavery, the emancipation of women, and perhaps even the end of apartheid, could all have been achieved without the aggressive behavior of militants. Typically, the church also fails to acknowledge the levels of inequality within itself. Many may still need to express or deploy aggressive behavior in order for Kingdom values to be established.

Presently in the Church of England, the fear of conflict and aggression on issues of sexuality and gender makes it very difficult to air strong feelings; the neuralgic anxiety is that the manifestation of feelings leads to the loss of poise in ecclesial polity. And yet we live in a world and within a church that are shaped by human failings, and if we truly love these institutions then we will inevitably be angry about the ways they fall short. So what we Anglicans do with our strong feelings, and how we handle the aggression that moves for change, will depend on whether we can see them as a sign of life and growth, or whether we suppress them for fear they will rock the boat too hard.

In the church, the desire to avoid conflict both in parochial matters and in relationships in the diocese can often be a recipe for atrophy. When situations arise which cannot be ignored, the scale of feelings aroused can surprise and disappoint those who believe that if we all try to love each other, we will all agree. To truly love is to take seriously the desire to deepen relationships and work against all that limits and devalues human worth. So discovering how to acknowledge and give voice to strong feelings – in ways that can enable radical working together for the growth of all – is a challenge that the church needs to heed. In his ministry, Jesus consistently listened to the voices of the marginalized. Indeed, not only did he listen, but he assimilated such voices into his ministry, and often made the marginalized central, and placed those who were central on the periphery, thereby re–ordering society, forcing people to witness oppression and the response of the Kingdom of God to despair, anger and marginalization.

So in the church, we need to allow the experiences and stories of the oppressed to challenge and shape the way we hold power and broker relationships. Churches and the wider Anglican Communion *do* need to continually learn from the veritable panoply of liberation theologies: that marginalized people should not simply be made welcome in the church, but that their anger and aggressive desire for justice might be allowed to reform the manners of the church. Learning to listen to narratives that convey strong, powerful feelings, rather than seeking to dismiss such stories as "uncultured" or as "bad manners", is a major, costly and on–going process for ecclesial polity and its pastoral praxis.

The task for the church, therefore, is to find ways that do not suppress or block out strong feelings of anger, or hurt and the aggression it arouses, but to help discern how to channel the energy they bring into the work of the Gospel. This means listening to the experiences that lead to aggression and anger, and seeing them as far as possible from the perspective of those with less power. It means humility on the part of those who hold power, and an acknowledgment of the fear of losing power and control. It means a new way of looking at power relationships that takes the Gospel seriously in their equalising and levelling.

Windsor, therefore, is to be commended for the attention it pays to experiences and feelings. In recognizing their vital role in ecclesial polity, Eames and his colleagues on the Commission have understood that experiences and feelings need to be heard and received. The debate on sexuality (perhaps more so than that of gender?) is one that cannot be exclusively resolved by arid academic disputations. But this in itself raises a question about how the process of deliberation is to be furthered.

Paula Nesbitt, in her reflections on the Lambeth Conference of 1998, shows how the Anglican Communion has been unable to avoid being gradually split: caught between increasing cultural diversity on the one hand, and the need to provide coherence and identity on the other. She notes how successive Lambeth conferences have moved sequentially from being grounded on traditional authority (that is, the establishment of churches and provinces during the colonial era), to rational authority (which presupposes negotiation through representative constituencies for dominance over meeting outcomes), to (finally) negotiated authority (but which normally lacks the power to stem the momentum of change). She notes that these kinds of authority, when pursued through the four "instruments of unity"[2] in the Anglican Communion, are usually capable of resolving deep disputes. They enable complex inter–action and conversation, but they do not lead to clear and firm resolutions. Correspondingly, Nesbitt argues that a new, fourth authoritative form has emerged within the Anglican Communion, which has in some senses been present from the very beginning, and is now tied up with the identity of scripture. She writes of this authority:

> [it] could be used to countervail the relativism of cross–cultural alliances without affecting their strategic utility: symbolic authority. The symbol, as a locus of authority, has a tangible and timeless nature. Where the symbol is an authoritative part of the institutional milieu, either traditional or rational authority must acknowledge its legitimacy...scripture is an authoritative symbol ...[3]

Nesbitt points out that the symbolic authority of sacraments may create shared bonds and enhance communal cohesion, but they are normally unable to regulate or negotiate conflict. But in contrast,

---

2 The four instruments of unity are the Archbishop of Canterbury, the Lambeth Conference, the Anglican Consultative Council, and the Meetings of the Primates. In turn, these "instruments" generally consider how issues fall within the "Anglican Quadrilateral": Scripture, Tradition, Reason and Culture.

3 P. Nesbitt, *Religion and Social Policy* (New York: Rowman & Littlefield, 2001), p. 257).

Scripture, when canonized as complete or absolute, becomes symbolic of a particular era or set of teachings and beliefs. However, unlike sacraments, the use of scripture as symbolic authority can be constructed and constituted according to selecting those aspects or passages that address an issue at hand. Furthermore, scripture as symbolic authority can be objectified or absolutized, which transcends cultural boundaries in a way that other forms of authority can less easily do. The appeal of scriptural literalism provides an objectification of authority that is independent of the influence or control of dominant perspectives, social locations, and circumstances. As symbolic authority, it can be leveraged against cultural dominance as well as provide common ground for cross–cultural alliances ...[4]

In other words, with scripture raised almost to the level of apotheosis, a cross–cultural foundation for authority exists that can challenge the dominance of rational authority, which is normally associated with highly–educated elite groups from the west or first world. Scripture, given symbolic authority, becomes an important tool in the hands of southern (non–elite) Christians who are seeking to counter–legitimate more conservative perspectives.

As Nesbitt notes, "scriptural literalism as symbolic authority represents the easiest and most accessible form of counter–legitimation across educational or cross–cultural divides".[5] And as Lambeth Conferences, like the Anglican Communion itself, have become increasingly diverse in their cultural expression, symbolic authority has risen to the fore. So at present, the only contender for being a focus of symbolic authority is the Bible, since cross–cultural negotiation only leads to sterile relativism: and so long as this situation continues, the dominance of groups, like Reform, within the Church of England looks set to continue.

---

4 Nesbitt, *Religion and Social Policy*, p. 257.
5 Nesbitt, *Religion and Social Policy*, p. 258.

We should note that the only other alternative to the Bible – the Communion itself becoming or attaining the status of symbolic authority – has so far failed, mainly because the very resourcing of that requires a looser, more elastic view of truth–claims, and a necessary tolerance towards competing convictions. Typically, those who press for the Communion as a natural focus for symbolic authority tend to be liberal catholic. But the lack of clarity that this tradition embodies is largely unacceptable to conservative evangelicals. Could it be, then, that a scripturally–based polity is set to triumph over one that configures itself through a trilateral or quadrilateral, or through the Communion itself? At present it is hard to make easy predictions. The Bible, not unlike a sophisticated computer, can only give an answer that is proportionate to the sophistication of the question it is asked. The current problem in the sexuality debate is that Anglicans have yet to learn to be deeply demanding of the scriptures. The present moment of crisis in the Communion lies not so much with the answers Anglicans have found as with the questions we have yet to ask.

Coda

It is said that Henry Scott Holland once stood on the hill at Garsington shortly before his death, and gazed over the valley to Cuddesdon College and parish church, where he had asked to be buried. He noticed a flock of starlings flying past, and remarked how like the Anglican Church they were. Nothing, it seemed, kept the flock together – and yet the birds moved as one, even though they were all apart and retained their individual identity. In an increasingly diverse and cosmopolitan world, of which the Anglican Communion is a part, I suspect that we are going to have to get better at moving together, whilst also at the same time respecting each other's particularity. Birds of feather still need to flock together, even though each creature is individual.

There is no doubt that Anglicanism currently stands at an important crossroads for its future identity. Windsor is merely a signpost at this juncture (albeit an important one): it anticipates the process that is to come, but it cannot predict the outcomes. However, we might say that the there are two very different versions of the Communion and its future that are beginning to emerge.

The first sees Anglicanism in concrete terms. The polity will be governed by law, and scripture will be its ultimate arbiter. Here, Anglicanism will become a tightly defined denomination in which intra–dependence is carefully policed. Diversity of belief, behavior and practice will continue, but they will be subject to scrutiny and challenge.

The second sees Anglicanism as a more reflexive polity; one that has a shape, but is able to stretch and accommodate considerable diversity. Here the polity will be governed by grace, not law, and the Communion itself will continue to operate as both a sign and instrument of unity. Anglicanism will continue to be a defined form of ecclesial polity, but one that tolerates and respects the differences it finds within itself.

Personally, I pray and hope for option two. But I also pray that I will not be divided from my sisters and brothers who favor the first option. I pray that in the midst of our common and diverse struggles, we will discover ourselves afresh in the learning church, within that community of peace we still know as the Anglican Communion. I believe that this may well stretch the Communion to its limits, and test its viability vigorously. But I believe the stretch will ultimately be worth it. For in reaching out just beyond ourselves, and moving outside our normal boundaries and comfort zones, God's own hand is already waiting to clasp our feeble groping.

An earlier version of this paper appeared in *Conversations*, 2005.

16

UNDERSTANDING
SEXUAL DIVERSITY

Anthony P. M. Coxon

Windsor was not, of course, primarily about authority in the Anglican Communion, nor even about seeking a compromise which would avert schism (though it was certainly concerned with those issues). It was primarily about two other things: the tolerability of homosexuals – primarily male homosexuals, since lesbianism does not seem to worry Primates to the same extent – in the ordained ministry, and whether the church could be seen to countenance blessing two persons of the same gender in their wish to live faithfully together. In a word, it was about the problems caused by homosexuals – not covert practitioners, it should be added, who have always been present and tolerated at the highest levels of the hierarchy, but explicitly by "self–confessed" ones who ask for more than toleration. In this essay, I shall argue, *inter alia,* that Windsor and the Primates' responses are, at best, grossly simplistic (and at worst crucially mistaken) in their conception of "homosexuality" as a social category, and that many of the implicit assumptions about the nature of homosexuality are based on manifestations of contemporary western cultures that are untypical in the world context.

Terminology and definitions
To ensure consistency of meaning, some terminological distinctions

need to be spelled out at the outset, because use of the generic and undifferentiated term "homosexual", treated as unproblematic in so many church reports, turns out to be, in fact, far from unproblematic. The somewhat quaint and antiquated term "homophile" (used in earlier documents and reports) will be eschewed. If its use is prompted by a desire to include those with same–sex predilections who do not engage in same–sex behavior, the latter can be explicitly described more adequately as "celibate" or "non–practicing" homosexuals, as the case may be. Rather than use the term "homosexuality" in a vague way, we need to distinguish between these terms: "MSM" – males who engage in sexual behavior with other males; "homosexual" – which includes more general aspects of sexuality, and "gay" meaning those who identify with that social label, implying as it does a sexual identity and a social category.

The nature of homosexuality

In 1978, the Lambeth Conference called for a "deep and dispassionate study of the question of homosexuality, which would take seriously both the teaching of Scripture and the results of scientific and medical research." This admirable goal was never fufilled. Ten years later, it was augmented by a further request that: "such study and reflection [should] take account of biological, genetic and psychological research being undertaken by other agencies, and the socio–cultural factors that lead to the different attitudes in the provinces of our Communion." To my knowledge, no such integrative studies have been commissioned (except, significantly, by the Episcopal Church of the U.S.A and by the Anglican Church of Canada), and the form of the bishops' request itself reveals clearly a medicalized perspective with its pre–supposition that homosexuality is a condition needing to be explained with a specific (medical) aetiology (incidentally implying that bisexuality or heterosexuality do not).

It is also significant that the injunction to bring to bear relevant scientific information and research restricts the appropriate disciplines first to the natural sciences (possibly psychology, no doubt in its behaviorist manifestation), and this is extended to include the social sciences (sociology and anthropology, one assumes). To these disciplines is relegated merely the residual role of explaining why different *attitudes* towards homosexuality prevail in the Anglican Communion. Moreover, the implicit assumption is that homosexuality is all of a piece – a culturally *invariable* phenomenon – and whilst such an anglo– (or western–) centrism is understandable for English bishops' reports, it will not do when pronouncements are made which are intended to have wider (and especially non–western) relevance. For if "the homosexuality question" actually differs widely by culture then their "answer" might well only apply to a particular culture, and looking through western glasses will be, at best, misleading and, at worst, distorting.

This might be considered unimportant, were it not for the fact that the continuing scientific search for aetiological explanations of homosexuality (genetic, hormonal, neurological; see for instance overviews by Byne 1995, and Harrison 1994) are hardly conclusive.[1] Although evidence from dizygotic twin studies consistently points to a genetic component in sexual orientation among western males (Bailey and Pillard 1991) and between Xq28 chromosome markers and male homosexuality (Hu, Papatucci, *et al* 1995), there are no parallel findings for female homosexuality. The only environmental variable consistently correlated with male homosexuality is birth–order (Blanchard and Bogaert 1996). This research suggests that the likelihood of a man becoming homosexual increases in proportion to the number of his older brothers.

What of the social sciences? There have been rapid developments in the last few decades in theory, research and applications relating to sexuality, especially in social anthropology and sociology. In particular, it has become clear that conceptions of the body

---

1 Probably the most encyclopedic reference to research in the aetiology of homosexuality is: http://www.fsw.ucalgary.ca/ramsay/gay–lesbian–bisexual/4a–genetic–biology–gay.htm (at March 9 2005).

and procreation, as well as sexuality itself, are a social (and often a historical) construction. They need to be seen not only in a given cultural setting, but also as an interactional and relational negotiation (Bell and Weinberg, 1978, Blackwood 1986, Foucault 1980, Gagnon 1977, Greenberg 1998). Much of this research and theorizing has been necessitated by the AIDS pandemic because sexual (and, originally, male–to–male) transmission was early identified as a major risk factor. As a consequence, we now have extensive, and more reliable estimates of the prevalence of sexual behavior (of all sorts) in many countries.[2] These are probably the most reliable data we have on the prevalence of all sexual behaviors, and of stated sexual preference (but see below).

Problems of definition, estimation of prevalence, and generalizability of research on homosexuality are all of a piece, and are all crucially related to the difficulties of obtaining genuine probability samples of MSM, on the one hand, and truthful replies about same–sex behavior, on the other. Many earlier western studies had to rely upon opportunistic samples (for example, Kinsey 1948) which tended to over–estimate prevalence,[3] and it is only within the last ten years that resources for developing national sampling frames have been available. Methodological improvements, such as random–walk methodology for obtaining probabilistic samples (based upon contact networks and anonymised and controlled interviewing) mean that reliable estimates are now possible – in the western world. The combined impact of these developments has resulted in a major shift of focus and forms of explanation in the study of sexualities rendering older behaviorist schemes redundant. This shift has immediate consequences for the church's study of sexuality. But little, if any, of this information appears to have informed the thinking of the Lambeth Conferences and the pronouncements of Primates.

---

2 The British national study is NATSAL1&2: National Survey of Sexual Attitudes and Lifestyles, reported in Wellings, Field, & Johnson *et al* (1994, 2001). The U.S. study is reported in Lauman *et al* 1994.

3 The famous "1 in 10" male homosexual estimate comes from a partial Kinsey estimate – this number had been exclusively homosexual for a period of at least three years between the ages of 16 and 55.

Does this matter? Indeed it does. The presupposition, especially of Church of England reports and of Lambeth and Windsor pronouncements, is that (male) homosexuality is a largely unproblematic category. It is important to rehearse some of the more relevant social science material in order to show just how deficient and culturally biased Anglican presuppositions actually are, and how little they are able to bear the weight of the recommendations they are invoked to support. What, then, are these new findings?

The first is that sexual activity between persons of the same gender occurs in all known societies. In this restricted sense, homosexuality is universal. A useful early summary of anthropological cross–cultural evidence of this universality is given in Ford and Beach (1948), based on the Human Relations Area files (http://www.yale.edu/hraf/), and subsequently supplemented by a wide range of cultural – and historically – specific studies. Obvious qualifications are necessary to the claim that homosexual behavior is universal, since wide variation marks out most of what can be said about human sexuality. However trends can be discerned, and generalizations and contrasts made, and these are relevant to our purpose.

Second, same–sex activity is extensive in other animal species. Bagemihl (1999) summarises some 450 vertebrate species where same–sex genital contact occurs regularly. Such sexual activity is mixed (homosexual and heterosexual); in some species same–sex activity is only between males, in others only between females, in others both genders. In some species, homosexual bonds are short–term, in others life–long. As well as acting as a counter–assertion to the claim that homosexuality is "unnatural" – at least in the sense that it does not occur in Nature – it also suggests that it may well have an evolutionary function. As Bagemihl comments: "If it has a genetic basis at all, it has some broad adaptive significance, and is not an aberrant condition just a few species happen to be stuck with" (ibid, p. 70). Other extensive studies in evolutionary biology (see, for example, Roughgarden 2004) also indicate the existence of sexual diversity among many mammalian species.

Returning to the domain of human same–sex (and particularly male–male behavior), it is important to note that it seems to be proscribed in many societies, and where this is so, sex between men will consequently often be socially invisible – or at least the reported prevalence rates will be artificially low. Indeed, the very existence of such behavior will often be denied, (and not only by archbishops in the African continent) and/or ascribed (like sexually–transmitted diseases before them) to western foreign influences or importation.[4] The apparent absence of same–sex behavior was strengthened by those nineteenth– and early twentieth–century anthropologists' accounts which made no mention of homosexuality. It was only later discovered that less selective accounts were present in the anthropologists' field–notes, but were excluded from publication on the grounds that they might prejudice public attitudes to indigenous peoples, whose interests they sought to promote (Coxon 1992).

Third, homosexuality is culturally and historically variant. The cultural and historical manifestations of male and female homosexuality are increasingly well–documented,[5] but the forms and characteristics vary considerably. Most markedly of all, modern western forms relate the stigma of homosexuality to the gender of the partners: for a man to be known to engage in (or even to have engaged in) sexual activity of any sort with another male – sometimes even if only once – is sufficient to attract the label of "homosexual". This definitional link of homosexuality simply to same–*gender* sexual activity is culturally and historically peculiar. In most historical and cultural contexts (including in earlier epochs in the west), it is the *role* that is adopted which makes same–sex behavior either proscribed, condemned, or viewed as deviant.

---

4. There is more than semantic issues involved here. In some languages and cultures, there is no orientation–free generic word for sexual behavior, and male same–sex behavior is referred to as "fun" or "play" – such as *maasti* ("mischief") in Hindi. In a period when men naturally slept together, the same was clearly the case in Europe, when men who were surprized in their activity and brought before the courts often made no connection in their own minds between their acts and the serious church warnings about the dire sin against nature.

5. http://www.infopt.demon.co.uk/bibanthr.htm (at March 9) is a useful updated resource.

Specifically, the distinction is between whether a man *penetrates* (anally or vaginally) or *is penetrated* that marks out the behavior as tolerated or not. To penetrate with the penis is a masculine, male–dominant thing to do, even if to another man. But to be penetrated, in contrast, marks out a man as a deviant, being like a woman and hence betraying his gender. This distinction is a particular feature of "Latin" or "Mediterranean", and also of many Indian and African societies. It will not escape biblical scholars that the use of the two crucially important words in New Testament references to same–sex behavior: *malakoi* and *arsenokoitai* in I Corinthians 6:9 and I Timothy 1:10, are rendered respectively in different versions in very different ways as "catamite" and "sodomite" in the Jerusalem Bible, as "effeminate" and "abusers of mankind with themselves" in the Authorized Version, as "Sensual" and "given to unnatural vices" in the Chicago Bible, as "effeminate" and "liers with mankind" in the Douai versions, and as "homosexuals" without further specification) in the Revised Standard Version (see McNeill 1976). These are not in any sense translations, but modern re–constructions of what the translators have largely read into the terms, but they undoubtedly contain strong echoes of – or may even have specifically refered to – precisely this penetrator/penetrated distinction. The phrase, "liers with man as with women" has precisely this connotation.

Obviously not all societies judge male homosexual behavior in precisely this way, but the linkage to generation in the case of Greek homosexuality,[6] and to dominance and humiliation in the case of Rome (and many contexts of military victory) shows the centrality of sexual role and masculinity in evaluation of same–sex activity. In other contexts, the divide between penetrative and receptive role is even more marked. The colloquial terms sometimes rendered as "homosexual" are nothing of the sort: they refer exclusively to the receptive role (such as *bichas* – "worms" – in Brazil) and only to those engaging in passive anal

---

6 See Dover 1978. The older/insertor and younger/insertée contrast means that an older partner wishing to be penetrated by a younger would be thought of as laughable.

intercourse, and often only to those exhibiting "feminine" traits. Their "active" sexual partners are felt neither to impugn their heterosexual status, nor their masculinity. In yet other cultures this "feminization" extends to cross–dressing and trans–gendering, and even to the creation of a specific "third–sex" role (for example, the Indian *Hijra* and the American Indian *Berdache* "men women").[7]

Even the prevalence of male–to–male anal intercourse differentiates sexual cultures both symbolically and actually.[8] In some cultures *only* anal intercourse counts as sex between men, in others any sexual activity does. In many societies, as we have seen, the role which a man adopts in anal intercourse is critical and crucially linked to its blameworthiness. Even today, when many western MSM do not include it in their repertoire (whether due to disinclination or fears of HIV transmission), it is still the most "gendered" of sexual behaviors (Coxon *et al* 1993). Indeed, the role will often be *the* differentiating activity in many gay men's identity. Much more significant is the fact that (in the western world) if a MSM engages in anal intercourse, then he will almost certainly engage in both forms, either regularly, or at some time during his sexual career. Perhaps the most significant difference compared both to heterosexual activity and "role–based" homosexuality is that approximately twice as many sexual sessions of homosexual men are "reciprocal" (taking the active and passive roles in turn) than are "role/power" based, where each partner adopts a consistent role throughout (Coxon 1996).

A further important differentiating factor between western and other cultures is the notion of homosexual *identity*. In many cultures and periods there is no "sexual identity" as such, and therefore no "gay identity", or even an appropriate language in which "gayness" can be

---

7 See Blackwood 1986, and Coxon 1995, for further anthropological detail.
8 Heterosexual anal intercourse, either for pleasure, or as an effective means of birth–control, is largely ignored here, though it too was a topic of prurient interest in the medieval Penitentials (Brundage 1987) as well as among modern sex researchers. Its relevance is discussed in Halperin 1999. There is a certain symmetry in the fact that in the west, about one–third of MSM do *not* include anal intercourse in their sexual repertoire, whilst about one–third of heterosexuals do. In terms of the amount of such activity, by far the greatest volume is among heterosexuals.

described. The very notion of a gay *identity* is culturally specific to the modern western culture; indeed, the idea that homosexual behavior forms the basis for a social role, and especially functions as a primary organizing role (McIntosh 1968), is simply inconceivable in many cultures. The attempt, therefore, to engage in cross–cultural discussion on the topic is difficult, depending as it does on the stock of concepts available in that culture. Once again, terms and concepts particular to the modern western terms do not map in a one–to–one manner, and it is often necessary in indigenous discourse to import the western term "gay" to describe lifestyles and identities which do not have a natural equivalent in the culture concerned, even when extensive male same–sex behavior may be prevalent.

Nowhere is this more evident than in the relationship between (heterosexual) marriage and sexual behavior between men. As in the case of homosexuality identity, the idea of exclusively homosexual sexual activity is the exception rather than the rule. In societies where the virginity of the woman at marriage is paramount, or marriage is delayed, or sexual activity before marriage is proscribed, male–to–male sex (at least before marriage) can be the rule rather than the exception – it often does not "count", as in the famous instance of "ritualised homosexuality" in Melanesia (Herdt 1984), where all boys in an age–set reaching maturity have to be inseminated orally by an older man as part of tribal initiation. Even until recent times in the west, co–existence of same–sex and opposite–sex activity was far more common than exclusively same–sex activity, and for this reason bisexuality is in many ways more culturally typical than homosexuality.

Yet, bisexuality is even more taboo among church authorities than is homosexuality, and it is instructive to enquire why. At root, I surmise, bisexual behavior attracts what used to be referred to as the invert/pervert distinction. What is meant is that if a person *can* relate sexually to a member of the opposite sex, then not only ought he or she to do so, but not to do so is thought morally pernicious. He or she is regarded as freely *choosing* "the wrong" – is perverted – as opposed to not being able to help his or her sexual orientation, and therefore not being culpable, and so is an invert. Extending this point, an invert is expressing a "permissible" version of homosexuality, whereas anyone capable of opposite–sex sexual activity is *ipse facto* sinful. In recent times, the number of "[heterosexually] married homosexuals" has decreased considerably in the west in the wake of gay liberation and the liberalizing of attitudes towards homosexuality, but in plenty of other societies marriage is in effect still mandatory and same–sex activity pre–dates or parallels heterosexual activity.

Social and church attitudes to homosexuality

In Europe, social and religious attitudes towards homosexuality are changing rapidly. In Britain, one of the most remarkable examples of large–scale attitude change has been with respect to tolerance of homosexuality. Reporting on the 2002 *British Social Attitudes*, Geoff Evans says that: "In 1985, 70% of people though it was "always" or "mostly" wrong. Now under half (47%) think this, while a third (33%) says it is "not wrong at all" ... Britain is likely to become increasingly tolerant over time and older, less tolerant, generations will die out and be replaced by more tolerant ones".[9] Moreover, the most significant variables affecting this change are age and education. Evans continues: "one of the less obvious pay–offs from higher education seems to be more liberal views on these issues. So tolerance should increase as the numbers of people entering higher education grows".

And racial and homophobic prejudice certainly does vary dramatically by age and education: Under a quarter (23%) of the under 30s think homosexuality is "always wrong", compared with almost two–thirds (60%) of the 60 plus group. Fewer than one in five (17%) of graduates think homosexuality is "always wrong", compared with more than half (54%) of people with no qualifications. Nor is this finding restricted to Britain or Europe. A study comparing 29 national

---

9 http://www.natcen.ac.uk/natcen/pages/news_and_media_docs/bsa1_pr.doc (March 2005).

samples with comparable question–frames and sampling (Kelley 2001) reaches virtually identical conclusions. In this case, however, he is not only able to look at the variation across the 29 nations but also assess directly the effect of religiosity. In 1999, by far the most tolerant country was the Netherlands with the median position well in the "not wrong at all category" (70% points), followed by northern European nations (62–51), British and Commonwealth countries (46–41), then follows the significantly less tolerant USA with the median category in the "almost always wrong" (31 points), and a tail of Latin American countries who are the least tolerant on average.

As to the effect of religion (in these largely Christian or post–Christian countries) the author comments, "Religious beliefs make a huge difference to tolerance", reducing the level of tolerance by a massive factor (28%), and regular church–going in many cases reduces the tolerance level yet further. To some extent the major effect of religiosity on tolerance of homosexuality may be due to the fact that adherents and believers are on average considerably older than the rest of the population, which itself would increase intolerance, but, even when such variables are partialled out, it is clear that a major, significant and substantive effect of religiosity is intolerance.

Conclusions

Understanding the complexity of human sexuality is no small matter. But before we begin to make judgments about sexual behavior, it behoves us to at least understand not only the various meanings of sexuality, but also its sheer range and diversity. To its credit, Lambeth in 1978 recognized this, and set before the Communion the goal of "deep *and dispassionate* study". The years between 1978 and 2004 have been largely wasted years in which the Communion has consistently failed to inform itself of the latest results of scientific knowledge, and to try to integrate that knowledge with theological insights. Windsor needs to be seen, first and foremost, as the result of the consistent failure by the church to fulfil its own self–declared goals.

Windsor's deficiencies must be exposed, in order that the church may learn from its mistakes. First, there is no evidence that the Commission understands the phenomenon with which it is actually (even at least indirectly) dealing, and which, after all, occasioned the "crisis" to which Windsor is supposed to be a response. To be frank: there is nothing in Windsor, or in the statements by Lambeth, or by the Primates that suggests they know what they are talking about – at least empirically and scientifically.

Second, the language and concepts used to address issues in homosexuality is western–centred, taking contemporary gay western characteristics and lifestyles as presuppositions. But such assumptions are culturally bound and unrepresentative. Because of this bias, what emanates from Winsdor is also bound to be perceived differently (and judged as irrelevant) by those in other cultural contexts.

Third, the issues viewed as divisive within the Anglican Communion are also primarily western concerns, not easy to make sense of, or understand as pressing, outside current western society. In particular, the possibility of a same–sex union may be inconceivable in the experience of homosexuality in many cultures, and probably only becomes credible against the back–cloth of modern gay culture. A serious, resourced (rather than a symbolic or hoped–for) attempt to actually engage with (social) sciences and with other relevant professionals, and with members of the organized gay community, as well as networks of MSM is necessary to develop a theology (or theologies) of sexuality, and it needs to be a Communion–wide enterprise.

Fourth, churches need to know and take account of people's *lived* experiences. It is all very easy for the church to pronounce here or condemn there, but to do so without actual understanding is to belittle the people the church should seek to serve. A good maxim here is: before judgment – understanding. Windsor exhibits no understanding of *why* Anglicans see homosexuality differently, or why ECUSA or New Westminster took the actions they did. Being part of a Communion should require greater understanding – on all sides.

Finally, as I have wrestled, as an academic and a sociologist, for more than four decades with the immensely diverse accounts of sexual experience, I have often wondered how much *theological* sense can be made of the apparently bewildering range of sexualites that I have studied and encountered. I understand how people can look at this variety and feel fearful and threatened. At one level, it appears threatening to Christian values of love and fidelity, and especially to the ideal (for an ideal it certainly is) of life–long monogamy. But there is, I think, a deeper insight to be encountered – and one that should challenge us all. It is this: the very God, celebrated in narrative and ritual and art and music, is a diverse God of Father, Son and Holy Spirit. And this is the God who has created diversity, and even rejoices it in.

References

Bailey, J. M., and Pillard, R. C. (1991). "A Genetic Study of Male Sexual Orientation". *Archives of General Psychiatry*, 48, 1089–1096.

Bancroft, J. (1994). "Homosexual Orientation: The Search for a Biological Basis". *British Journal of Psychiatry*, 164, 437–440.

Blackwood, Evelyn (ed) (1986). *The Many Faces of Homosexuality: Anthropological Approaches to Homosexual Behavior.* New York: Harrington Park Press.

Blanchard, R., and Bogaert, A. F. (1996). "Homosexuality in Men and Number of Older Brothers". *American Journal of Psychiatry,*153:27–31.

Bagemihl, Bruce (1999). *Biological Exuberance: Animal Homosexuality and Natural Diversity.* New York: St. Martin's Press

Brown, Peter (1988). *The Body and Society: Men, Women and Sexual Renunciation in Early Christianity.* London: Faber & Faber.

Brundage, James A. (1987). *Law, Sex and Christian Society in Medieval Europe.* Chicago: Chicago University Press.

Byne, W. (1995). "Science and Belief: Psychobiological Research on Sexual Orientation". *Journal of Homosexuality*, 28:3/4, 303–344.

Cecco J. P. and Parker P. A.. (1995). "The Biology of Homosexuality: Sexual Orientation or Sexual Preference?" *Journal of Homosexuality*, 28:1/2,1–25.

Coxon, A. P. M. (1992). *Homosexual Response Studies: International Report.* Geneva: World Health Organization, Global Programme on Aids.

Coxon, A. P. M. (1995). "Homophobia", "Same–Sex Relations", "Sexuality" in P. A. B. Clarke and A.

Linzey (eds), *Dictionary of Ethics, Theology and Society*. London and New York: Routledge.

Coxon, A. P. M. (1996). *Between the Sheets: Sexual Diaries and Gay Men's Sex in the Era of AIDS*. London and New York: Cassell.

Coxon, A. P. M., N. H. Coxon, P. Weatherburn, *et al* (1993). "Sex Role Separation in Sexual Diaries of Homosexual Men". *AIDS*, 7(6), 877–882.

Dover, Kenneth J. (1978). *Greek Homosexuality*. Cambridge, MA: Harvard University Press.

Ford, C. S., and F. A. Beach (1951). *Patterns of Sexual Behavior*. New York: Harper and Row.

Foucault, Michel (1980–87). *The History of Sexuality, Vol 1: An Introduction*. (1980, Harmondsworth: Penguin Books), Vol 2: *L'Usage des plaisirs* (1987, Paris: Gallimard), Vol 3: *Le Souci de Soi* (1988, Paris: Gallimard).

Gagnon, John H. (1977). *Human Sexualities*. Glenview, Ill.: Scott Foreman.

Greenberg, David E. (1988). *The Construction of Homosexuality*. Chicago: Chicago University Press.

Halperin D. T. (1999). "Heterosexual Anal Intercourse: Prevalence, Cultural Factors, and HIV Infection, and Other Health Risks". Part I, *AIDS Patient Care STDS*, 13(12), 717–30.

Hamer, D. H., Hu, S., Magnuson, V. L., Hu, N., and Pattatucci, A..M. L. (1995) "A Linkage Between DNA markers on the X Chromosome and Male Sexual Orientation". *Science*, 261:321–327.

Harrison P. J. (1994). "Is Homosexual Behaviour Hard–wired? Sexual Orientation and Brain Structure". *Psychological Medicine*, 24, 811–816.

Herdt, G. H. (ed) (1984). *Ritualized Homosexuality in Melanesia*. Berkeley: University of California Press.

Hu, S., Papatucci, A. M. L., Patterson, C., Li, L., Fulker, D. W., Cherny, S. S., Kruglyak, L., and Hamer, D. L. (1995). "Linkage Between Sexual Orientation and Chromosome Xq28 in Males But Not in Females". *Nature Genetics*,11:248–256.

Kelley J. (2001). "Attitudes Towards Homosexuality in 29 Nations". *Australian Social Monitor*, 4 (1), 1–22.

Kemph B. T., Kasser T. (1996). "Effects of Sexual Orientation of Interviewer on Expressed Attitudes Toward Male Homosexuality". *Journal of Social Psychology*, 136:3, 401–403.

Kinsey, A..C., Pomeroy, W. B., Martin, C. E. (1948). *Sexual Behavior in the Human Male*. Philadelphia: W. B. Saunders.

Lauman, E. O. *et al* (1994). *The Social Organization of Sexuality: Sexual Practices in the United States*, Chicago: University of Chicago Press.

McIntosh, M. (1968). "The Homosexual Role". *Social Problems,* 16, 92–193 reprinted with postscript in E. Stein (ed) *Forms of Desire: Sexual Orientation and the Social Constructionist Controversy*. London and New York: Routledge.

McNeill, S. J., John J. (1976). *The Church and the Homosexual*. Kansas City: Sheed, Andrews and McMeel.
Roughgarden, J. (2004). *Evolution's Rainbow: Diversity, Gender, and Sexuality in Nature and People*.

Berkeley CA: University of California Press.

Tielman, R. A. P., M. Carballo, and Aart C. Hendricks (eds), *Bisexuality and HIV/AIDS*. Buffalo, NY: Prometheus.

Wellings, K., Field, J., Johnson, A. *et al* (1994). *National Survey of Sexual Attitudes and Lifestyles I*. London: Penguin, 1994, and Erens B., McManus S, Field J., Korovessis C., Johnson A. M., Fenton K., *et al.* (2001) *National Survey of Sexual Attitudes and Lifestyles II: Technical Report*. London: National Centre for Social Research.

West, D. J. (1977). *Homosexuality Re–examined*, 4th revised edition. London: Duckworth.

17

AFRICAN PERSPECTIVES ON EPISCOPACY AND SEXUALITY

Kevin Ward

Introduction

Soon after the publication of Windsor in October 2004, Bishop Griswold, presiding bishop of the Episcopal Church of the USA (ECUSA), reflected on the stance of his church in relation to the issues, which have precipitated the present "crisis" in the Anglican Communion:

> It is important to note here that in the Episcopal Church we are seeking to live the gospel in a society where homosexuality is openly discussed and increasingly acknowledged in all areas of our public life.[1]

In Africa, personal issues of sexuality, whether heterosexual or homosexual, have not been debated with such openness, though the church has long debated issues concerning social norms of marriage. Griswold's reflection highlights the need, which Windsor also acknowledges, of pastoral sensitivity to the differences of culture. This does not lead to a cultural relativism; rather it emphasizes the need for caution and sensitivity in all discussions of our common humanity and

---

1 Presiding Bishop Griswold, "Remarks on Windsor Report", 18 October 2004, http://aacblog.classicalanglican.net/archives.

sexuality, expressed in diverse social realities. The same can be said of episcopacy. The office of a bishop has varying meanings in England, America and Africa, not least in its popular accountability. One of the weaknesses of Windsor may be that its understanding of episcopacy is expressed in so abstract and ideal a form, that the actual place of a bishop in the community, with all the pressures and demands which that creates in different places and times, is not adequately expressed. Since it was the election of a bishop that has provoked the present crisis in Anglicanism, this essay will begin with an examination of the issue of episcopacy in African Anglicanism.

Episcopacy in Africa

Before the 1960s there were few black African Anglican bishops, and those who were bishops were mostly suffragans: "half–bishop" was James Johnson's contemptuous response when he refused such a position in 1892, having been the outstanding Christian minister in Lagos for a generation.[2] Things did not substantially change until the very end of the colonial era. But rapidly, the Anglican episcopacies of most independent African nations became overwhelmingly African. This was a time of rapid expansion of the church, when Christians for the first time became a majority in much of sub–Saharan Africa. There was popular demand for local dioceses and, overwhelmingly, the expectation was that bishops should be the "sons of the soil", representing and articulating the needs of the local area. In areas of strong Anglican presence, like Nigeria and the countries of East Africa, dioceses proliferated. Independent, democratic governments curtailed traditional power, but confidence in central government also waned, as political leaders failed to deliver good government or were toppled by army coups. Church leaders became even more important in their role as "fathers of the people", ensuring that resources were directed to their

---

2 Johnson was a West African Creole of Yoruba extraction, the son of freed slaves and brought up in Sierra Leone where he was ordained. Eventually he did become an assistant bishop on the Niger Delta. E. A. Ayandele, *The Missionary Impact on Modern Nigeria* (London: Longmans, 1966), p. 228.

locality and defending the local community against violence and arbitrary government.

In this situation, the election of bishops itself became a highly contested arena: the stakes were high. The ethnic origin of the candidate was often an important factor, as were regional or class issues. Identification with, or opposition to, the regime in power might also be important in securing election. The intensity of local involvement is often manifest in intense campaigning, overt or covert. With a limited electorate (usually lay and clerical members of the diocesan synod), opportunities for influencing electors are abundant. In East Africa, the term "decampaigning" has entered the political and religious vocabulary, to describe negative campaigns aimed at undermining candidates. This might involve accusations of sexual impropriety as well as corruption. Local politicians and notables are often drawn into the conflict – indeed they sometimes are at the center of disputes, anxious to have a compliant church figure at the top. Elections are usually confirmed by the respective House of Bishops, but the decision may be contested in the secular courts. Once a bishop has been installed, antagonisms abate. But problems can resurface. If the political regime changes, a bishop may be identified with a former, discredited regime, and this can undermine his general authority, as happened in Rwanda.

Despite the high level of popular involvement in an election, once elected a bishop finds himself in a position of high responsibility with few constitutional restraints. It is difficult to avoid developing an authoritarianism that may be essential to functioning as a bishop in such circumstances. The deployment of clergy is almost entirely in his hands, and transfer to a remote parish or unpopular job can be used as a weapon to ensure clerical compliance. This ensures conformity, but builds up resentment. The laity is less amenable to control. An unpopular bishop can generate strong centrifugal tendencies, with marginalized or far–flung regions of the diocese demanding separation and the creation of their own diocese.

Uganda provides a good example of these trends. The first Ugandan Archbishop, Erika Sabiiti, had had a somewhat tumultuous career, as Bishop of Ruwenzori and as Archbishop of Uganda. He was unpopular for a variety of reasons: he was an outsider to Ruwenzori; he belonged to the Hima pastoralist group, a minority which had long held a political and social dominance which were resented; he belonged to the *Balokole* Revival group[3], which was seen by "ordinary" Christians as inflexible and overly moralistic; and, despite his claim to stand aside from politics, he was commonly identified with opposition to the ruling political party. Despite this, the depth of his personal faith, and his incorruptibility, made him an outstanding leader, whose courage and plain speaking at the time of the murder of Archbishop Luwum in 1977 was much admired.[4] Subsequent Ugandan archbishops have found their authority compromised within the church by a change of regime.

Episcopal problems can have a more local origin. In Busoga, in eastern Uganda, the diocese was rendered ungovernable for almost a decade in the 1980s and 1990s, with the bishop denied access to his cathedral and forced to abandon his residence, because his presence was unacceptable to a substantial, or at least highly vocal, section of the community. Parts of the diocese refused to send collections to the diocesan centre. At one point a rival bishop declared himself elected as new bishop. The archbishop had to intervene and appoint an episcopal administrator to run the diocese. But peace and unity was only restored when the bishop himself chose to retire and a new one was appointed, a Musoga (that is, a local person like his predecessor) but someone who had not worked in the diocese before and who was able to begin the work of reconciliation between the different factions.[5]

More recently, the diocese of Muhabura, in southwest Uganda, has been without a bishop since the election in 2001 became mired in

---

3 The *Balokole* (literally: "Saved People") has been the most important single spiritual movement within east African Anglicanism.
4 Kevin Ward, "The Church of Uganda Amidst Conflict", in H. B. Hansen and M. Twaddle, *Religion and Politics in East Africa* (London: James Currey, 1995), pp. 72–105.
5 Cf. Paul Gifford, *African Christianity: Its Public Role* (London: Hurst, 1998), pp. 67–75, and T. M. Kisitu, "A Historical Study of Conflicts in Busoga Diocese", unpublished PhD dissertation, Edinburgh, 2002.

controversy. Eventually, the archbishop was forced to annul the election, which led to litigation. In 2003, the High Court found that the election had been in order and demanded that the archbishop proceed with the confirmation and ordination. Regarding such a decision as *ultra vires,* the Church of Uganda did not act on this decision, and the diocese remains without its own bishop. Interestingly enough, the failure to elect a bishop has not diminished the numerical growth of the diocese – in some ways the popular feelings aroused in this case has energised local identification with the Church of Uganda.[6]

In the 1980s, disputes centred on episcopacy reached even more serious proportions in the Sudan. Archbishop Elinana Ngalamu's ten year term of office came to an end in 1986 and the Provincial Synod decided that he should retire. The archbishop, though a sick man, refused to accept the validity of this decision. A schism ensued in which Ngalamu consecrated a rival set of bishops. The dispute exacerbated complex tensions within the southern Sudan, at a time when the south as a whole was engaged in the long struggle with the Khartoum Government, divisions which the North was able to exploit. Archbishop Robert Runcie was involved in attempts to achieve reconciliation. But the schism was only resolved when Archbishop Elinana died. His appointees were eventually accepted as assistant bishops in 1992 and became diocesans in their own right in 1996. The Episcopal Church in the Sudan (ECS) could hardly sustain 24 dioceses, but it was considered a price worth paying to bring about unity.

> Many in the ECS used the term 'miracle' to describe the remarkable transformation in attitude that made reunification possible in 1992. Certainly, after several years of extremely bitter conflict, the rapid resolution in 1992 is an indication of how central Christian values of forgiveness and reconciliation survived despite everything, and could be drawn on with

---

6 Much of the information for this ongoing issue comes from the Uganda press, *New Vision* and *Monitor*, available on the web.

integrity when the decisive moment arrived. Nevertheless, deep wounds had been caused by the 'crisis'.[7]

Amidst all the political issues which exacerbated episcopal conflict in both Sudan and Uganda, there are the also important personal issues including, personal rivalries, the reluctance to give up power and influence, the need continually to satisfy community aspirations, the expectations of the extended family, and fears about survival in retirement given the lack of pension provision.

These are persistent issues relating to the exercise of episcopal power in Africa, which are not likely to go away. At times Anglicans have wondered whether some central authority, external to the conflict, might provide an instrument to heal division. Catholic centralism in Rome has certainly limited the scale and number of disputes, though it has not prevented conflict over episcopal appointment altogether. When the choice is seen as insensitive to local aspirations, or where the bishop has lost confidence of the clergy or the faithful generally, conflict can and does emerge, with the same mix of ethnic and regional cleavages evident. But, however much Anglicans may admire the control and efficiency of the Catholic Church, there is little desire for any diminution of the local autonomy which Anglicans prize so highly. The Primates meeting at Newry in February 2005 reaffirmed this strongly:

> While we welcome the ministry of the Archbishop of Canterbury as that of one who can speak to us as primus inter pares about the realities we face as a Communion, we are cautious of any development that would seem to imply the creation of an international jurisdiction that could override our proper provincial autonomy. [8]

---

7 Roland Werner, William Anderson and Andrew Wheeler, *Day of Devastation, Day of Contentment: The History of the Sudanese Church across 2000 Years* (Nairobi: Pauline, 2000), p. 634–638. The quotation is on p. 635.
8 The Anglican Communion Primates Meeting Communiqué, February 2005, para 10. http://www.anglicancommunion.org.

It seems unlikely that any of the suggestions in Windsor, or indeed the proposed covenant, would make any effective contribution to healing divisions like the ones we have described. The African Anglican Church is well aware of the need to develop robust institutions of provincial authority. However, there has been a welcome for intervention at the pastoral level – Archbishop Runcie's concern for the ECS is particularly noteworthy in this regard. But, ultimately more important was that sense of "forgiveness and reconciliation" which meant that the parties in Sudan could not, ultimately be satisfied with "walking apart". In this case the Anglican "bonds of affection" did triumph over the centripetal forces, which can strain the Anglican system to breaking point.

The question arises: why is the election of a gay bishop in a single diocese, constitutionally elected and with strong popular support within his diocese, a more serious crisis than the ones described in Africa, which seem potentially and actually much more subversive of the life of the church in the community? And why does it preclude the kind of solutions that have brought reconciliation and unity in the Sudan? Windsor states:

> Granted that local churches are often best placed to respond to pastoral needs within their own context and to understand the issues that arise in their particular culture, no part of the church can ignore its life in communion with the rest (16).

But, why cannot the proper interest and concern of the wider church be exercised in the same spirit of concern and desire to assist? This leads to the issue of sexuality in an African context.

African Anglicanism and marriage discipline

Unlike Europe and America, the church in Africa has never been in a position to impose its own vision of marriage on society as a whole. Christians at first portrayed the sexual mores of traditional African society as lax and unbridled. One of the marks of the early converts was their acceptance of a strictly controlled sexuality and the adoption of monogamy, celebrated by a church wedding. This was meant to distinguish Christians from the rest of society, of which they were a part. Much early mission education for girls had, as one of its goals, the preparation of young women to be Christian wives. The church soon evolved from this small, tight–knit community in which such strict discipline could be effectively monitored and controlled. With large–scale conversion, it became difficult, if not impossible, to maintain the radical distinctiveness of marriage discipline. Even though the church could never accept polygamy as a way of life for a Christian, it began to see the value of some of the other traditional marriage norms. It began to insist on the fulfilment of traditional forms of courtship and of marriage contracts before it would bless a couple's wedding in church. In the meantime, the disruptive effects of modernity began to impinge on African family life. Migrant labor, urbanization, the loosening of chiefly or parental authority, the delay in marriage which schooling necessitated – all created a situation in which traditional marriage discipline eroded, but without effectively establishing the predominance of a Christian ideal. The church itself had long ceased to consist of small faith communities based on individual decisions to break with traditional values. Instead, it became itself a deeply rooted local institution, with a mass following. The boundaries between traditional and Christian culture became blurred. A smaller proportion of the baptized felt it important or necessary to seek a church wedding.[9] The complexity of modern living has gradually, but inexorably, weakened the moral guidance of both traditional society and the church. External respect is paid to both. But the reality for many young people is that it is impossible rigorously to follow either set of values. The sexual choice and lack of authoritative norms in Africa is every bit as great as in western secular societies. But, in Africa, the crisis does not stem from an

9 Adrian Hastings, *Christian Marriage in Africa* (London: SPCK, 1973).

erosion of Christian values, but partly from a failure of the church to establish those values in the first place, not least among its own membership.

Where the church has always been rigorous is in its insistence on a strict marriage discipline for its employed workers, lay and clerical. In colonial times advancement in church work was slow and laborious. Faithfulness within a monogamous marriage was one of the prerequisites for progression. Catechists and evangelists were often only ordained when they were mature in years and respectability.[10] From the 1960s this ponderous progression of clerical advancement was often criticised. In the new Africa, it was argued, education must be the most important criterion. As a result of this, younger men (and later women) were admitted to ordination when they were still in their 20s. Sometimes bishops have insisted on young people being married before ordination. But this has rarely been followed systematically, and there has been an increase in unmarried clergy, most of who eventually do get married. Another issue, especially in rural dioceses, is to ensure that young married men get properly married in church and so regularize their status before ordination. These criteria apply, *e fortiori,* to bishops. By the time someone is under consideration for the episcopate, he will have long been married. Allegations about sexual misconduct might well feature during campaigning – often malicious attempts at "decampaigning" which can be disregarded. But sometimes the aura of respectability essential to a bishop will fade and marital problems will assume an importance, especially if the bishop becomes unpopular for other reasons.

If the clergy are expected to evidence clear Christian marriage standards, the Christian community as a whole recognizes two classes of Christians. In most Anglican churches, anyone whose style of life does not meet the high standards of Christian marriage will not be expected to take holy communion. This often means that a majority in a

---

10 Cf. Kevin Ward, *Called to Serve: A History of Bishop Tucker College* (Kampala, 1989).

congregation are not communicants. Full membership often resides in special groups of particularly devoted church members, such as members of the Revival Fellowship, or of the Mothers' Union (MU), though even here there is diversity. In some of the older established areas, Christian marriage is sufficiently common to make sense of restricting membership of the Mothers' Union (MU) to the "ring wife". But in less established areas, the MU could not function unless it had a wider admission policy. In Uganda before 1973, couples that did not have a recognized Christian marriage would not be allowed even to bring their children for baptism. The new Canon on Baptism opened up baptism to the children of all who asked. This was hotly resisted by members of the strictest Revival group, the *Bazukufu* (the Reawakened). For a time they refused to take holy communion from a priest who had baptised *abaana eby'ensi* (literally: "the children of the world"). Attempts to open up communion to all church members, irrespective of their marriage status, have not met with wide success. Such a policy was often seen as favoring rich polygamists who exercised undue influence in the church because of their financial power. Ordinary Christians often saw no reason to dilute the official teaching of the church, even though they had no intention, or saw no possibility, of conforming their lives to those higher standards.[11]

This formalization of double standards has often been recognized as pastorally restrictive, inimical to "the radical holiness to which all Christ's people are called" (11). But, by and large, the African church has not found a way of satisfactorily dealing with the dichotomy.

The church in Africa is highly aware of the complexity of sexual issues – the problems of youthful experimentation, casual relationships, prostitution, polygamy, unstable family life, violence against women. They have never been blind to the fragility of marriage and its diversity; nor to the widespread failure of Christians to model a

---

11 Kevin Ward, "Same–Sex Relations in Africa and the Debate on Homosexuality in East African Anglicanism", *Anglican Theological Review*, Vol. 84/1, Winter 2002, pp. 81–111.

Christian life. Anglicans are divided into those who emphasize strictness and drawing the boundaries of acceptable behavior narrowly, and those who are more tolerant of a diversity of practice, and are not overly concerned by the failure of individuals to conform. A large proportion of Christians accept the strict standards at face value, but then mitigate the severity by tolerance and flexibility. The HIV/AIDS crisis has greatly intensified the stakes in the field of sexual morality, but has not fundamentally altered the ground rules of the debate.

Homosexuality as a "crisis" for Anglicanism

Given the complexity of establishing a viable Christian sexual ethics in Africa, not least in African Anglicanism, one might have expected a larger measure of realism and proportion in confronting the issue of homosexuality. Why should this issue be so "divisive and destructive" (4)? Africa is not characterised by the depth of its homophobia. In fact, there are indications of permissive and relaxed attitudes in traditional cultures – homosexuality being seen as a transitional form of sexual experimentation, rather than a state of being, of minor importance, so long as it did not conflict with the universal obligation to marry and bear children. In colonial society, homosexuality was associated with the enforced separation of men and women resulting from single sex Christian schools and migrant labor. Again, it was not seen as a permanent life option. Christianity, in its concern for women, emphasised that marriage should not be seen primarily as a genealogical or economic strategy, but should be grounded in relationships of equality, affection and mutual respect. These are also the qualities that gay Christians who are serious about committed human relationship are likely to emphasize.

African Christian leaders are less likely than they were a few years ago to dismiss homosexuality as foreign. Homosexuality has in fact a long history in Africa. But African men and women are only beginning consciously to identify themselves as "homosexual" and to articulate their sexual identity in new, more public ways. Outside South

Africa, these explorations remain highly tentative and are fraught with danger. One of the sad things about the present Anglican "crisis" is that it has engendered a homophobic reaction in many parts of Africa which was absent before. British colonial laws criminalizing male homosexual activity, hardly utilized during the colonial period and for long ignored in independent Africa, are invoked to persecute individuals and incipient gay and lesbian action groups. Moreover, the destructive nature of the Anglican "crisis" encourages neither theological reflection, nor imaginative pastoral concern within Africa. The authoritarian, "chiefly" tendencies within episcopacy assert themselves to destructive effect, and stifle debate. Gay people themselves are too weak to insist on their voice being heard, and lack the organization and the skills to argue their case theologically. The Primates' Communiqué spoke movingly of the continued and unreserved commitment "to the pastoral support and care of homosexual people":

> The victimisation or diminishment of human beings whose affections happen to be ordered towards people of the same sex is anathema to us. We assure homosexual people that they are children of God, loved and valued by him, and deserving of the best we can give of pastoral care and friendship.[12]

But, as yet, outside South Africa, there is little sense of how this can be implemented in Africa itself. Archbishop Henry Orombi of Uganda, in a press release to the Ugandan *New Vision* newspaper on 3 March 2005, after returning from Northern Ireland, seemed to offer little hope for engagement with gay Christians:

> We see homosexual practices as unbiblical and against the teaching of the Church. Only Jesus who makes a difference to people can transform them not debates ...

---

12 The Anglican Communion Primates Meeting Communiqué, para. 6.

The Church of Uganda is committed to offering the gospel to those struggling with homosexuality. Jesus told the woman caught in adultery, "Go and sin no more" and not "go and sin some more". For the North Americans pastoral care means providing services for the blessing of same–sex unions. For us in Uganda pastoral care means leading people into fully transformed life that Jesus promises to those who call upon his name.[13]

In discussing *adiaphora* (things about which a difference of interpretation can be tolerated), Windsor uses this criterion:

That which embodies and expresses renewed humanity in Christ is always mandatory for Christians; that which embodies the dehumanising turning–away–from–God which Paul characterises with such terms as 'sin', 'flesh', and so on, is always forbidden. This, of course leaves several questions unanswered, but at least sketches a map on which further discussions may be located (39).

But many African bishops are already clear that homosexuality (not to mention homosexual practice) is dehumanising: "unbiblical and inhuman", as an open letter of the Uganda House of Bishops put it in 2000.[14] Archbishop Akinola of Nigeria has equally likened homosexuality to a form of slavery.

There has been little attempt to justify the premise that homosexuality is so "inhuman", "sinful" and "enslaving" that debate about it is ruled out without further ado. Even if homosexual practice is sinful, in what way is it more sinful than other forms of sexual relationship of which the church does not approve? As we have seen, the African church does in practice tolerate a variety of relationships within

---

13 Reported in *Church Times*, 11 March, 2005.
14 Public letter of Bishops meeting at Lweza Conference Centre, 20–24 November, 2000. Published on the (American) Integrity website: http/www.integrityusa.org.

the Christian community, even when it does not approve of those relationships – in particular, permanent, committed sexual relations which fall short of Christian marriage for one reason or another. The church challenges people in such relationships and encourages them to seek full Christian marriage. But they do not abandon those who fail to respond. The recognition that homosexual relationships might fall into that category, while hardly satisfactory, would at least go some way in assuring homosexuals that they were not being "dehumanized" or "victimized". It would also be some kind of reparation for the damage, which the Anglican Church has directly or indirectly caused by appearing to support state or societal oppression of people because of their sexuality.

Such a step would still leave the African bishops free to express the unacceptability of gay bishops. In that sense, it would not end the present "crisis", but it would serve to give some proportion to the issue, placing it alongside the other debates about human sexual relationships with which the African church has wrestled from the beginning, knowing that there are no easy answers. It would enable a critical dialogue with the American churches rather than breaking of "the bonds of affection" (5), which threaten to disintegrate the communion as a worldwide body. As Windsor acknowledges: practice on divorce and remarriage varies widely throughout the Communion. "The fact of divorce and remarriage would therefore not seem *per se* to be a crucial criterion." (51). Despite the particularly clear and uncompromising stand of many of the African Anglican churches on marriage and divorce, it has not come anywhere near endangering a common sense of Anglican identity. Equally, there seems no reason why a difference in attitude to homosexual practice should be a "crucial criterion".

In the end, however, it is unsatisfactory simply to accept difference of practice in the area of sexuality as irredeemably culturally specific. A radical critical dialogue also needs to take place within the African church, involving Africans who understand themselves to be gay or lesbian and who feel excluded and marginalized, and a much larger group of Africans who would not define themselves as "homosexual", but who have engaged in same–sex activity. Such a dialogue must be based on a re–engagement with the Bible, in which the church acknowledges that it does not control the Bible. The Bible challenges the prejudices and presuppositions of all who listen. It cannot be used as a tool to condemn a particular category of people, simply for who they are. One of the problems for the East African revival, and this seems to inform Archbishop Orombi's press statement, has been its tendency to divide church people into the saved and the unregenerate, "true Christians" or "sinners". Homosexual people are sinners, but they rightly reject the idea that they are sinners because they are homosexual. They look to the Christian community to guide them positively about how to lead the Christian life as homosexuals, not despite their homosexuality. They are looking for ways in which they can respond joyfully and with fulfilment to the command of Genesis 1 that "it is not good for man to be alone". Like Job, they long for an advocate, a deliverer, who will argue their cause against the pious friends who condemn them. This is a great missionary challenge for the church in Africa, as elsewhere. It looks for new ways of hearing the message of the Bible, ways that reach back to the revolutionary voice, which it had on first contact with African societies, the profound existential questionings that it provoked for the early Revivalists. It will go beyond the narrow conception of the Bible as a book of rules, or as a catena of texts strung together to justify a belief or practice already arrived at.

Conclusion

A devastating recent event was the suicide on 19 January 2005 of the young black South African novelist, Sello Duiker, whose novel about being black and gay in South Africa *The Quiet Violence of Dreams*[15], was a work of such integrity and profound insight. Duiker saw himself as representing South African youth, and their multiple identities, racial

---

15 K. Sello Duiker, *The Quiet Violence of Dreams* (Cape Town: Kwela, 2001).

and sexual. His publisher and friend, Annari van der Merwe, said in an obituary:

> He was blessed with equal measures of gentleness and kind–heartedness on the one hand, and unflinching honesty and a fearless pursuit of what he saw as essential human experience on the other. If he had one shortcoming, it was an inability to protect himself from life.[16]

In the light of the complexity of sexual identity and the difficulty of all people, heterosexual and homosexual, to achieve satisfactory relationships which both meet basic human needs, and which honor and respect the mystery of the other person, it is equally appalling this issue should have become such a battleground. In the early years of the twentieth century, the Anglican Church avoided both the authoritarianism of the Catholic Church in its harassment of "modernists" and the schism of American Protestants in their disputes over the fundamentals of the faith. African Anglicanism, while basically conservative in its views of scripture, avoided at that time falling into the sterile polarization of "liberal" and "orthodox". It would be a tragedy if this dispute about sexuality became the stumbling block, which destroys the Communion. It goes against those virtues of hospitality and respect for human difference, which in much of east and southern Africa is known as *ubuntu*, a willingness to debate and discuss issues with vigor but without rancour. Windsor argues that, "The Anglican Communion cannot again afford … the crippling prospect of repeated worldwide inter–Anglican conflict such as that engendered by the current crisis (49)". But it seems unlikely that its recommendations concerning the creation of institutional processes or the signing of a binding covenant, will resolve differences of the kind involved in the present crisis.

---

16 Obituary: Sello Duiker Remembered 21 January 2005; www.iafrica.com.

Africans are often praised or blamed for instigating this "crisis". For some, it is the "revenge" of an African Anglicanism long discontented by the way its voice has been ignored or sidelined in the structures of the Communion. But, in retrospect, the "crisis" may come to be seen as having more to do with the unresolved polarization of American Christianity, of which ECUSA is the latest victim, than the supposed "conservatism" of the African church. In fact, the African church is well used to living with plurality and diversity, both in its relation to the wider society and within its own structures. The immediate issue for the survival of Anglicanism is not how best to devise procedures and legally binding agreements, but how to generate that humanization and *ubuntu* – that concern for human dignity and respect, that desire for community and solidarity – which has been a defining characteristic of the church in Africa.

18

The Many Faces of Anglicanism

Martin Stringer

Having read through the Windsor Report many times, I cannot help but be reminded of an encounter I had some twenty years ago with Sam Van Culin who was at that time General Secretary of the Anglican Consultative Council. I had recently come back from a "gap year" following my undergraduate studies, working for the Anglican Church in Tanzania. I was invited to London to be involved in the liturgical preparations for Lambeth 1988, and I was chatting to Sam before or after a meeting. He asked me what I thought it was that defined the Anglican Communion; what was distinctively "Anglican" about it? I answered with the naïve confidence of a twenty something doctoral student: "A shared history of British colonialism". My knowledge of the Communion at that time was still fairly limited, and things have changed dramatically within all the Anglican churches in the last twenty years. However, I could not get that comment, that simplistic summation of worldwide Anglicanism, out of my mind as I read this latest Report.

What struck me most forcefully was the stark, arid, institutional image of the church that was being presented in its pages. It talks of instruments of unity, consultative councils, synods, conferences, and commissions. Even when it begins to talk of "communion", the central notion it chooses for its underlying ecclesiology, this becomes a dry theological concept that exists more in impairment than in any kind of ongoing reality. The Report does talk of "culture" and "enculturation" in passing, and makes some important points about the limits of enculturation in practice, but the reality of ordinary Anglican Christians, living out their everyday lives, struggling to understand how the Gospel relates to them and their social context, or what their church means to them, is seriously lacking. This is characteristic of practically all "official" ecclesiastical documents. However, this is a serious omission in Windsor, which may be central to the very future of the Anglican Communion itself.

In this paper, I want to redress some of that balance. I want to go to various corners of the Anglican Communion, to meet real Anglicans living and worshipping in different parts of the world, and to draw together some reflections that may help to shed a different light on this issue than that which is presented in the Report itself.

Tanzania

I was born in Tanzania where my parents were Anglican Missionaries. I left when I was eighteen months old, and visited again in the early nineteen eighties. I had plenty of opportunity to observe different aspects of the Anglican Church in the country, including two theological colleges, two episcopal consecrations, a tour of the north of the country, and nine months working for a church–funded hospital in the foothills of the Usambara mountains. I have continued to try and keep close contacts with the people and the church, and have a great deal of affection for both.

Looking at the Anglican Church in Tanzania, however, highlights a number of points that need to be recognized if we are fully to understand the difficulties faced by the Anglican Communion today. First, we need to understand the history. Tanganyika only came within the sphere of British influence following the First World War. Before that, its colonial heritage was German. This did not, however, stop Anglican missionaries working in the country from the end of the nineteenth century. One of the principal bases for Anglican missionary activity was on the Island of Zanzibar, where the Anglican Cathedral is built on the site of the old slave market. From here the Universities Mission to Central Africa (UMCA) launched expeditions into the south and east of Tanganyika, and into what are now Zambia, Zimbabwe and Malawi. UMCA was a missionary society that was firmly within the catholic wing of the Anglican Church, and the missionaries exported the full panoply of catholic theology, ritual and sentiment with them into the African context. In fact, it is commonly recognized that the anglo–catholics in the colonies could avoid most of the censure and prejudice that they suffered in England and could in most cases be more catholic than would ever have been allowed in the home country. The life of Frank Weston, Bishop of Zanzibar, clearly exemplifies this.

The northeast of Tanganyika, however, was untouched by UMCA and was evangelised by the Church Missionary Society coming down from Uganda and Kenya. Where UMCA was catholic, CMS was firmly on the protestant, or evangelical, wing of the Anglican Church. They exported a love for the Book of Common Prayer, a commitment to biblical teaching and a distrust of hierarchy, ritual and excess. The current Anglican Church in Tanzania now combines both these traditions, but with a clear and distinct geographical divide. In many of the places that I visited in the nineteen eighties, the worship of the east and the south still had the feel of nineteen twenties anglo–catholicism. Everything was in Swahili, but the hymns came straight out of the *English Hymnal* and the vestments, the incense, and the ceremonial, were clearly Anglican despite the very different context. In the north east, the worship was also trapped in something of a time warp, but this time of early nineteen fifties evangelicalism, with great shows of enthusiasm, traditional mission hymns, and long, powerful biblical preaching. Both were exciting and enthusiastic in their own way, but neither could really be described as "enculturated".

The point I wish to make is valid for practically the whole of the Anglican Communion in the old colonies, and goes back to my initial comment to Sam Van Culin. The form of Anglicanism that was exported to the colonial, or mission churches, was either one that was strongly and uniformly catholic, or one that was strongly and uniformly evangelical. In both cases, the missionaries in Africa, India or wherever, were able to go further in their catholicism or evangelicalism than they were allowed, or felt comfortable doing in England. And in both cases the churches exhibited a purer form of both these traditions than was ever seen, except in the most extreme churches, back home. These were also traditions that placed a strong emphasis on mission, on biblical teaching, on strict moral behavior, and on the centrality of the Gospel, in the lives of the people. Putting it bluntly, the liberal, middle of the road Anglican would never have seen the point of mission, and therefore left the conversion of the empire to the more conservative extremes. While an over–simplification, it underpins a reality that cannot be ignored. The mission and colonial heritage of Anglicanism has left conservative churches, and conservative Christians, scattered throughout the empire, and these churches are now coming back to challenge its liberal heart.

The second point comes out of my surprise; I might even say shock, while working at the hospital in Muheza. I discovered, almost by accident, that the local Anglican priest, like the majority of his congregation, took his baby son to a local herbal healer before he brought the child to the hospital for attention. The vast majority of the cases seen at the hospital came from failed, mostly harmful, effects of local healing. This drove the English doctors mad. Of course we can talk of "enculturation" in this context, or the value of local healing traditions alongside those of western medicine. As an anthropologist, I am aware of all these arguments and have some sympathy with most of them. The reality on the ground, however, was that most of the local, native practices were harmful, especially to children, and seriously hindered the work of the hospital and its staff. These native practices, however, were endorsed, and engaged in, by the local Anglican priest and his family, despite a public rhetoric from the pulpit against the very spirits that animated the local healing practices.

The major crisis facing the Anglican Church in Tanzania in the early nineteen eighties was a crisis of education. They needed desperately to find people capable of running the theological colleges and priests able to fill the role of bishop. There was a severe shortage of suitably qualified candidates and, much against the better judgement of the archbishop of the time, they had to look to Britain for both theological educators and, in the case of the southern dioceses, for a bishop. This was far from ideal and everybody in the church at the time recognized this.

That, however, was twenty years ago and things have clearly changed in the field of theological education throughout the Anglican Communion. My current position as head of a theology department in Birmingham University, which has inherited some of the pioneering work of the Selly Oak Colleges, provides a vantage point from which to observe those changes. Selly Oak has traditionally trained potential leaders from across the Anglican Communion through schemes that have brought aspiring leaders and potential academics to Birmingham to gain an MPhil or a PhD in mission studies. In recent years, however, we have seen this market decline and dwindle to little more than a trickle. At one level, this is excellent news as it means that our work has been realized. We have trained people to go back to Tanzania and other churches around the world to take up the training of clergy and theologians locally. The missionary societies no longer need to send such people to us. This has to be positive, even though it does affect our own long–term profitability. We have also noted that many mission societies are choosing to send potential academics to other universities and theological institutions that are nearer to the home church, say in South Africa.

There is, however, a down side. In Selly Oak at the height of its popularity and reputation, we had colleges that represented all forms of churchmanship, and most of the mainline churches. CMS and USPG (the successor to UMCA) both had colleges, as did the Methodist church, the Baptists, the Quakers, the URC, and others. It was a place where people from different nationalities, cultures, and church backgrounds could mix and interact and, hopefully, learn from each other in a spirit of tolerance and positive engagement. The colleges even chose to set up a Centre for the Study of Islam and Christian–Muslim Relations that was about twenty years ahead of its time, and is now considered to be a beacon of interreligious education in a post 9/11 world. The students have taken the underlying ideology of the colleges that encouraged debate, toleration and dialogue, to all corners of the world including Tanzania.

If, however, the future education of clergy, church leaders and theological educators, is going to happen more locally and in colleges chosen by the churches themselves, is there not a danger that the conservative evangelical or catholic traditions are simply going to be reinforced without the outward looking perspective of a center, such as Selly Oak? This is not, of course, a call for the renewal or revitalization of Selly Oak as such, nor am I saying that it is only in England that such tolerant intercultural study can be undertaken. I am simply pointing to a factor important to understanding the global Anglican Communion as it moves into the twenty–first century, and yet which is missed entirely within the body of the Report itself.

North East Brazil

Let me now take you to another corner of the Anglican Communion, to Recife in North West Brazil. A couple of years ago I had a student from Recife, an Anglican priest, who was interested in the nature of enculturation and the liturgy in this part of South America. What struck both my student and myself was just how little contact there was between her own understanding and experience of Anglicanism, and the situation she found in England. She had been brought up in a free evangelical context, even within what might be described as a pentecostal tradition, and after moving into the Anglican Church in Recife she had found herself completely at home. Free, non–liturgical, enthusiastic, passionate worship was the order of the day. On seeing the

Anglican Church in Britain, however, she could not have felt more alienated. There was nothing familiar to her home context whatsoever. What is more, despite wanting to study the enculturation of worship, I found out that she was not even aware of the presence of a Portuguese liturgy within Anglicanism, and had hardly ever used a formal liturgy of any kind for worship in her own church. There was nothing here that could be encompassed by my flippant comment about "British colonial heritage" as the basis for Anglican identity.

If we look at the history of Anglicanism in this region, however, we do find that at one level its roots are firmly based in the British colonial, or at least ex–patriot, context as the original Anglican community of the region had serviced the British and American ex–patriot community. The other strand of the church's history, however, came from US Episcopalian missionary activity of a decidedly pentecostal nature. Once again, we see the place of those with a drive for mission, from the extremes of the home church, planting and supporting the mainline churches of other parts of the world. This church looked to the States for its support and its spiritual sustenance, not to Britain, or to other parts of the Anglican Church in Brazil. The particular strand of the Episcopalian tradition that the church looked to had institutionalized itself in this isolated corner of Brazil. By all accounts, it is a thriving and highly successful church with a strong worshipping tradition (although whether that can be described as "Anglican" may be open to question) and a deep commitment to work with the poor and oppressed.

When I was working on the committee to prepare liturgical matters for Lambeth 1988, I remember that I was surprised to learn that even at this time there was a strong part of the Anglican Communion that spoke and worshipped in Portuguese. This was remarkable in part because there is no historic association between Portuguese speaking parts of the world and British or American colonialism, and because we do not often think of Portuguese as a significant international language. The Portuguese synod that met at that time included representatives from Brazil, Angola, Mozambique and Portugal. It was the presence of a significant Portuguese Protestant Church at these meetings, and as part of the Anglican Communion, that first alerted me to the fact that there are in fact elements, and traditions within the Communion that have nothing to do with the British or American missionary endeavour. This is important to remember and something that is also lost sight of in the institutional language of the Windsor Report.

Vermont, USA

Thirdly, I want to take you to a tiny rural Anglican Church not far from Brattleboro, Vermont. My partner and I were staying with friends in the region and on Sunday morning we braved the rainstorms and the mountain roads to attend a small church nestled among the forested hills of South Vermont. Our friends were officially Presbyterian but had chosen to attend this Anglican Church because of the congregation's liberal stance on social issues. This particular morning the newsletter had announced a "garden service", but the rain had already ruled that out. The church had no priest of its own and a Canon from the diocese had come to take the service. In the spirit of the "garden service", and despite the rain, he appeared at the front of the church wearing a brightly patterned Bermuda shirt, shorts, and a stole, and proceeded to lead the service. It was informal, cosy and welcoming, with a special mention for visitors and friends, including my partner and myself. The sermon, however, consisted of a commentary on the recent meeting of the synod of the Episcopal Church at which the election of Gene Robinson as bishop of New Hampshire had been endorsed. The Canon had been at the synod, and he was able to give us a first hand account of events in an up beat and celebratory fashion. This was the "good news" – clearly welcomed by that small rural community in Vermont.

What struck me most about this particular service, with all its incongruities, and despite its clear Anglican shape, was that, of all the situations I have described so far, this event comes closest to the true "enculturation" of the liturgy as defined by Shorter, Chupungco, and other writers. In Tanzania, we worshipped with full catholic regalia or a solid prayerbook tradition in the heart of Africa. In northeast Brazil, American pentecostalism provided the theological and liturgical language for this Anglican Church of the slums. In Vermont, however, we had a "garden service", Bermuda shirts, informality, liberal theology, and cookies in the hall after the service. This was Anglicanism enculturated into the heart of Democrat America. Does this make the situation in Vermont any more authentic, or more in need of attention, than the ex–colonial (or neo–colonial) situations of Tanzania or Brazil? I do not think so. It is simply an observation that needs to be noted, and one that is often forgotten in wider debates about enculturation.

The other point, of course, is that the "culture" of Vermont was not the majority culture of the States. The re–election of George W. Bush has shown that. Our friends and their colleagues within this congregation are committed Democrats and on the far left of the Democratic Party. They were vehemently opposed to the war in Iraq, they campaigned for justice for the Palestinians, they argued for the rights of Muslims and other minorities within the States, and expressed a range of beliefs and values that would be expected from this kind of population, including an open and accepting view of same–sex relationships. We could describe these people as being part of a "subculture", albeit a significant minority in the country as a whole, and probably the majority in southern Vermont. The point, however, is that the church in that place fully reflected its own specific "culture". Nobody who opposed their values would choose to associate with this particular congregation.

Windsor asks whether there are in fact values and practices within any culture that Christianity should choose to challenge rather than to accept. This is an interesting question to address to the church in Vermont. Nobody in that congregation would probably see any contradiction between the Gospel and any of the liberal values that they endorse. In fact my friends, and others in the congregation, are university and theological lecturers, are highly intelligent, and work in this area for a living, writing about the theological underpinning of just such liberal values. However, we still need to ask the question: Can we stand back enough from this tight, cosy relationship between culture and theology to ask where the boundaries of theological acceptability can be drawn?

Conclusions

The fundamental issue, as I hope I have demonstrated, is the relationship between theology and culture. One important question is whether homosexuality is itself a theological or a cultural issue. Windsor follows the majority view of conservatives, and many liberals, who assume that homosexual practice is a theological issue. This is based primarily, it appears, on the fact that homosexuality is mentioned, albeit obliquely and with considerable controversy, in the Bible. If the Bible mentions a subject, it is assumed that it must be theological. While recognizing that drawing a clear boundary between the theological and the cultural is often very difficult, I would beg to differ in this case.

If we take the African situation as an example, it is evident that the majority of social and cultural groups still retain a very negative view of homosexuality in all its forms. This is rooted in the deep cultural values of many different societies and is based, principally, on the view that the person (primarily the male person) is remembered into the future through his (or occasionally her) descendents. Children are an essential part of the maintenance of the family name, necessary for the memory of the ancestors and understood as a gift from God. This attitude has been transferred into the churches of Africa and underpins a virulent homophobia in many African societies. It happens to be the case that a conservative attitude to homosexual practices rooted in a particular interpretation of the Bible supports this fundamental prejudice, but this does not mean that the position itself is primarily theological as opposed to cultural.

Despite a growing literature, we have only begun to scratch the surface of the relationship between theology and culture. We have, for example, the simplistic distinctions as set out by Richard Neibhur, which I still find presented in many undergraduate and postgraduate essays: Christ with culture, Christ against culture, Christ above culture, and so on. All these categorizations, like much of the enculturation literature from Alward Shorter onwards, assume that there are two specific kinds of things, "culture" and "theology" (or "Christ", or "the Gospel"), that have to interact, but are clearly distinguishable. This is highly dubious. Apart from the fact that we have to question whether we can properly talk in terms of "cultures", it has long been recognized that theological discourse cannot exist outside of one or more cultural discourses within which it has been expressed. The two elements cannot, in any abstract sense, be distinguished.

This makes any attempt to place the question of homosexuality on either the cultural or theological side of the argument enormously difficult. But if we talk not of "theology" or "culture", as if they were two distinct things, but begin to talk about "theological discourses" (or "Christian discourses") and "cultural discourses" then we may begin to see a way forward. There are fundamental features to all discourses that would claim to be defined as "Christian". There is, of course, great variety between one Christian discourse and another, and an almost infinite number of such discourses if we take the concept down to the individual level. Fundamentally, however, there has to be a limit beyond which we have to recognize that a certain discourse cannot be called "Christian". There are an infinite number of discourses that have their roots in sources that are clearly not Christian, and I would include both the discourses of anti–homosexuality in Africa, and those of the American left on various issues, within this category. Both the African Church and the American Anglicans can claim that their particular discourse is "Christian", but this is a case of giving a discourse from a fundamentally different source a dubious credibility by including certain Christian elements within it. Neither, in my view, can be said to be a truly Christian discourse in and of itself.

This takes me back to Windsor and the question of the Anglican Communion. The Church of England may not be unique, but it is only one of a very small number of churches whose core narrative about itself is not rooted in a doctrinal Christian discourse. The Church of England is the church in, and for England, and the hope was always that every citizen of England would be a member. This national identity was maintained, despite empirical evidence to the contrary, through four or five centuries and still exists in a more or less explicit form today. The church has always had to hold within itself many different and divergent theological discourses in order to sustain its underpinning national discourse, and to a large extent it has been successful. This can even be said to be the particular gift that Anglicanism offers to the wider church, the ability to encompass diversity of theological opinion while maintaining unity of institution.

As Anglicanism spread throughout the world, on the back of British colonial activity, this aspect of the church accompanied it, even though many of the individual churches planted in different parts of the world maintained a greater theological unity than the home churches. This comes back to the point I made right at the beginning of the paper. What is it that defines the Anglican Communion as a church? It is not any specific or unique theological discourse; it is the shared common heritage in British colonial history. The Anglican Communion has to recognize this fundamental point, and the great gift of theological and cultural diversity that inevitably flows from it.

Anglicanism should not be bludgeoned, or bribed, into holding onto a theological discourse at the expense of many of its members. Diversity is its life, and while it may be difficult to maintain that life in the reality of today's global context, it should never simply let it go. Apart from anything else, it should never let a small matter such as differing cultural attitudes to homosexuality get in the way of a greater unity of purpose.

What is more, because of its inward looking institutional brief, Windsor does not begin to encompass, or even recognize, that essential

Anglican diversity. The members of the commission should have been given the chance to experience the many different faces of the Anglican Communion, those I have recounted in this paper and the many others that I have not had the good fortune to experience. If they had met real people, real Anglicans living and worshipping in Africa, South America, Asia and North America, as well as England and other parts of Europe, then they may have wanted to say something very different.

Windsor ends by making recommendations about what church committees should, and should not, do. This will never solve the "problem", whatever we conceive it to be. If the issue is fundamentally historical and cultural, then the church needs to find a way to put the reality of Anglicanism in different parts of the world back into the debate, to engage with real people, and real situations rather than abstract ecclesial notions. The church needs to find a way of helping Anglicans from different places to meet and engage with each other, to study together, and to share each other's lives and values. There needs to be a greater movement of people around the Anglican Communion; not just primates or church bureaucrats. It is only when the people of Vermont get to see the reality of the church in Tanzania, or those in Tanzania experience the congregations in the slums of Recife, or those in Recife visit Vermont, and so on, that the sense of an "Anglican identity" may begin to emerge in reality rather than as an academic ideal.

The tendency and temptation in theological education today, primarily for financial reasons, is for local churches to become increasing isolated by only talking to like–minded people. That has to change if the Anglican Communion, with its rich heritage of diversity–in–unity is ever going to provide a truly prophetic voice for the future, and so move beyond its "British colonial heritage".

PART IV

JUSTICE FOR GAYS

19

"IMPAIRED" COMMUNION: SOME QUESTIONS

Adrian Thatcher

How is communion impaired? The Lambeth Commission on Communion was mandated to examine and report "on the canonical understandings of communion, impaired and broken communion, and the ways in which provinces of the Anglican Communion may relate to one another in situations where the ecclesiastical authorities of one province feel unable to maintain the fullness of communion with another part of the Anglican Communion" (8, para 1). It was asked to make "practical recommendations (including reflection on emerging patterns of provision for episcopal oversight for those Anglicans within a particular jurisdiction, where full communion within a province is under threat) for maintaining the highest degree of communion that may be possible" (8, para 2). The circumstances leading to the Commission are well known.

Well, what are the canonical understandings of communion? Unfortunately, as the Commissioners note later (and in parentheses) "impaired communion is not a generally recognized canonical category" (19, para 29). "The Anglican Communion does not have a Pope, nor any system which corresponds to the authority structure and canonical organisation of the Roman Catholic Church" (23, para 42). So much, then, for any objective canonical understanding of communion, real, impaired, or imagined. Neither was there ever a serious possibility of an objective understanding of impairment within the Commissioners' remit. That is because impairment of communion happens when "ecclesiastical authorities of one province *feel* unable to maintain the fullness of communion". We are in the realm of feelings, the feelings of some Anglicans about the actions of some other Anglicans. It is not a matter of doctrine, nor of canon law: it is a matter of feeling. Certain feelings are compromising "the fullness of communion". Indeed, even a feeling, not about impaired communion, but about the mere *threat* of it, suffices to generate agonized inquiries about "degrees" of communion that may be possible. But there are no yardsticks for measuring degrees (like protractors), because we are not dealing with measurements, or canon laws, or doctrines. We are dealing with feelings.

Before we inquire into what feelings of which Anglicans impair communion, it is important to note that we are dealing with subjectivity through and through. Impaired or "broken" communion exists at first in the public world simply by being announced. Statements of broken communion are like Gilbert Ryle's "avowals" ("I am fed up, happy, sad, disgusted", etc.)[1] which express feelings. As Ryle says "We expect them ... to be spoken in a revolted and a resolute tone of voice respectively. They are the utterances of persons in revolted and resolute frames of mind."[2] A less emotive philosophical example is Wittgenstein's discussions of the "mineness" of toothache. Toothache is not the private language by which one names sensations (in his view). Rather (and famously) "a great deal of stage-setting in the language is presupposed if the mere act of naming is to make sense".[3] Now Anglicans reporting impaired communion are also reporting pain-behavior, but of a religious kind. And in this case too "a great deal of stage-setting in the language" is required if we are to make sense of their screams.

---

1 Gilbert Ryle, *The Concept of Mind* (Harmondsworth: Penguin Books, 1963), pp. 98-9, 195-6. First published in 1949.
2 Ryle, *The Concept of Mind*, p.175.
3 Ludwig Wittgenstein, *Philosophical Investigations* (Oxford: Basil Blackwell, 1972), Section 257, p. 92e.

One doesn't normally question avowals (or pain expressions) provided they are taken to be statements about "me", the avower, not about the world beyond me. Declarations of impaired communion are best understood in this way. We are told, correctly, that "several provinces and dioceses in the Communion have included in their reactions to developments in New Hampshire, either by primatial announcement or by synodical vote, a declaration that a state of either impaired or broken communion now exists between them and those who have taken the actions in the Episcopal Church (USA)" (18-19, para 29). Impaired communion exists by being announced, by being avowed. It is a feeling, not a state of affairs in the world or the church.

Those who are allegedly responsible are not asked whether they agree to this new state of impairment, nor whether they harbor similar feelings about communion being broken. That seems odd, if a situation of full communion existed between them prior to it becoming impaired. The Commissioners agree that these impairments are feelings when they say "Whilst these declarations may express natural frustrations and conscientious reactions to abnormal circumstances, they have left many Anglicans without a clear sense of who is now in communion with whom (personally and ecclesially)". Expressions of frustration fit neatly into the category of avowals. Of course there is no clear sense of who is in communion with whom because the basis of not-being-in-full-communion is based on feelings – nothing else.

I do not wish to minimize feelings. Without them, we have no moral sense and become diminished. Feelings alone are important enough, apparently, to impair communion, break up the Anglican Communion, and cause schism. The Commissioners note that there are "question marks" over the "ecclesiological legitimacy" of these statements, and over "the constitutional authority under which some were issued". Precisely. They are feelings. But are we not already noticing something else odd? These feelings are being accorded the same status as the events that apparently triggered them. No one has sought to analyze them, assess them, confront them, verify them. That too is characteristic of avowals. These avowals are announced by their utterers into the ecclesial world and a Commission is set up to deal with them. Impaired communion, like war of old, exists by being declared. Thus spoken into the Anglican world, no one questions them.

They must, therefore, be very strong feelings. But the strength of any feeling is no guide to its legitimacy or veracity. Hatred is a strong feeling, and sometimes the strength of a feeling is a key to its distance from considered analysis. Now, it is possible that the strength of feeling against recent attempts among Anglicans to create a more inclusive church in the USA and in Canada is because many straight Christians have a strong feeling about what they imagine the sexual behavior of men loving men, and women loving women, to be. That feeling is disgust. These Christians cannot bear these feelings.

The possibility exists that a loathing of lesbigay people and their sex lives is the real source of impaired communion. Heterosexuals are disgusted by them. The body of Christ is polluted by them. Wherever the boundaries of that body are to be located, "practicing" homosexuals are to be located outside of it. Communion, we are told, is inseparable from the "radical holiness to which all Christ's people are called" (11, para 3), and Gene Robinson is thought not to be holy because (presumably) he goes to bed with his male partner. Unspeakable. Unholy. Is this why he can't be invited or admitted "to the councils of the Communion" (53, para 133)? Because he pollutes the body? Even his consecrators cannot represent the Communion. Has he infected them too? Has their effectiveness as official spokespeople been impaired, like the communion they have allegedly broken?

Anglicans will not at any price discuss the possibility that our Communion is deeply set in a nexus of homophobic attitudes. Since it may be these, and not the consecration of Bishop Gene, that is impairing communion, the proposals of the Windsor Report are not going to begin to address the big issue that divides Anglicans, and most churches throughout the world.[4] An example of the refusal even to admit the possibility of homophobia within Anglicanism is the "discussion document" of the House of Bishops of the Church of England, *Some issues in human sexuality: A guide to the debate*, released in December 2003.[5] Sadly, it has been necessary to point out that that portentous document is not a guide, because it leaves out some of the very features of the landscape that wary travelers will want to know about. (Neither should the exchanges it describes be dignified by the title 'debate').[6] One of its main omissions is any serious discussion of homophobia and the possible influence of that on biblical interpretation.[7] (Another is the lack of discussion of the theology of sexuality.)[8] The unwillingness to discuss this precludes the possibility that the use of scripture to proscribe sexual relationships between same-sex couples belongs to that long and sad history of oppressive readings of scripture, such as the use of the narrative of the cursing of Canaan's children (Genesis 9:20-9) in the legitimation of racism; the use of the baying crowd in Matthew's crucifixion narrative (Matthew 27:20-6) to justify the charge of deicide levelled at Jews; or the use of the Bible to support slavery, the subordination of women, despotic evil regimes, the beating of children; what Stephen Pattison has named "abusive theology".[9] All it takes is a few godly men, in positions of power, who are familiar with the surface text of scripture and are convinced that they alone are right. The possibility is not allowed to enter into the "debate" that the reading of certain biblical passages purporting to deal

---

4 On the extent of the churches' difficulties over sexuality, see Adrian Thatcher, "Authority and Sexuality in the Protestant Tradition", in Joseph A. Selling (ed), *Embracing Sexuality: Authority and experience in the Catholic Church* (Aldershot: Ashgate, 2001), pp. 127-48.

5 House of Bishops' Group on Issues in Human Sexuality, *Some Issues in Human Sexuality: A Guide to the Debate* (London: Church House Publishing, 2003).

6 See Adrian Thatcher, "Some Issues with "Some Issues in Human Sexuality", *Theology and Sexuality*, May 2005, forthcoming.

7 There are six references to homophobia in 350 pages of text.

8 See below.

9 Stephen Pattison, "'Suffer Little Children': The Challenge of Child Abuse and Neglect to Theology", *Theology and Sexuality*, 9 (September 1998), pp. 36-58, 44.

with lesbigay unions by many Christians actually belongs to this tradition. That is not even to say that it does so belong: only that the basic, painful issue is deftly circumvented, and so occluded in advance. Anglicans can have their "debate", accompanied by their episcopal "guide". But they won't be allowed to see the putative ugliness of much of their own internal landscape.

It is difficult to mention homophobia without loss of charity, so let's try. In England, Scotland and Wales, homosexual acts between men were not de-criminalized until 1967. Homosexuality was not removed from the register of psychological illnesses of the American Psychological Association until 1973. The sense that there is something criminally, medically and morally wrong about homosexual love-making is deep-seated, and readily explicable. Recognition that committed relationships between same-sex couples could be a genuinely holy life style, an icon of Christ's love for the church, was bound to be slow in coming, especially among elderly Christians uncomfortable with even talking about sexuality. The term is often used accusingly and therefore unproductively. If anyone is in the grip of feelings they find difficult to deal with or talk about, the last thing they need is to be set back on the defensive. That said, the term is appropriate to attitudes which express disgust about sexual difference, because these are not rational (or empathic), and the *phobia* part of homophobia expresses this. I am disgusted by Christians who luxuriate on the seared flesh of cows, but I don't announce that I am in impaired communion with them. Neither can the Commissioners complain if this medical term is used. Their report contains copious references to "illness", "diagnosis", "symptoms", and so on.

The Commissioners want "Christians of good will" to be "prepared to engage honestly and frankly with each other on issues relating to human sexuality" in accordance with the notorious resolution 110 of the 1998 Lambeth Conference (57, para 146). While that resolution called for "an ongoing process of listening and discernment", that Conference was hardly noteworthy for its contribution to the listening that it advocated. (It should not be forgotten that 148 bishops were moved to apologize to lesbian and gay Anglicans for the treatment they received at the Conference and pledged "that we will continue to reflect, pray, and work for your full inclusion in the life of the Church"[10]). Neither can the thousands of gay clergy who are closeted by the church they serve suddenly be expected to be honest and frank about their situations. These appeals to goodwill, discussion, dialogue, debate, and so on just don't allow that what the Communion has to deal with may not be rational at all. Prejudice can be rendered respectable by the appearance of debate and discussion, and further disguised by it. That is why sincere calls for healing and reconciliation among Anglicans are unlikely to be efficacious. It is possible they operate on the wrong level, and prevent the deeper questions being put. Decades of vacillation have compounded the problem.

I have asked how communion is impaired, and answered that question by reference to feelings. That designation led away from doctrinal and canonical matters to the unspoken question whether what needs to be dealt with is deep prejudice against a minority of people whose challenge to sanctified heterosexual normativity is thought to disable them from full membership of the body of Christ. This suspicion is itself fuelled by another feature of the Anglican literature on sexuality; what might be called the phenomenon of culpable ignorance.

Culpable ignorance is akin to ignorance of the criminal law in relation to a particular offence I did not know I had just committed. It is no defense. A worse form of culpable ignorance is not *wanting* to know; that happens when one's adverse judgment about another person or group of persons is impaired by the lack of knowledge that one seeks to sustain. We have already noted the ignoring of homophobia. Unfortunately other examples abound. Official discussion material that

---

10 *The Lambeth Conference 1998: A Pastoral Statement to Lesbian and Gay Anglicans from Some Member Bishops of the Lambeth Conference August 5, 1998.*

accompanies *Some issues in human sexuality* contains the group exercise: "Ask members of the group each to recall a homosexual (or, if they prefer, transsexual) individual they know (or know of)".[11] The text makes it clear that (once again) lesbigay people are to be discussed in their absence by Christian straights who willfully avoid the inconvenience of talking *with* them and being challenged by their own ignorance. So it was at Lambeth 98. Imagine talking about Muslims, instead of with them, by means of this flawed procedure, worse even than gossip. Or think instead of the hundreds of books, articles, testimonies, journals, life-stories that were not read or heard by that Conference even as it advocated being a listening church. Or the indignation of the Commissioners that nobody from New Westminster or ECUSA "has made a serious attempt to offer an explanation to, or consult meaningfully with, the Communion as a whole about the significant development of theology which alone could justify the recent moves by a diocese or a province" (20, para 33). Where has "the Communion as a whole" been for the last 25 years? Or consider the treatment of theology in *Some Issues*. When the bishops finally get round to discussing the theology of sexuality, they briefly refer to *three* authors (Norman Pittenger, Rowan Williams and Eugene Rogers) and veto any insights they might have with the supine question "what are we to make of their arguments ...?"[12] They don't make anything of them, for with that flat rhetorical question the chapter ends.

I worry that for all the smooth talk, the Commission, the Reports, statements, lengthy discussion documents, calls for restraint and macro-political proposals for councils and covenants, more basic issues are being ignored, and these are the ones that need to be painfully addressed. There is a tradition of Bible reading that has oppressed countless people over the centuries, finding God's will in the very

---

11 Joanna Cox and Martin Davie, *A Companion to Some Issues in Human Sexuality* (London: Church House Publishing, 2003), p. 22.
12 Cox and Davie, *Some Issues*, para.3.6.37, pp.115-6.

cruelty it inflicts. The feelings of today's avowers of impairment may stand in this tradition, and if so they ought not to be given the means of legitimizing it. Given the pallid tenor of the official documents, resistance rather than reconciliation may be necessary.

The gay-friendly side of the Christian churches does not issue avowals of impairment of communion. But this same side, in its desire for an inclusive church must (*logically* must) also strive to keep the Communion together, since there would be little point in arguing for an inclusive church that drove other Christians out. The impairment from this side of the divide is differently read. From this side some Christians may be attempting to deal with their feelings of disgust generated by the sexual practices of a minority of other Christians by condemnation, or exclusion, or denial of full membership or episcopal office. They are dealing with difference by converting it to otherness. A more fruitful way of handling this sorry impasse may lie, not with accommodation, but with the examination of the feelings that are causing the pain. "Perfect love banishes fear" (1 John 4:18b). While none of us can yet love perfectly, we could all aspire to loving one another without fearing that God may have differently made us.

From this side we don't even claim to be right; we would like to rejoice in the diversity of the body of Christ and we believe that prejudice corrupts love. We are suspicious of the religious *hubris* that leads to avowals of impairment. If we think some of our brothers and sisters are afflicted by prejudice, we must be doubly aware of the possibility of prejudice in ourselves. In the end, we think the treatment of lesbigay Christians by the Anglican establishment is a constriction on the love of God revealed in Christ and so a betrayal of the gospel. That is a platform for proper "debate" and "dialogue", and it takes us away from the flimsiness of avowals and the unreliable (and possibly destructive) feelings they express.

20

WE HAVE BEEN HERE BEFORE

Sean Gill

I have read and wrestled with the Windsor Report as a practicing Anglican, church historian and homosexual. Although practice rarely makes perfect in this world, all three of these dimensions of my life have been immensely fulfilling, and have helped to shape the form of my response. Thus I shall, firstly, offer some comments as a historian on the report's understanding of the development of the Anglican community in the past and its bearing on the situation in which the Communion now finds itself. Secondly, I shall consider what the document reveals about the nature of contemporary Anglicanism. Lastly, I shall relate the aims and tenor of the report to my experience of being a Christian in a committed same-sex relationship stretching back over twenty years.

The writers of the Report paint a picture of a church in an unprecedented state of crisis over the issues of ordaining a practicing homosexual bishop and performing services of blessing for same-sex couples, and one which justifies taking urgent action that will involve significant changes being made to its organizational structures and ethos in the direction of imposing more uniformity of belief and more centralized control. As the Report puts it:

> The depth of conviction and feeling on all sides of the current issues has on occasions introduced a degree of harshness and a lack of charity which is new to Anglicanism. A process of

dissent is not new to the communion but it has never before been expressed with such force nor in ways which have been so accessible to international scrutiny. (5)

At the same time, Windsor makes several passing references to the Communion's history that suggest that the current situation is not in fact as novel as they would have us believe. As they indicate, the first Lambeth Conference of 1867 was mired in controversy: "The question of controversial teaching by a bishop of the emerging South African Church, William Colenso, the Bishop of Natal, was manoeuvred on to the agenda by pressure from participating bishops; in some ways, this was to be a foretaste of what would follow in international gatherings of Anglicans, when controversial topics arise." (42)

Colenso's case is more instructive that this passing mention might imply. Bishop Gray of Cape Town had attempted to excommunicate him from the Anglican Communion for holding liberal theological opinions about (amongst other things) biblical interpretation, but Colenso refused to accept his removal from the office of Bishop of Natal. The controversy engaged the secular as well as the religious press over a number of years. Media attention is not after all such a modern phenomenon. Epithets applied to Colenso by his fellow Christians – including some bishops – included "heretical," "blasphemous," "abominable," "blind," "ignorant," "half-informed," and the more eye-catching "instrument of Satan."[1] Accusing the Archbishop of Canterbury of "theological and intellectual prostitution," as one Anglican dean has reportly done because of Rowan Williams' supposed failures to withstand liberal heresy over homosexuality, may be deeply offensive and unfair, but it hardly represents a new and higher – or rather lower – degree of harshness and uncharity in Anglican discourse.[2]

---

1 G. Parsons, "Rethinking the Missionary Position: Bishop Colenso of Natal," in John Wolffe (ed), *Religion in Victorian Britain, Volume V, Culture and Empire* (Manchester: Manchester University Press, 1997), pp. 135-175, 142.
2 *The Guardian*, 13 October, 2004.

Even after the Colenso affair, relations between the Anglican Church at home and the churches in Africa continued to generate very public and often vituperative disharmony. The publication in 1912 of the volume of liberal theological essays *Foundations: A Statement of Christian Belief in Terms of Modern Thought* resulted in a situation described by the historian Keith Clements, as: "one in which the Church of England was riven by doctrinal controversy as never before or since, to the extent that many despaired of the future of the Church and warned darkly of its disintegration."[3] The African contribution to this decade-long fracas was provided by the formidable anglo-catholic missionary and subsequent Bishop of Zanzibar, Frank Weston, who warned that liberal theological opinions at home were endangering the progress of Christianity in East Africa in its competition with Islam – an accusation that strikingly parallels that made by a number of contemporary African bishops over the consequences of accepting same-sex relationships in the western part of the Communion. As for the expression of strident disagreement, Weston was no shrinking violet describing his opponents as in a state of mental chaos and without faith of any kind.[4] Now my purpose in referring to these events is not simply to prove that we have been here before. Even if true, that fact does not diminish the seriousness of the current situation nor entail the conclusion that nothing needs to be done about it. What is more relevant is to ask what was, and still is, at stake in the way in which theological differences in general, and the acceptance of new theological insights in particular, were dealt with in the Communion in the past. To return for a moment to Colenso. In conventional accounts the bishop has too often and too conveniently been dismissed as being the cause of his own misfortunes on account of his stubbornness, naïvety and insensitivity to the views of others.[5] The truth is that he was right about

---

3 Keith Clements, *Lovers of Discord: Twentieth-Century Theological Controversies in England* (London: SPCK, 1988), p. 49.
4 Keith Clements, *Lovers of Discord*, pp. 62-63.
5 For the traditional view, see Owen Chadwick, *The Victorian Church Part II* (London: Adam & Charles Black, 2nd ed., 1972), pp. 90-95. More sympathetic is Jeff Guy, *The Heretic: A Study of the Life of John William Colenso 1814-1883* (Pietermaritzburgh: University of Natal Press, 1993).

issues that mattered then and still matter now and had attempts to exclude him from the Anglican Communion been successful the church would have stifled debate and fresh thinking with consequences that would have been detrimental both theologically and morally. As John Rogerson has shown, Colenso's refusal to accept untenable beliefs about the historicity of the Pentateuch made his the most significant contribution to the development of a properly informed study of the Old Testament by any nineteenth-century English scholar.[6] Later, his equally unpopular support for the independent Zulu kingdom north of Natal, whose people he saw were being deliberately provoked into conflict by colonial officials in order to annexe their land, was also of enduring significance for the church. As one of the most recent historians to consider his life and work has concluded:

> For Colenso – in his own blunt, uncompromising manner – had already engaged, in his own day and way, with both the relationship between Christianity and other religions and with the implications of Christian discipleship in the realms of social justice and racial oppression. It was to take most of the Christian churches the better part of another century before they even began seriously to confront such issues.[7]

We should also note other striking parallels with the current situation. For many overseas bishops, one major reason for the calling of the first Lambeth Conference was to find a way to condemn what the Bishop of Ontario called Colenso's "theological aberrations," and the crisis provoked Bishop Tait into asking his fellow bishops whether they should be required to take a canonical oath of obedience to Canterbury and to establish structures to guarantee unity and discipline in the Communion. In the event it proved impossible to draw up any binding

---

6 John Rogerson, *Old Testament Criticism in the Nineteenth Century* (London: SPCK, 1984), p. 232.
7 Parsons, "Rethinking the Missionary Position", pp. 135-175, 172.

canons and to his credit Archbishop Longley refused to allow a formal condemnation of Colenso.[8] In the judgement of W. M. Jacob, in his scholarly account *The Making of the Anglican Church Worldwide*, the importance of this decision lay in the fact that "liberal and critical thought about the Bible and the Christian tradition were not condemned."[9] Part of Anglicanism's genius and distinctiveness arose, he concluded, (as recently as 1997!) from the fact that in the past: "It has avoided endorsing systematic theologies which risk prematurely freezing Christian faith in propositional forms which inhibit further exploration."[10] It is also worth recalling that the question raised in 1867 is again posed in the Windsor Report: "Should the Lambeth Conference, as the gathering of the chief pastors and teachers of the churches have a 'magisterium', a teaching authority of special status?" (44) The quotation marks here are revealing – presumably designed to allay fears that this would entail precisely the kind of stifling of disagreement and of exploratory theology which Anglicans rightly reject when they see it in operation in the exercise of the magisterium of the Roman Catholic Church.

What conclusions, then, should we draw from this brief foray into the history of the Anglican Communion? Clearly, it is not intended to resolve the disputed questions that led to the calling of the Lambeth Commission on Communion. The fact that Colenso was right about the need for fresh thinking about biblical criticism and the injustices of colonialism does not establish the correctness or otherwise of contemporary arguments for the acceptance of the goodness of same-sex relationships. What it should alert us to is the danger of attempting to discipline, or silence by exclusion, those who advocate unpopular or innovative theologies. Our history shows that today's heresy has too often become tomorrow's Christian truth.

---

8 For a detailed account of this story, see Randall Davidson and William Benham, *Life of Archibald Campbell Tait* (London: Macmillan and Co., 1891), pp. 332-397.
9 W. M. Jacob, *The Making of the Anglican Communion Worldwide* (London: SPCK, 1997), p. 170.
10 Jacob, *The Making of the Anglican Communion Worldwide*, p. 299.

I want, secondly, to say something about what Windsor tells us about the current spiritual health of worldwide Anglicanism. My first point follows on from my reading of Anglican history and the lessons we should draw from it. Over the past few years there has been considerable discussion about whether Anglicanism can be said to have a distinctive identity at all and if so how it is to be defined.[11] Paul Avis, one of the leading scholars in this field, has argued that Anglicanism has a definable ecclesiology derived from its three-fold inheritance as catholic, reformed and informed by the exercise of reason and scholarly enquiry. His definition is worth quoting since it seems to me to apply with particular force to our current situation:

> Anglicanism sets out to offer a rational faith. It believes that its position in Christendom as a church that is both Catholic and Reformed can be justified by an appeal to sound learning. Its catholicism is not enslaved to tradition nor is its reformed character in bondage to biblical literalism. It is notably receptive to new insights deriving from 'secular' disciplines – receptive not in the sense that it is prone to embrace these without resistance, but in the sense that it gives scope and freedom to its clergy, as well as to its laity, to pursue such insights and to promote them without undue fear of ecclesiastical discipline or censure. In due course (though it never seems soon enough) it adapts to those insights (as we are seeing today with regard to the feminist critique of sexism, androcentrism and patriarchalism in the tradition).[12]

The decisions taken by the American and Canadian branches are the outworking of just the process that Avis seeks to delineate. In

---

11 For a good recent introduction to this debate with a useful descriptive bibliography of important works in the field see Paul Avis, *Anglicanism and the Christian Church: Theological Resources in Historical Perspective* (London: T& T Clark, revised ed., 2002).
12 Paul Avis, *The Anglican Understanding of the Church. An Introduction* (London: SPCK, 2000), pp. 40-41.

this respect one of the puzzling features of Windsor is its demand that the American Church give theological reasons for its decision to ordain Gene Robinson as part of a wider charge that it has acted without due time for thought and reflection. In fact the opposite is nearer the truth. Since the liberation of gay people from the fear of imprisonment or blackmail in the 1960s, scholars both inside and outside these groups have produced a large body of theological work, much of it informed by new insights in the social sciences into human sexual orientation and the socially constructed nature of sexual identities.[13] The current crisis within Anglicanism has not descended from heaven like a thunderbolt out of a clear blue sky. The American and Canadian decisions are the logical outcome of nearly forty years of theologically informed reflection and debate.

Of course it would be wrong to suggest that Avis's ecclesiological paradigm is the only one in the field. An alternative model is suggested by Stephen Sykes, one centered upon the primacy of scripture as set out in the Chicago-Lambeth Quadrilateral of 1888 with its claim that the Bible is "the rule and ultimate standard of faith."[14] This position goes to the heart of the current controversy since the opposition to the actions of the American and Canadian Anglican churches derives primarily from fundamentalist interpretations of scripture. But like Avis, Sykes rejects the claim that such a hermeneutic can form any part of an authentic Anglican identity. Even if Anglican liturgical and ecclesiological practices and creedal statements must necessarily be judged by scripture, the way in which Sykes suggests this needs to be done gives no warrant for the conservative case:

> All these activities invoke the priority of Scriptural symbols over later Christian thought, though there is no

---

13 For a brief overview, see Sean Gill, "Why Difference Matters: Lesbian and Gay Perspectives on Religion and Gender," in Ursula King (ed), *Gender, Religion and Diversity. Cross Cultural Perspectives* (London: Continuum, 2004), pp. 201-211.
14 Stephen Sykes, *Unashamed Anglicanism* (London: Darton, Longman and Todd, 1995), p. xvii.

objection in principle to the presence of the latter in a subordinate position. The fact that the symbols are part of a system of communication, that they must proclaim and embody 'the Gospel', implies that they are in need of revision since cultures have their own symbol systems, some of which make it impossible for the Gospel to be heard.[15]

Several of the proposals in Windsor therefore represent a triumph for a fundamentalist reading of scripture wholly at odds with core Anglican values, and will also seriously damage the community's tradition of living with diversity, whilst also running the risk of stifling the possibility of creative theological change in the future. This is true of the requirements that the Episcopal Church be forced to express regret over the consequences of its actions. Even more serious is the Primates' decision to implement the Report's recommendation that ECUSA and the Canadian Church be made to withdraw from one of the instruments of unity, namely the Anglican Consultative Council – a decision that has no legal force since both provinces exercised their autonomy of decision making in perfectly constitutional ways. The same is true of the demand that ECUSA cease ordaining to the episcopate those in same-sex unions until an Anglican consensus is achieved (53-54). On the latter point, talk of a covenant which sets out a broad range of essential theological requirements that all must adhere to, presents the same danger of stifling dissent and theological development. In fact, the whole approach of the Windsor Report and the way in which the Primates are seeking to implement it is wrong-headed and fraught with danger for the future health of Anglicanism. Those who cannot live with the wide degree of theological pluralism and praxis, which has long characterised the Anglican Communion, cannot be prevented from leaving, and were some conservative

---

15 Sykes, *Unashamed Anglicanism*, pp.117-118.

evangelical churches to do so this would indeed diminish its life. What is unprecedented is not the fact of difference and disagreement, but the attempt to institutionalize the silencing by exclusion of those who are unable to conform to a conservative theological agenda.

Equally disturbing is Windsor's account of the relationship between the Communion and issues of justice and integrity. Early on its writers argue that:

> Perhaps the greatest tragedy of our current difficulties is the negative consequence it could have on the mission of the Church to a suffering and bewildered world. Even as the Commission prepared for its final meeting the cries of children in a school in southern Russia reminded us of our real witness and ministry in a world confronted by poverty, violence, HIV/AIDS, famine and injustice (6).

This expression of exasperation is in line with the repeatedly voiced view of leading Anglican bishops that constant disagreements about the rightness of same-sex relationships distract the church and the wider public from focussing on the "real" issues of world poverty and debt relief. As David Hope, the Archbishop of York opined:

> There is a cacophony of factions drowning out the Good News of Jesus Christ. We have got world problems of poverty, hunger, Aids, the war on Iraq, the environment – large questions – and here we are, almost preoccupied with the gay issue. We need to look beyond ourselves.[16]

One obvious rejoinder to this claim is that it looks like an attempt to distract attention from difficult and unpalatable truths at

---

16 *The Guardian,* 2 November, 2004.

home to issues that pose fewer uncomfortable challenges to the Church of England. More seriously, it ignores the fact that ending discrimination against gay and lesbian people is as much a justice issue as those listed above, and the pressing need is for Anglicanism to set its own house in order. So long as sections of the Communion both advocate and actively practice discrimination of this kind, its moral credibility to be heard on its own chosen list of justice issues will rightly be compromised. The cries of children in a school in southern Russia should indeed be heard, but what of those gay men who face imprisonment, social ostracism, and physical violence - many of them in parts of Africa where the official voice of Anglicanism continues to demonize them? Same-sex relationships remain illegal in twenty-nine African states including Nigeria.[17] The bracketing of gay relationships with bestiality by its Archbishop, Peter Akinola, who has been at the forefront of the attack on the American Episcopal Church, will do nothing to change this situation.

Of course, the Windsor Report repeats the standard response to such criticism arguing that the Anglican Communion should hold that "any demonising of homosexual persons, or their ill treatment, is totally against Christian charity."(58) Rowan Williams made the same point in his 2004 Lenten Letter to the Primates of the Anglican Communion warning them against the use of intemperate language on the grounds that "in many countries such persons face real persecution and cruelty."[18] Such concern cuts little ice with those driven by irrational fear and hatred. The riposte from the fundamentalist group, Reform, was predictable and typical dismissing the Archbishop's intervention as "presumably a gesture to the gay community who love to peddle this line that they all feel under enormous pressure and they are all being persecuted which is not true."[19]

---

17 "The legal status of homosexuality in Africa" at www.afrol.com/Categories/Gaybackgr_legalstatus. htm.
18 *The Sunday Times*, 28 November, 2004.
19 *The Sunday Times*, 28 November, 2004.

The reality is that deeply engrained bigotry, ignorance and hatred against the gay and lesbian minority cannot be countered without a paradigm shift in attitudes that not only totally repudiates homophobic theologies and practices, but actively seeks to replace them with positive ones. In a recent collection of articles on the worldwide Anglican Communion James Keetile, a black heterosexual man from South Africa articulates this shift drawing on his own experience:

> Many of our people were socialized to accept homophobia as a way of life. The debate is often clinical rather than humane. Many think being heterosexual is more important than being human. I want to suggest the second, fundamental challenge facing the Church is to change some of these stereotypes that have been institutionalised. Is there any possibility for an openness to the work and guidance of the Holy Spirit in a Church that has institutionalised its views and prejudices? In a democratic, non-sexist society which South Africa has become, homosexuals rather than being some how a menace to the values of society and family, should be regarded as part of God's creative plan. They have special qualities and gifts and a positive contribution in the building and healing of our nation.[20]

The recent actions taken by the American and Canadian churches represent further important stages in this vital process of reformulation of Christian theology and praxis.

One important reason for urgent action along these lines is the uncomfortable truth not faced by the authors of the Windsor Report, nor by the subsequent meeting of Anglican Primates, that it is not possible to remain even-handed, or worse still to give sustenance to

---

20 James GaOfenngawe Keetile, "A South African reflection on the issue of homosexuality in the Anglican Communion," in Andrew Wingate *et al* (eds), *Anglicanism: A Global Communion* (London: Continuum, 1998), pp. 207-11, 208.

theologically inspired homophobia, and avoid responsibility for the consequences. Rowan Williams himself made this point very sharply when he criticized the appeal to gender specific symbolism made by opponents of women's ordination in the Church of England. "If we want to argue the women's issue in symbolic terms," he wrote, "we need to see what we are doing in the society we are in." The result he concluded had been to reinforce patterns of inequality and to systematically devalue human female experience – all of which is equally applicable to the lives of gay and lesbian people.[21]

Here the parallel with the Christian churches' record of anti-semitism is telling. The primary responsibility for the Holocaust, in which both Jews and gay men were victims, lay with the Nazis and their murderous ideology of racism and eugenics. Nevertheless, since 1945 the churches have come to recognise that two thousand years of persistent denigration and demonization of Jewish people was a necessary, if not sufficient, cause of what happened. The result has been an almost complete theological re-conceptualisation of Judaism on the part of both Protestantism and Catholicism.[22] In so far as there has been a comparable transformation in attitudes to gay and lesbian people in some parts of the world, this has been a consequence of secularisation and the spread of Enlightenment values and has owed very little to the Christian churches. The tenor of Windsor suggests that little is likely to change in this respect in the future.

This last point can be explored from a slightly different angle. One of the hopes expressed by the Report is that the current review of systems of canon law operative within the Communion might be one further means of imposing a greater degree of order if not unity upon its constituent provinces (47-48). Since one of the members of the Commission is Michael Doe, himself an authority on Anglican canon

---

21 Quoted in Sean Gill, *Women and the Church of England from the Eighteenth Century to the Present* (London: SPCK, 1994), p. 263.
22 The literature on this subject is huge, but for a short accessible introduction, see Carol Rittner *et al* (eds), *The Holocaust and the Christian World* (London: Kuperard, 2000).

law, it might be worth considering his views on the Communion's approach to human rights which he has expressed elsewhere.[23] Doe notes that whilst the rhetoric of human rights has been expounded at a number of Lambeth Conferences – culminating in the 1998 declaration that the churches should be model communities in which discrimination plays no part (not applicable to its gay members) – the actual canonical practices of churches throughout the Communion have not reflected this. As he notes: "The specific Lambeth Conference call for individual church members to promote human rights in civil society finds no echo in the laws of any church."[24] One reason he adduces for this situation is that the Christian concept of human rights derives from a very different theological framework from the secular model which has driven legislative changes in the western world since 1945. But the main reason he advances for this divorce between ethics and canonical practice should give us pause for thought:

> First, insofar as it exists to facilitate and to order the domestic life of churches, the purposes of canon law itself are spelt out in the legal texts of churches without mention of human rights: typically, laws function simply for 'The order, good government, and efficiency of the Church'. Anglican jurisprudence generally is utilitarian.[25]

If this is true then little can be expected from the forthcoming review of the Communion's systems of canon law. Utilitarianism of this kind, which puts the demands of institutional functioning and survival before human well-being and justice is the *raison d'etre* of the Report and is deeply embedded in the mind-set of much of the church's leadership. The Communion's response to the rights of its gay and

---

23 Norman Doe, "Canonical Approaches to Human Rights in Anglican Churches," in Mark Hill (ed), *Religious Liberty and Human Rights* (Cardiff: University of Wales Press, 2002), pp. 185-206.
24 Doe, "Canonical Approaches", p. 205.
25 Doe, "Canonical Approaches", p. 201.

lesbian members and to those churches, which have taken prophetic action on their behalf, is the best available measure of the sickness unto death of contemporary Anglicanism.

Finally, how do my own personal experiences inform my response to the Report? Do they leave any grounds for optimism that the theological and ethical demise of Anglicanism can be arrested? I was born in 1951, came from a poor working-class background and had the great good fortune to benefit from the provision of free university education, and from the decriminalisation of homosexuality that was part of the socially transformative ethos of the 1960s, now so derided by the Christian right. Even though I was fully aware of my sexual orientation from the beginning of my teenage years, the internalization of guilt and insecurity from having been brought up in a climate of social and legal hostility took their toll. A wariness about coming out for fear that it might hinder my career was a further consideration.

Two things have since reduced these experiences to distant, though not altogether comfortable memories. The first has been meeting my partner from whom I have received the healing power of unconditional love and acceptance in a faithful relationship over many years. The second has been the continued transformation of social attitudes and the process of legal reform that has just culminated in the Civil Partnerships Act that removes a number of our fears about our legal right to take full responsibility for each other in the event of sickness, and our ability to cope with the financial consequences of one of us dying.

But what of our faith? We are both committed Anglicans, one of our many shared bonds. In my own life, I have a sense of regret that I was unable even to test whether I had a vocation to the priesthood unless I was willing to deny the importance and value of the deepest relationship in my life. As a university lecturer in a department of Theology and Religious Studies I have amongst my friends former students, now clergy, who live their lives in fear and secrecy because of their sexuality and relationships. The Church of England claims to believe in Christ's words that the truth shall make you free. I know of no public organization in which hatred, ignorance, dishonesty and hypocrisy over the issue of same-sex relationships have been so routinely institutionalized. In my professional life and that of my partner, it would now be unthinkable for us to be subjected to the kinds of derogatory and dehumanising statements that are the accepted theologically sanctioned coinage of much Anglican discourse. Not surprisingly, the only hostility we have experienced in recent years has been religiously inspired, most woundingly in the refusal of two of my partner's relatives to allow him to attend the baptism of their second child if I were present.

Of course these attitudes are not representative of a large number of Anglican clergy and laity, as the American and Canadian churches have shown. Here at home, many of our closest friends come from the church at which we worship, most of them heterosexual couples. With them we have a sense that our relationship is not simply "tolerated", but is celebrated and affirmed like any other. Parents, living and now dead, have reacted in the same way. Later this year we will be able to publicly attest to our relationship in a civil partnership and hold a small celebration with our friends. We have toyed with the idea of a service of blessing and thanks, but are aware that any Anglican priest who performed it would run the risk of censure or worse.

The unwillingness of the Church of England to take the vital affirmative step of unequivocally ordaining clergy without reference to their sexuality, so graphically illustrated by the treatment of Jeffrey John, leave us both feeling betrayed and unwilling to commit ourselves fully to the life and work of the church. Even worse are the implications for continued membership of a church in which the role of reason, scholarship and reflection upon human experience are being swept away in a tide of bigotry and prejudice. These are the only terms I can use when I see the way in which so many conservative evangelical opponents of an inclusive church have nevertheless been willing to accept the application of modern theological insights to the issue of interpreting texts about the subordination of women and their unfitness to exercise priestly functions in the Church that are as unequivocal as any reference to homosexuality. If I might adapt some words of the nineteenth-century Anglican, Benjamin Jowett, as a gay man I shall continue to believe in God in spite of what many of the clergy tell me. Sadly, the Windsor Report and its results only increase my sense of internal exile.

21

GOD'S GOOD NEWS FOR GAYS

Philip Kennedy

The most arresting and intriguing aspect of debates about same-sex relations among Anglicans presently is their ecclesial and social prominence. Sex dominated Anglophone news commentary on Christianity in the opening years of the twenty-first century. Since 2003, no topic has received more attention in Anglican circles and in news reports sparked by them than the question of whether people may enjoy sexual relationships with friends of their own sex, and the concomitant issue of whether priests and bishops may live, in an ethically blameless way, with partners of the same sex. Why have such matters proved exceptionally engrossing and taxing for Anglicans today?

Contemporary Roman Catholics share with Anglicans public quarrels over sex, but they differ in that more often than not they bemoan the sexually predatory behavior of some of their unmarried priests, and they lament the conspiratorial incompetence of some of their bishops who have been caught out protecting miscreant priests rather than nurturing victims of priestly lasciviousness. Among Anglicans, though, clerical homosexuality rather than sexual abuse occludes most other issues in public fora. Gene Robinson's ordination to the episcopate in 2003 attracted international media attention. In the same year, Jeffrey John's coerced resignation from candidature as the Bishop of Reading was gossiped about throughout the United

Kingdom, causing glee for some and gloom for others.[1] Recently, televisions have barked news of bishops disagreeing with each other about homosexuals, and newspapers have carried anguished stories of different Christian groups excoriating each other for either wicked indulgence or ignorant bigotry on the issue of homosexual liaisons.

Meanwhile, the world at large is bedevilled by pervasive and debilitating poverty, genocidal mayhem, ecological enfeeblement, AIDS, weapons trading, terrorism, and capitalistic profiteering that allows corporate chief executive officers to feather their nests with the finest baubles loot can buy while slum dwellers feed their children stewed rats. The toys of the rich on this planet stand in execrable contrast to the deprivations of the poor. Suffering, not sex, overwhelms the preoccupations of the world's malnourished economic underdogs. In such a setting, why have impassioned disagreements over psycho-sexual relations of males with males, and females with females, eclipsed death-dealing dangers as an issue of paramount concern for the public face of contemporary Anglicanism? The answer to that question can be given in two words: the Bible. The ecclesiastical struggle over homosexuality is, in part, a tussle over the status and authority of the Bible. The way the Bible is regarded separates modern theology from pre-modern theologies as it divides opposed parties among Anglicans on the matter of gay clerics' relationships.

The status and authority of the Bible in the modern age will be pondered below, but first, two other prominent features of the current Anglican brouhaha over same-sex engagements can be noted. Apart from public prominence, the second most noteworthy and fearsome feature of present debates is their frequently vitriolic nature. In Matthew's Gospel, Jesus warns his listeners that if they insult a brother or sister by saying "You fool", they will be "liable to the hell of fire" (Matthew 5:22; NRSV). The admonition not to call anyone a fool has

---

1 For the controversies surrounding Gene Robinson and Jeffrey John, see Stephen Bates, *A Church at War: Anglicans and Homosexuality* (London and New York: I. B. Tauris, 2004).

been drowned out among some Anglicans in a cacophony of bilious vituperation. "Fiendish heretic", "faggot priest", "destructive lunatic liberal", and "blockheaded fundamentalist evangelical" are some of the current labels of abuse that make "You fool" look decidedly polite!

A third mark of current altercations over homosexuality among Anglican, and other Christians, is a widespread unfamiliarity with tools that modern theological, biblical and historical research offer to lead safely and calmly to the conclusion that neither God nor Jesus can be credited with the notion that gay liaisons – emotional and bodily – are evil, distorted, sinful, dirty, or depraved. Neither God nor Jesus can be convicted of gay bashing. The same could hardly be said for many of their devotees.

Jesus and fools

The thesis proposed by this chapter is simple to state and easy to demonstrate: Jesus, viewed as God's Good News for and among suffering human beings, has never been remembered as a denouncer of male-male, or female-female sexual couplings. There is not the slightest extant fragment of biblical or historical evidence that can link homophobia and homohatred to Jesus as he lived in Galilee and Judea. Therefore, no denunciation of gay associations can technically be called *Christ*ian, that is, directly reflecting Jesus *Christ*. Difficulties for gay people today do not come from God or Jesus, but from human beings who are repelled by homosexuality for a host of reasons. Because there is no historical basis for viewing Jesus as a vilifier of people sexually attracted to others of their own sex, his life and teachings are good news, not bad breath, for gays. He cannot be added to the list of shrill denouncers and decriers of same-sex intimacy.

On sexual relations between males and between females, Jesus as recorded in the Bible is entirely silent – with one possible and remote exception. The very word used for "fool" (*Raca*) in the warning not to say "You fool" to a brother or sister, might have been a term of abuse for an effeminate male in Jesus' environment.[2] It no doubt had a variety of usages, one of which might have been to abuse males deemed to be unmasculine. If that is so, and it is uncertain that it is, then the only known reference of Jesus to people forming a minority with regard to sexuality and gender warns of the fires of hell for anyone who abuses them. Had Jesus stood up in defence of individuals mocked for their bodily, sexual demeanour, he would have been entirely consistent with his practice of siding preferentially with outcasts and victims of vilification.[3] For the Bible, the associates of Jesus are variously called "the poor, the blind, the lame, the crippled, the lepers, the hungry, the miserable (those who weep), sinners, prostitutes, tax collectors, demoniacs (those possessed by unclean spirits), the persecuted, the downtrodden, the captives, all who labor and are overburdened, the rabble who know nothing of the law, the crowds, the little ones, the least, the last, and the babes or the lost sheep of the house of Israel".[4]

In the light of which, it becomes all the more implausible to imagine that Jesus would have wished to slight those whom the self-styled righteous besmirch as sexually deviant.

A kaleidoscope of horrors

While the life of Jesus can be interpreted as God's Good News for gays, the same cannot be said for churches that functioned long after his death. Throughout Christianity's extended life its churches have often proved to be much more than verbally abusive of what are now commonly called gay people. They have frequently been violent and

---

2 See Louis Crompton, *Homosexuality and Civilization* (Cambridge, Mass., and London: The Belnap Press of Harvard University Press, 2003), p. 111, and W. Dynes, W. Johannsson, and W. Percy (eds), *Encyclopedia of Homsexuality*, 2 vols (New York: Garland, 1990), II, p. 1093.
3 On the life of Jesus and his association with poor and marginalized people, see John P. Meier, *A Marginal Jew: Rethinking the Historical Jesus*, Vol. 1: *The Roots of the Problem and the Person* (New York: Doubleday, 1991); John Dominic Crossan, *The Historical Jesus: The Life of a Mediterranean Jewish Peasant* (Edinburgh: T & T Clark, 1991); Sean Freyne, *Jesus: A Jewish Galilean: A New Reading of the Jesus-Story* (London and New York: T & T Clark International, 2004), pp. 136-149; and K. C. Hanson and Douglas E. Oakman, *Palestine in the Time of Jesus: Social Structures and Social Conflicts* (Minneapolis: Fortress Press, 1998).
4 Albert Nolan, *Jesus before Christianity* (Maryknoll, New York: Orbis, 1978), p. 21.

vicious persecutors of same-sex friends hapless enough to fall into the hands of their persecutors. Some scholars like to scan human history in search of shining examples of Christian tolerance of same-sex liaisons. David Greenberg, for instance, reports how Pope Urban II, when told at the end of the eleventh century that the man named to become the bishop of Orleans was the lover of the archbishop of Tours, did nothing to stop the installation of the new bishop.[5] John Boswell attracts attention for arguing that same-sex unions occasionally received ecclesiastical blessings in pre-modern Europe.[6] He also concludes, wrongly, that "the peculiar horror which has been associated with male homosexuality in western culture and the correspondingly violent condemnation of it were products of the twelfth century".[7]

From the Christian emperor Justinian in the sixth century until the eighteenth century, Christian communities around Europe regularly put homosexuals to death by burning, beheading, flaying, drowning, or hanging them. The ancient Christian thinkers Tertullian, Eusebius, and John Chrysostom all argued that same-sex relations deserve the penalty of death. The fabricated *Collection of Capitularies* prescribed the death penalty for sodomy in the ninth century. It was written by Benedict of Levita in 857, but ascribed to the emperor Charlemagne, and thereby enjoyed the emperor's authority. In medieval Europe, secular laws often invoked the authority of the Bible to execute homosexuals. Bologna adopted the death penalty for sodomy in 1259. Padua followed suit in 1329; Venice in 1342; Rome in 1363; Cremona in 1387; Milan in 1476; and Genoa in 1556. King Ferdinand and Queen Isabella of Spain actively sought out sodomites to be burned. In the hundred and

---

5 David F. Greenberg, *The Construction of Homosexuality* (Chicago and London: The University of Chicago Press, 1988), p. 270.

6 John Boswell, *Same Sex Unions in Premodern Europe* (New York: Villard Books).

7 R. I. Moore, *The Formation of a Persecuting Society: Power and Deviance in Western Europe, 950-1250* (Oxford: Blackwell, 1990), p. 92. See too, John Boswell, *Christianity, Social Tolerance and Homosexuality: Gay People in Western Europe from the Beginning of the Christian Era to the Fourteenth Century* (Chicago: The University of Chicago Press, 1980).

twenty-five years after Calvin taught in Geneva, there were thirty burnings, beheadings, drownings, and hangings of homosexuals in that city. Scores of men and boys were hanged for homosexual activity in Georgian England. Before the advent of modernity, women in Europe were also vulnerable to execution if convicted of lesbianism.[8] The history of churches' treatment of gay people has for over a thousand years been a history of hatred, persecution and death. To this day, standard Christian textbooks devoted to moral theology and commenting on homosexuality are usually trite treatises because of their complete silence on the long-standing brutality meted out to homosexuals by churches, whether Roman Catholic, Anglican, or Protestant. For homosexuals, the history of the Christian church has been a kaleidoscope of harrowing horrors. Their fortunes have now changed. Physical violence has mutated into rhetorical violence, although there are still nine countries today where homosexual behavior is punishable by death.[9]

Homosexuality and the Bible

The principal reason why many Anglicans today denounce sexual activity between people of the same sex is because the Bible apparently condemns men who engage sexually with males, and females who do the same with women. The word "homosexuality" was coined in the nineteenth century and is thus not mentioned anywhere in the Bible. However, biblical texts such as Leviticus condemn the practice of a man lying with a male as with a woman as an abomination deserving of death (Leviticus 18:22 and 20:13). Whatever term is used, the Bible does provide for executing males who engage sexually with other males.

---

8 For detailed explanations of the persecutions and executions mentioned in this paragraph, see Crompton, *Homosexuality and Civilization*, pp. 141-143, 159-160, 245-247, 324, and 539. Crompton describes the history of homosexuality in the west as "a kaleidoscope of horrors" (p. 539). The same phrase aptly designates the history of "Christian" treatment of homosexuality.

9 Jessica Williams, *Fifty Facts that Should Change the World* (Cambridge: Icon Books, 2004), p. 53. The nine countries are Mauritania, Sudan, Afghanistan, Pakistan, the Chechen Republic, Iran, Saudi Arabia, the United Arab Emirates, and Yemen.

The executions of homosexuals in Europe during the Middle Ages, the Reformation, the Inquisition, and the seventeenth century, were normally sanctioned by appeal to the authority of the Bible. Before the modern age in the eighteenth century, it was widely believed by Christians that Moses wrote Leviticus. Indeed, pre-modern Christians thought that Moses wrote the Pentateuch, the first five scrolls of the Bible. Since the Pentateuch records an encounter between God and Moses on Mount Sinai, any text composed by Moses would naturally be regarded as being or inspired by God.

In an oft-cited text, Hans Frei instructs that "Western Christian reading of the Bible in the days before the rise of historical criticism in the eighteenth century was usually strongly realistic; i.e. at once literal and historical, and not only doctrinal or edifying. The words and sentences meant what they said, and because they did so, they accurately described real events and real truths that were rightly put in those terms and no others".[10]

Modern theology and biblical criticism

Strongly realistic readings of the Bible have been greatly unsettled and frequently undermined since the emergence of modern theology and biblical criticism. In this chapter, the phrase "modern theology" designates a discourse about God that arose in the eighteenth century and continues today. What is described as "modern theology" in this chapter would easily and rightly be recognized as "liberal theology" by others.

Modern theology in the sense being employed here has six defining features. First, it is enthused by the intellectual and cultural legacy of the French Revolution and the Enlightenment. It celebrates a world of religious tolerance, freedom of speech, democratic decision-making, equality of human dignity and gender, and open, unfettered

---

10 Hans W. Frei, *The Eclipse of Biblical Narrative: A Study of Eighteenth and Nineteenth Century Hermeneutics* (New Haven and London: Yale University Press, 1974), p. 1.

debate. Second, it engages the philosophy of Immanuel Kant, and like him, esteems the use of reason above all else in discussions of God. Kant's monograph of 1793, *Religion within the Limits of Reason Alone*, captures the spirit of a modern philosophical approach to the analysis of religious ideas. After Kant, modern theology does not assume that the Bible is a revelation of God simply because someone says it is.

Third, modern theology is informed by the findings of modern empirical sciences. It rejects the defunct cosmology and biology assumed by the Bible and all pre-modern theologies. Unlike their predecessors, modern theologians know that the universe is expanding and that the earth is roughly four and a half billion years old. They know that there are about a hundred thousand million stars in the Milky Way galaxy, and that there are about a hundred thousand million galaxies in the universe. Pre-modern theologians were unaware of such states of affairs and spoke of God as if the earth were the centre of the universe and about six thousand years old. Fourth, modern theology is not confined to churches and is practised in state-funded secular universities as well as in monasteries, convents, seminaries, and local church communities. Fifth, modern theology relies on the insights of modern biblical criticism or analysis, which has its roots in the sixteenth and seventeenth centuries, but rose to prominence in German-speaking universities in the eighteenth and nineteenth centuries.[11] The distinctiveness of modern biblical scholarship resides largely in its method of studying the Bible as an historical document composed entirely by human beings in their specific historical contexts. Finally, modern theology relies on hermeneutics, the methodological investigation of the meaning of language, especially as it is codified in texts.

Hermeneutics raises the difficult question of how best to interpret texts today that were composed in languages and places

---

11 Consult Roy A. Harrisville and Walter Sundberg, *The Bible in Modern Culture: Barach Spinoza to Brevard Childs* (Grand Rapids, Michigan: Eerdmans, 2002); and Thomas Albert Howard, *Religion and the Rise of Historicism* (Cambridge: Cambridge University Press, 2000), pp. 17-20.

unknown to many contemporary readers. Most people read the Bible in translation not realizing that the translators they rely on interpreted words as they translated them. Frequently, biblical translators make false assumptions about words they interpret. A significant example that is relevant for current debates about homosexuality is the Hebrew word *kadesh* (plural *kedeshim*). This word appears about six times in the Hebrew Bible, for example, in 1 Kings 14:24. It means literally, "consecrated one" or "holy man". However, the translators of the King James Bible translate the term *kadesh* as "sodomite".[12] Hence the following translation: "And there were also sodomites in the land: and they did according to all the abominations of the nations which the Lord cast out before the children of Israel" (1 Kings 14:24). The translation of the New Revised Standard Version renders the same verse thus: "there were also male temple prostitutes in the land. They committed all the abominations of the nations that the Lord drove out before the people of Israel". For "consecrated one" these two translations offer "sodomite" and "male temple prostitute". The translators may have assumed that a consecrated or holy man must have been involved in temple prostitution that involved homosexual behavior. The point is: the translations differ significantly from the original texts because of the hermeneutic strategies of the translators.

Modern biblical scholarship undermined the view that the Pentateuch can accurately be read in a strongly realistic way, that is, as literally and historically descriptive. The seventeenth-century philosopher, Benedict Spinoza (1632-1677), clearly demonstrated that Moses could not possibly have written the first five scrolls of the Bible, because one of them, Deuteronomy, describes Moses' death and burial at the age of a hundred and twenty years (Deuteronomy 34:5-8). A dead man is unable to describe his own death and the grief of others after his

---

12 For a prudent discussion of the word *kadesh* in the Bible, see Louis Crompton, *Homosexuality and Civilization*, pp. 39-43.

death.[13] Therefore, someone else must have written Deuteronomy or at least its conclusion documenting Moses' demise. Julius Wellhausen (1844-1918) was able to show in the late nineteenth century that different people wrote the Pentateuch in its current form in diverse epochs, and that it did not appear before the end of the fifth century BCE, that is, hundreds of years after the death of Moses. Its different sections were originally written between the ninth century BCE and around 400 BCE.

The Bible's immorality

There is not a word in the Bible that was not written by a human being. Many of its words were penned by people thoroughly at ease advocating violence in extremely aggressive times and places. For instance, Deuteronomy 20:13-14 instructs victorious Israelites to kill their vanquished male adversaries and carry off their women and children as booty. By modern western post-Enlightenment ethical standards, the Bible advocates immoral practices. For example, Deuteronomy 22:13-21 rules that a woman who is found not to be a virgin after her marriage is to be stoned to death, whereas if a man falsely accuses his wife of not being a virgin he is to be fined one hundred sheckels of silver. Chapter 23 of the same text discriminates against children "born of an illicit union" (Deuteronomy 23:2). Chapter 25 commands: "If men get into a fight with one another, and the wife of one intervenes to rescue her husband from the grip of his opponent by reaching out and seizing his genitals, you shall cut off her hand; show no pity" (Deuteronomy 25:11-12).

Stemming from patriarchal societies, the entire sexual ethic of the Bible can be judged immoral or askew because such societies regarded women as the property of men in an unequal power-association under men. In ancient societies, like Rome, significant

---

13 See Benedict de Spinoza, *A Theologico-Political Treatise* (New York: Dover Publications, 1951; originally 1670), p. 124 (Ch. VIII).

distinctions were not so much made between heterosexuals and homosexuals, but between dominant and subordinate sexual partners. A dominant male partner could treat subordinate women (*feminae*), girls, (*puellae*), young men or boys (*pueri, adulescentuli,* or *iuvenes*), as he willed with complete disregard for the wishes and dignity of the subordinate partner.[14] The Bible's teaching that a male who lies with a man as with a woman must be put to death reflects the common notion in the ancient Near East that a mature man (*vir*) should not suffer the indignity of being treated as a subordinate sexual partner like a slave, woman, girl, or boy. The notion of the sexual coupling of equal partners belongs to late western societies, not to the Near East of three thousand years ago. The Bible's teaching that men who relate sexually with each other ought to be put to death is universally ignored by Christians and Jews today. It does not come from God. Its author was a human being entirely unknown to anyone alive at present. Leviticus 20:13, like every other text, has a context, a pretext, and a subtext. The Levitical text condemning to death men in same-sex liaisons was penned in an historical context that was prone to allow dominant human beings to exploit and humiliate subordinate people in a society that was generally violent, patriarchal, and exploitative of slaves. Leviticus can only be ascribed to God at the risk of turning God into a brutal patriarch.

The language used of God in the Bible is profoundly colored by the violent and aggressive historical context in which it was composed. Violence is by far the most frequently attested type of divine behavior mentioned in the Bible. Raymund Schwager points out that "there are six hundred passages of explicit violence in the Hebrew Bible, one thousand verses where Yahweh expressly commands others to kill people, and several stories where God irrationally kills or tries to kill for no apparent reason (for example, Exodus 4:24-26)".[15]

---

14 See Craig A. Williams, *Roman Homosexuality: Ideologies of Masculinity in Classical Antiquity* ((New York and Oxford: Oxford University Press, 1999), esp. pp. 17-19; and Merry E. Wiesner-Hanks, *Christianity and Sexuality in the Early Modern World* (London and New York: Routledge, 2000), pp. 22-27
15 Walter Wink, *The Powers That Be: Theology for a New Millennium* (New York: Galilee Doubleday, 1998), pp. 84-85.

Jack Nelson-Pallmeyer finds it very difficult to harmonize Jesus' vision of God with a great deal of what the Bible says of God. He concludes that "the overwhelming portrayal of God in the Bible is as a brutal killer and punishing judge".

This God "orders people to execute children who curse their parents; sends forth she-bears to maul children who insult a prophet; punishes disobedient people by reducing them to cannibalism; orders the murder of all men, women, and children after a battle; drowns nearly all of creation and humanity in a punishing flood; sends imperial armies to slaughter sinful people; promises eternal punishment for those who do not feed the hungry; and demands human sacrifice, recants, and then requires the bloody sacrifice of Jesus as atonement for human sin and as a means to reconciliation".[16]

One would have thought that the prevalence of so much violent rhetoric in the Bible draws immediate attention to its human rather than divine authorship.

The Windsor Report

The authority of the Bible stands at the center of current debates about gays among Anglicans. The Report singles out two questions currently troubling Anglicans: "whether or not it is legitimate for the church to bless the committed, exclusive and faithful relationships of same-sex couples, and whether or not it is appropriate to ordain/or consecrate to the episcopate, persons living in a sexual relationship with a partner of the same sex" (16).

The Report notes that when Gene Robinson was consecrated as a bishop in 2003, and when the Canadian diocese of New Westminster approved rites of blessings for same-sex unions, "The overwhelming response from other Christians both inside and outside the Anglican family has been to regard these developments as departures

---

16 Jack Nelson-Pallmeyer, *Jesus Against Christianity: Reclaiming the Missing Jesus* (Harrisburg, Pennsylvania: Trinity Press International, 2001), p. 20.

from genuine, apostolic Christian faith" (18). Be it noted, though, that homosexual relations have nothing whatsoever to do with genuine, apostolic Christian faith. The faith of the Apostles was in the Creator-God Yahweh, and in Jesus Christ whom they confessed as Lord, Messiah, and Master. The faith of the Apostles was not fetishistically focussed on sex, let alone gay sex. The Apostles followed their master in seeking out the lost, the loveless, and the lonely. Would that contemporary Anglicans focused their hearts and minds on the Apostles rather than New Hampshire and New Westminster. The very notion that homosexuality relates to "genuine, apostolic Christian faith" is indicative that the authors of the Windsor Report are gripped in the vice of the libidinally supercharged Zeitgeist of the contemporary west. The *Fides quae creditur* ("The faith which is believed") of the ancient church is focused on God and Christ, not sex.

Windsor also notes that condemnation of Robinson's consecration and the rites of blessing has come from the Russian Orthodox and Oriental Orthodox churches, and the Roman Catholic Church, meaning the Vatican's curia, has warned of serious new difficulties having been created for ecumenical relationships (18). Both Orthodox churches and the Vatican condemn homosexual behavior in the clearest of terms. In doing so, however, they condemn what is not yet understood. In short, they speak from a vantage point of opinion, not assured and widely shared knowledge. To date, there is no agreement among scientists as to the aetiology of homosexuality. Theories variously nominate the cause of homosexuality as a matter of inherited genes, parental influence, social conditioning, endochrinological imbalances, neurophysiology, neuropathology, or neuropsychology. Those churches that condemn homosexual activity condemn that which is, to date, inadequately understood.

Considered as a whole, Windsor rests on a massive blunder. It is a mistake to appease and apologize to Anglicans offended by gay couples in order to maintain church unity. In the timely words of John Shelby Spong, the Lambeth Commission decided mistakenly that they were dealing with an issue of disunity, when they were in fact dealing with the evil of prejudice. That was clear when their solution was to invite those churches that have banished their homophobic prejudices to consider apologizing to those parts of the church that were offended by their inclusiveness. That would be like asking those nations that have thrown off the evil of segregation to apologize for hurting the consciences of the segregationists. It was an inconceivable request. Whenever growth occurs there is always conflict and dislocation. The world would still be practicing slavery, child labour, and second class status for women, had not a new consciousness confronted our prejudices in a movement that always destroys the unity of the old consensus.[17]

Sexual orientation

A distinctive feature of modernity is that it has witnessed a wide-ranging progress in knowledge over a large field of disciplines. Modern psychiatry, psychology, biology, physics, medicine, sociology, cultural studies, and historical research have generated knowledge and understandings unavailable to pre-modern people. More is known of the Bible now than in any previous age. More too is known about sex and sexuality. The function of the human ovum, for example, was only discovered in 1827 by K. E. von Baer.[18] An important example of modern progress in knowledge impinges directly on gays and the future of Anglicanism. Recent social science has discovered sexual orientation. The Bible and pre-modern cultures were unaware of sexual *orientation*, that is, "a *proclivity* or predisposition that is given and not deliberately chosen or subject to the will of the individual. Sexual orientations exist

---

17 John Shelby Spong, Foreword to Jonathan Clatworthy and David Taylor (eds), *The Windsor Report: A Liberal Response* (Winchester and New York: O Books, 2005), ix-xiv (pp. xii-xiii).
18 Uta Ranke-Heinemann, *Eunuchs for Heaven: The Catholic Church and Sexuality* (London: André Deutsch, 1990), p. 164.

on a spectrum that stretches between exclusively heterosexual and exclusively homosexual individuals".[19] In the ancient world of biblical authors, it was generally believed that there is only one sexual identity, which is heterosexual. Were homosexuals to be slighted, it would have been on the grounds that they violated their heterosexual identities by acting in a homosexual way.[20] Consequently, in view of new knowledge about sexual orientation, for homosexual people to behave according to their orientation, which is usually determined in childhood, is not to act unnaturally. Homosexuality is a normal form of sexual disposition and behavior. It is normal, though not the preferred disposition of most human beings. Liking to eat snails is also a normal human orientation, though by no means shared by the majority of human beings. Homosexuals have been known in every culture in every age. Some hide their identities. Others flaunt it. Some were executed, others venerated.

Conclusion

As painful as disagreement over homosexuality is for contemporary Anglicans, they can at least be admired for confronting their demons, unlike the leadership of the Roman Catholic or various Orthodox churches. Over the past quarter century Roman Catholics were governed by an autocratic papacy deaf to the findings of modern theology and biblical research.[21] Anglicans can also be commended for the courageous and intellectually honest way in which they have frequently approached controversial new developments within Christianity. An example of a laudable approach to a disputed question was the General Synod debate of 1992, which discussed the issue of

---

19 Dan O. Via, "The Bible, the Church, and Homosexuality", in Dan O. Via and Robert S. J. Gagnon, *Homosexuality and the Bible: Two Views* (Minneapolis: Fortress Press, 2003), 1-39 (p. 16). See, too, Christine Gudorf, "The Bible and Science on Sexuality", in David Balch (ed), *Homosexuality, Science, and the 'Plain Sense' of Scripture* (Grand Rapids, Michigan: Eerdmans, 2000), pp. 121-141 (p. 122).
20 Via, 'The Bible, the Church, and Homosexuality', p.15.
21 See Hans Küng and Leonard Swidler (eds), *The Church in Anguish: Has the Vatican Betrayed Vatican II?* (San Francisco: Harper & Row, 1987); and John Cornwell, *The Pope in Winter: The Dark Face of John Paul II's Papacy* (London: Viking Penguin Books, 2004).

whether women could be ordained to the priesthood. Every effort was made at the time to consider all sides of the debate. Every care was taken to listen to opposed voices.[22] Then the decision was made to ordain women. Exactly the opposite behavior transpired in the Roman Catholic Church during the 1990s. Its theologians were forbidden even to discuss the matter. To this day, Vatican officials decide what is to be said and done about women in the church without listening to women, by ignoring theologians, and by bullying bishops to comply. Exactly the same approach is taken to homosexuals: their experiences are not heeded, scientific insights are ignored, theologians are sacked if they challenge curial teachings, and bishops are once again tethered to Vaticanic documents while untold numbers of gay people suffer from evil prejudices. Anglicans may fret that their ranks are divided over homosexuality. Fret they might and disunited they are. Fools they are not.

22 See *The Ordination of Women to the Priesthood, The Synod Debate: 11 November 1992, The Verbatim Record* (London: Church House Publishing, 1993).

22

MAKE US PROPHETS AND PASTORS: AN OPEN LETTER TO GAY AND LESBIAN PRIESTS

Carter Heyward

Dear sisters and brothers in Christ

Ours is a special vocation in these times, one of accountability to God as She[1] is manifesting herself through the lives of lesbian, gay, bisexual, transgender, and other Anglicans who are being abandoned by the bishops of the Communion. The Primates' meeting in Northern Ireland in February 2005 makes abundantly clear that those who have stood with gay and lesbian Anglicans are almost as unwelcome today as we are in the councils of the church and in fact are considered quite "queer"[2] themselves. We Anglican priests who happen also to be lesbian or gay must step forward now to fill the breach created by the Primates' rejection of gay men, lesbians, and our allies. These bishops are barricading the doors against our participation, with them, in any genuinely mutual engagement and study of human sexuality. Despite

---

1 I tend often to use feminine pronouns for God as a tiny counter-balance to the massive weight of patriarchal Christianity, which as a matter of fact is the root of the church's virulent homophobia (and, more generally its erotophobia – fear of the erotic).

2 I'm using the term "queer" here to include not only "homosexual" persons but all bisexual, transgender, and others derided by the Christian majority on the basis of our sexual/gender identities and commitments; and moreover also those "heterosexual" persons who put themselves at risk in the church and world by standing publicly in solidarity with us.

their claims of "care and friendship" toward "homosexual people," the Primates' "bonds of affection" do not, in fact, extend to gay people and our friends, and so we priests must take the place of the bishops in extending pastoral, sacramental, and liturgical care to our gay, lesbian, bisexual, and transgender sisters and brothers. Although few of us would have chosen this vocation, it has been cast upon us by the bishops' abandonment of the *whole* people of God.

A little personal and church history may be helpful. In 1973, a week after my ordination as an Episcopal deacon - and five years before I realized I'm basically lesbian in my own sexual identity - I phoned the office of my bishop to say that I would be officiating several days later at the blessing of a committed "holy union" between two women. After a brief pause, Bishop Stuart Wetmore[3] spoke in his soft voice, "Well, Carter, the church blesses hounds and houseboats. I don't see why we shouldn't also bless committed, loving relationships between people. Thank you for alerting us. God bless you and these women – and we'd prefer, of course, that the press not get hold of this."

Thirty-one years later, in May 2004, I solemnized the marriage of two women in Massachusetts who were among the several thousand gay men and lesbians married within days of the state's new non-discriminatory law going into effect, which permits the civil marriage of homosexual couples on the same basis as heterosexual. In between these two liturgical events, like many Episcopal deacons, priests, and bishops in the United States, I have officiated or participated in dozens of same-sex blessings and also scores of ordinations and consecrations of lesbians and gay men to Holy Orders in the Episcopal Church, including the 2003 consecration of Gene Robinson as Bishop of New Hampshire, a holier man you'll never find.

I tell you these stories to illustrate that what Anglican leaders are portraying as a sudden crisis in the Communion, something that

---

3 The Bishop of New York, Paul Moore, was unavailable, and so I spoke with Bishop Suffragan Stuart Wetmore.

seems to have taken the world of Primates by surprise, reaches back in history. In fact, the ordination and consecration of gay men is hardly a new phenomenon, and those who pretend that it is, are choosing to keep their heads in the sand. As retired Bishop Suffragan Barbara C. Harris of Massachusetts is fond of pointing out, " 'De-Nile' ain't just the name of a river in Africa!" Denial is, in fact, one of the church's great sins.

Denial is what enables church leaders around the globe to imagine that homosexual bishops have not been attending the Lambeth Conference from its inception.

Denial is what allows any of us to assume that gay men and lesbians have not always been present in our common prayer and shared holy communion with us.

Denial is what allows bishops from the global South as well as the North to imagine that women who love women sexually and men who love men sexually are not seated in their own congregations, leading Bible studies, and singing anthems to the glory of God.

About 15 years ago, in one of my classes on a "theology of sexuality" at the Episcopal Divinity School in Cambridge, Massachusetts, a young man – white, conservative, and earnest – rose to denounce homosexuality as a "white Western phenomenon." A moment later, a black Roman Catholic Sister from Kenya raised her hand, "Actually, what you say is not true," she spoke patiently. "We do not use the same language for these relationships as you do. But these relationships are present. Believe me. And how do I know? Because I was blessed to be raised by two mothers who loved each other sexually and were life-partners."

But the Primates and most of our bishops, when they get together, tend to choose denial over such truth speaking. Hear, for example, what they said in response to the Windsor Report, "We wish to make it quite clear that in our discussion and assessment of the moral appropriateness of specific human behaviors, we continue unreservedly to be committed to the pastoral support and care of homosexual people.

The victimization or diminishment of human beings whose affections happen to be ordered towards people of the same sex is anathema to us. We assure homosexual people that they are children of God, loved and valued by him, and deserving of the best we can give of pastoral care and friendship."[4] If I were to address these Primates, I would say this:

> With all due respect, dear bishops, and regardless of what may be your good intentions, you are fast putting yourselves, as a collegium, outside the realm of being able to respond pastorally to gay, lesbian, bisexual, and transgender Anglicans. You are increasingly unable to be pastors to us not primarily because most of you believe homosexual activity is sinful, or that gay men and lesbians shouldn't be ordained, or that the church shouldn't bless lesbian and gay relationships. These are, after all, important ethical matters to be studied and debated by people of good faith who hold different views about matters of human sexuality, people like you, people like us. Such debate and dialogue is what makes Anglicanism at its best "comprehensive." So, it is not your lack of agreement with queer Anglicans that is the problem for us. It is your commitment to structures held in place to protect your own authority, structures like the proposed "Instruments of Unity," that do not permit, much less invite, any genuinely mutual relation with those to whom you offer your "care and friendship" that makes it impossible for us to take your spiritual or moral authority seriously. Where there is no room for mutual relation, there is no room for God.

Bishop Steven Charleston, former Bishop of Alaska and currently President of the Episcopal Divinity School, counsels wisely that the current crisis in Anglicanism is "a call to courageous self-

---

4 Communiqué from Primates' Meeting, Newry, Northern Ireland, February 20-5, 2005, para 6. [Material accessed on-line from Anglican Communion website, February 25, 2005].

reflection, careful historical analysis, and difficult cross-cultural dialogue." "It is," he writes, "an opportunity for us to come in from the extreme edges of emotional conflict to find a common center. It is an appeal to our leadership to lower the levels of invective and rhetoric so that the people of our Communion may listen to what others are trying to say."[5] Unfortunately, most Anglican bishops are failing to demonstrate Bishop Charleston's openness to mutually sharing and studying our histories, theologies, politics, and cultures with one another – homosexual and heterosexual Anglicans alike, women and men from different parts of the world and church, people of diverse cultures and traditions and biblical hermeneutics.

I believe, dear gay brothers and lesbian sisters, that we should say clearly to our bishops and other Anglicans that the problem with the Primates' quaint offering of "care and friendship" to us is not primarily that most of them are upset about Gene Robinson's consecration and the blessing of same-sex unions in the United States and Canada. The problem with their bid to care for us and other "homosexual people" is that, as a group, the Primates transparently are not interested in any genuinely mutual journeying with us toward a "common center." These men do not *want* a common center with lesbian, gay, bisexual, or transgender Anglicans or, for that matter, with any Anglicans who show solidarity with us, like the scores of bishops, including Bishop Steven Charleston and Presiding Bishop Frank Griswold (USA), who participated in the Robinson consecration. The Primates, on the whole, seem frightened of women who openly love women and they are probably terrified of men who openly love men. They do not want to get close enough to us to be touched by us, metaphorically or literally. Thus it is up to us, dear brother and sister priests, to work closely enough together and keep closely enough in touch with one another to

---

5 Bishop Steven Charleston, *The Middle Way: A Congregational Resource for Discussing the Lambeth Commission Report*, available on the website of the Episcopal Divinity School, www.eds.edu.

help the whole people of God work and pray their way through the fears and hostilities being set in place by the Primates of the Anglican Communion.

Whether we are Primates or priests, we can love only those to whom we are not afraid to listen and from whom we do not have to flee in fear. What, then, are we to make of the Primates' request, in February 2005, that "the Episcopal Church (USA) and the Anglican Church of Canada voluntarily withdraw their members from the Anglican Consultative Council (ACC) for the period leading up to the next Lambeth Conference [2008]"?[6] What is this supposed to accomplish? Is this supposed to help "restore bonds of affection" among Anglicans, asking two of its most controversial members to please go away long enough for everybody else to figure out what to do – without them? And then, lo and behold, to suggest that these same two troubling members be invited to the ACC as guests – that is, as outsiders, people who do not belong – to defend themselves, "to set out the thinking behind the recent actions of their Provinces"?[7] How can the message to US Episcopalians and Canadian Anglicans be anything other than that the Primates of the Anglican Communion really don't want us "inside" the church – even though, of course, as good Anglicans, they can safely and politely invite us as "outsiders" to explain ourselves without fear of their being polluted by our alien outsider ways.

The message to "homosexual people" from the Primates of the Anglican Communion is that queer people are alien, shameful, and wrong: Our lives are wrong – the ways we love, the relational bonds we form, the blessings we seek. Moreover, neither we, nor those who stand in solidarity with us are welcome in the councils of the Anglican Communion. Still they ask us to "be clear" that we are "deserving of the best [they] can give of pastoral care and friendship." Perhaps this *is* the best they can give, these Primates of ours. Whatever, it is a far cry from

---

6 Communiqué from Primate's Meeting, February 2005, para 14.
7 Communiqué, para 16.

what "homosexual people" either need pastorally or, if we have any self-respect, what we can accept from our bishops or anyone else.

This is the context, in which we are being called, as sister and brother priests, to take up the work of pastoral, liturgical, sacramental, and prophetic leadership and oversight in the Anglican Communion. It falls to us, dear colleagues, to step in where our bishops are stepping out; to present ourselves as overseers of the well-being of gay, lesbian, bisexual, and transgender Anglicans; to officiate at gay blessings and weddings; to make ourselves available to queer Anglicans in other pastoral, liturgical, and sacramental contexts; from time to time to allow ourselves to be named and consecrated as bishops (in any case, to stand in every way we can with Gene Robinson and any bishops who may "come out"); and to be public and enthusiastic in our solidarity with "homosexual people" and all others whom the church oppresses and silences on the basis of their gender or sexual identity.

Stretching way beyond what we may once have assumed to be the vocation of the ordained priesthood, we are called now also to be community organizers. This means we share a vocation to help bring together sister and brother deacons, lay leaders, the occasional brave bishop, as well as members of other Christian churches and faith traditions, in building a global movement which, for us Anglicans, can be faithful to the biblical witness, as informed by tradition and reason, and as illuminated by what Anglican professors Christopher Duraisingh, Kwok Pui-lan, and Ian Douglas commend to us as "postcolonial imagination."[8] Such imagination requires not only that there be dialogue – more than one voice – in the search for theological and moral truth; but moreover that the dialogue be "polycentric" and "multivocal" – involving many voices speaking from many different situations and locations as partners in seeking to discover what may be most faithful to the Bible.

---

8 See Christopher Duraisingh, "Toward a Postcolonial Re-visioning of the Church's Faith, Witness, and Communion" and Kwok Pui-lan, "The Legacy of Cultural Hegemony in the Anglican Church," in Ian T. Douglas and Kwok Pui-lan (eds), *Beyond Colonial Anglicanism: The Anglican Communion in the Twenty-First Century* (New York: Church Publishing Inc., 2001), pp. 337-67 and 47-70.

And this shared vocation requires us to be more even than organizers. We must also be educators, not necessarily academics, but priests whose special role at this time is, through our words and actions, to help educate the church through these turbulent, fear-based, hostile times. Good education is public instruction, education with implications for the whole community, not just a few. And so, we cannot hide our light under a bushel or go tip-toeing about our business, as if we gay-affirming Anglicans were called to live secret lives. This is no time to minister from the closet – unless, of course, we put others or ourselves at risk by coming out and ministering publicly as queer priests. For all of us, there are times and places when to be quiet, discreet, sometimes even secretive, is the better part of wisdom – and we need to pray that God will show us when we are in such situations and give us the serenity to maintain a quiet peace with ourselves and those whom we serve. Being able to discern different kinds and levels of danger and vulnerability and, therefore, how to conduct our ministries – publicly or privately, with fanfare or quietly, in each others' company or alone – can be especially important in the controversial arenas of sexual and gender identity, where emotions can be so explosive (witness the Lambeth Conference 1998), psyches fragile, and possibilities of violence ever-present.   Nonetheless, as priests and educators, we need to teach the church by witnessing to the truths we are discovering through our ministries with the marginalized. For example, queer Anglicans, like all historically marginalized and outcast people, have much to teach the Communion about this "unity of the church" which the Primates are so eager to protect. "With whom," we must ask, "are the bishops of the church seeking unity?" Unity with each other, which is fine, but at whose expense? How about unity with Nigerian women who love women and men who love men, who are hiding in fear for their lives? How about unity with the suicidal gay man in London and the gay teenager in South Carolina who has been bashed and left for dead at the side of the road? How about unity with Bishop Gene Robinson and his episcopal allies, such as the Primates of the Canadian and United States churches?

Pleading for "the unity of the church" has been, historically, a cry against justice movements that have threatened to change the church and society. In the United States, movements such as those for the abolition of slavery, civil rights, and women's rights have met fierce resistance from Episcopalians worried about "the unity of the church." Any authentic unity we can forge as Anglicans, any common ground that will pass the test of time, will require the making of justice and compassion, both moral qualities rooted in mutual respect. Such mutuality can only be fostered through awareness and respect for cultural differences. In each location – in every town, county, diocese, and province of the Anglican Communion – we need to learn to share cross-culturally stories of how we have experienced justice and injustice, healing and liberation. Across the barriers that seem to separate us – walls of nation, culture, and experience – we need to come together to bear witness to our diverse lives, as the Spirit weaves us together.

Such a brilliant theological, anthropological, and sociological tapestry, woven boldly with diverse threads, patterns, and colors, would truly reflect "the unity of the church." Our oneness in this Spirit would radiate an integrity and credibility that is probably unimaginable to most of the Primates who would abandon us instead to the reckonings of the Lambeth Conference and other "instruments of unity" – the Archbishop of Canterbury, the Primates' meetings, and the Anglican Consultative Council – all except the latter structured entirely around the authority of bishops.

It becomes our vocation as gay and lesbian priests in this historical moment to be chief weavers of this tapestry of Anglican unity. But does it really matter that we are gay and lesbian? What difference does our sexuality make to our vocation as Anglican priests? Being lesbian or gay matters because it signals a shared experience of exclusion and rejection, a common place of marginalization and silencing, in which the roots of our prophetic voices and pastoral sensibilities have been cultivated. Oppressed people can either identify with, and mimic, the oppressor or we can commit ourselves again and again to the struggles for liberation, for others and ourselves. Our choice, as lesbian and gay priests today, is either to make a truce with oppression or to take on the mantel of the prophet.

Dear sisters and brothers, let me say that we must never stop trying to help one another and other Anglicans make connections – moral and political links – between oppressive structures in the world and church. Gay, lesbian, and other queer Christians must not be silent or passive in the face of racism and sexism, economic exploitation and imperialism, war and other forms of violence being waged against the poor by the United States of America more than any other nation on the face of the earth. There is no good excuse for gay and lesbian people to see ourselves as the only folks who suffer at the hands of a fear-based world and church or as those who suffer most. It doesn't matter who suffers most. Any oppression in the name of Christ is too much. We priests are morally obligated to help make these connections.

I am told that some of the Southern Primates – choosing to remain ignorant about who Gene Robinson really is – view him the same way they view George W. Bush, as a symbol of Western imperialism. Perceiving Bishop Robinson through the lens of such a superficial analysis of the very real complexities of neo-colonialism and imperialism enables these men not to notice the stunning difference between the Bishop of New Hampshire and the President of the United States, which we can summarize in an image of prayer: While George Bush does indeed offer the imperial prayer that "God bless America," Gene Robinson prays that God bless all people, everywhere, Iraqis and Irish, Australians and Rwandans, homosexual and heterosexual, paupers and Primates, including those who distance themselves from him and judge him most harshly. The distinction between the two is almost as stark as that between the Caesar and the poor man from Nazareth.

Finally, dear colleagues, we need each other's support and solidarity. Few of us know many other gay and lesbian priests personally, and most of us are busy in this post-modern world doing too many things. May we be given the grace to slow down enough to take prayerful stock of this situation, this crisis in Anglicanism, and our place in it. May we be given the courage to publicly support our sister and brother priests in their justice work, both those whom we know and those whom we don't know. May we hold one another in prayer morning-by-morning and day-by-day. Fortunately, many of us in the North have advocacy organizations in the church, like Integrity and the Lesbian and Gay Christian Movement, to help us network. It is heartening to see bridges being built through these networks, between gay and lesbian people in the Northern churches and those in the global South who may not name themselves "gay," "lesbian," or "homosexual," but whose same-sex love is real and vibrant, if often hidden. Never again should we neglect to search for ways to share in building these global bridges so that we can learn together how to generate more fully mutual, polycentric, and multivocal relationships, through which God is always born again and gives rise to theological truths that none of us can discover simply on our own or among folks who are just like us.

So, let us pray, brothers and sisters, that God will make us prophets as well as the pastors and overseers so desperately needed among those who have been abandoned by the Primates. Bishop Robert DeWitt, who ordained me to the priesthood in 1974, often wrote: "keep your courage". May we do just that, and may God bless us one and all.

In sisterly solidarity
Carter Heyward

AFTERWORD

WHY GAYS REFUSE TO BE UNCHURCHED

Richard Kirker

Why do lesbians and gays remain in the Anglican Communion? It is a good question, and one that deserves an answer. The first thing to say is that not all Christian gays are content to stay in the church. Over the years, one of the saddest, but entirely understandable, things that I have witnessed is the slow trickle of gay people who decide that enough is enough. As one person recently wrote:

> Last Sunday, I spoke to my parish priest and told him that I thought my time was up in the Church of England. After 52 years, I finally get the message that we are not wanted. I reassured him that it was nothing to do with the local church or him personally, but that the message was now clear.

Behind this letter, and the many others I receive, are years of struggling to be faithful, and much personal anguish. There are limits to what any individual can bear, and clearly some have reached theirs. It is not for me to pass judgment, except to say that I shall miss them, and that I understand their position much more than they might know. But there are many people who have decided, as a matter of principle to stay, and refuse to be unchurched – and I am one of them. The question is: why should one want to remain in a church that is often so plainly homophobic, and which variously gives succor to those who seek spiritual support for their own prejudice?

Well, the first reason is that deep down we know that the church, as the people of God, is more than priests, bishops, even archbishops. Yes, we know they "rule" (I can't think of a nicer word) the church, but the chief point is that it doesn't belong to them. It belongs to all of us, all baptized Anglicans, not just the largely self-selected group that often dominates our meetings and synods. To give up now would be to give over the church to those who are determined that it should never change.

Second, although it is often inchoately expressed, there is a deep vein of spirituality that runs throughout the gay movement. Ours is not, and has never been, just a movement about nuts and bolts, about rights here and welfare there. Don't misunderstand me: these things are important. We spend our time campaigning for them, and we rejoice at even the small victories (and sometimes very small they are). But the movement for sexual emancipation, for justice, for the recognition of our full humanity – has always been, for some of us, about spirituality – about liberation and humanization at the deepest possible level. Most liberation movements have a spiritual side to them – in our case, however inadequately expressed, it runs deep. We know what fellowship in suffering means; some of us know what it means to be crucified.

Third, for many of us Jesus is a person of irresistible fascination, as one theologian said "the only truly unforgettable person in human history". Not least of all, Jesus was not a homophobe. As Lisa Isherwood has indicated in her essay, while not claiming Jesus as gay, his lifestyle was clearly a challenge to heterosexualist stereotypes. The "beloved disciple" is no figment of our imagination. Jesus unquestionably had loving relationships with people of the same sex. To suppose otherwise is to deserve the rebuke offered by supporters of D. H. Lawrence to his critics – namely that their Christianity would have put a fig leaf on Christ on the cross. But it is not only the freedom that Jesus offers from sexual stereotypes that attracts gays to this unforgettable man. Rather, he is unforgettable because his own life represents in a microcosm the journey gays almost daily have to make from slavery to freedom. Lesbians and gays know first hand the experience of treading the way of the cross, the way of humiliation and public rejection. They have been there, they have felt it, and for all its terribleness, they know the redemptive capacity of Christlike suffering.

Fourth, we remain in the church because we are a sign of what the church could become, and *should* become. It sounds paradoxical to go on working within a community that appears to deny one's deepest aspirations. But all human institutions are compromised: we are all fallible, sinful human beings. There is no perfect church. The best that can be said for it is that it is journeying to become what it should be. And that's where we come in. The church of tomorrow will not be the church of today, and we want to be part of that change, that progressive reformation.

Some looking at the church as it is have some difficulty in believing that it can change – that it has the power to transform even itself. But, in fact, at almost every point in its history there have been Christians working for reform and often paying a very heavy personal price for doing so. In particular, there have been numerous struggles for justice: for the emancipation of slaves (on which, incidentally, Anglicanism does not have a good record), for women's equality, against racism and apartheid – none of these movements enjoyed unequivocal support from the Anglican hierarchy in their time.

But, some will still press: how can one continue with an institution that is so homophobic? The answer is that it isn't *all* homophobic. That is the puzzle and the opportunity. Puzzle because so many people (especially outside the church – and even sometimes within it) think that churchpeople are all of one shade, whereas, in fact, we are many colors – there is great diversity. And opportunity, because

– despite Windsor – there are many signs that theologians and churchpeople are beginning to see gays as an issue of justice for the church. Who would have thought 20 years ago, for example, that there would one day be an openly gay Anglican bishop?

Many people refer to the 1998 Lambeth Conference and the 1.10 resolution on homosexuality (see appendix 1). Well, Lambeth certainly was a disappointment, to say the least. But that resolution[1] had two parts – the first declares homosexual practice as incompatible with scripture, while the second (paragraph 3) calls on the Communion to listen to the voices of lesbian and gay people. Of course that process has hardly yet begun, but if it *did* there would be hope for the church. This may help to explain why the Primates of North America and others whose provinces ordain lesbian and gay people can continue to assent to Lambeth 1.10, and how so many were able to vote for resolution 1.10 and, then, almost immediately sign the Pastoral Letter to Lesbian and Gay Anglicans (see appendix 2), which called for their "full inclusion" in the life of the Communion. By 30 October 1998, there were 182 signatories to that letter, including 8 Primates.

But, it may be protested: where is the dialogue? Well, the lack of dialogue *is* deeply worrying. Windsor is itself a symbol of that. Despite the repeated calls of the Instruments of Unity to listen to lesbian and gay Christians (emphasised by Windsor itself in paragraph 146), the Lambeth Commission somehow managed to avoid meeting the gay man at the heart of the "crisis", Bishop Gene Robinson. This demonstrates the way the Anglican Communion deals with its lesbian and gay constituency – we will talk *about* you, but we will not talk *with* you. The Commission's refusal to call Bishop Robinson is even more reprehensible in the light of their subsequent recommendation that he be isolated, so denying him due process. We are, with justification, deeply suspicious that the Commission's refusal to hear our voices, and listen to our stories, is because it does not wish to be convinced by them. As Archbishop Orombi of Uganda has made clear he wants to talk us down, not listen to us at all.[1] On the other hand, Windsor did reach one conclusion that offers hope. Many submissions to the Commission called on it to say that homosexual practice is, and always will be, contrary to divine law. The Commission refused to do that, and firmly states in paragraph 146 that the issue remains a matter for *continued* discussion.[2] Well, our hope is in continuing discussion, because we believe that truth is on our side, and that rational argument can prevail over prejudice.

But, it may be asked, given that the church is such a compromised institution, what can gays reasonably expect? The answer is that we look to the church to offer us what it offers all God's children: to baptize and confirm us and our children, to share the sacrament of Christ's body and blood in supportive fellowship with fellow Anglicans, to comfort us when bereaved, to give us a Christian burial that respects our partners and family, and to educate our children in a faith that does not see their mothers and fathers as corrupt or evil, or teach them that their parents are an abomination. In addition, we expect the church to bless our unions, and make demands upon us to live to standards that reflect Christ's union with his church. This is a demand - a discipline of love - that we are anxious to fully embrace.

In some parishes where we live what we look for is already a reality; Scotland's bishops have already made their welcome to homosexual people a matter of record. Wales hesitates to make such a bold declaration as the Scots, but the policy there is clearly the same. The English bishops know the reality on the ground is poles apart from their declared position, as the Primate of Canada recently indicated by saying that there were more blessings of same-gender unions in England than there were in Canada.

But our abiding concern is with the plight of lesbian and gay people in the 80 plus countries where homosexuals are still routinely

---

1 The Archbishop of the Church of Uganda, Henry Luke Orombi, ruled out any debate with homosexuals, saying they either repent and adopt the biblical teaching of sex, or go their own way. "I do not think there is a debate. When God gives his word, you either take it or leave it. We either agree with God or go our own way," – Orombi told journalists. *New Vision*, 4 March, 2005.
2 http://www.anglicancommunion.org/commission/documents/200406lgcm.pdf.

executed, tortured and imprisoned. No matter how balanced the recent statements emanating from Primates or Windsor appear to be, nowhere have we seen them make any clear and unequivocal condemnation of the civil laws that place homosexuals in such real, life-threatening jeopardy. Most of the laws that persecute homosexuals were originally placed on the statute books of these countries when England was the imperial power, so we could at least expect the English bench to put on record their regret for this baleful historical legacy. What happens in the west does have an impact on the world, and the election of a bishop in a same-sex union speaks loudly in places where other churches turn a blind eye to the persecution of gays. The Archbishop of Canterbury's Advent letter in 2004, recalled the recent homophobic murder of a gay man in London, but he didn't draw the obvious conclusion: that unless the church changes its thinking about gays, then gays will continue to suffer brutal physical assaults and their verbal equivalents.

Our goal remains full inclusion: the recognition that God is working in, and is visible through, gay relationships, and that they can be as much a testimony of God's presence in creation as the best of heterosexual marriages. It is quite clear to me what "full inclusion" means to lesbian and gay people. Despite many centuries of persecution, we have remained faithful to the Gospel imperatives; we are disciples of Jesus, baptized brothers and sisters in the Lord. Though we, too, are repentant sinners, yet we hold that our sexuality is part of our redeemed and reborn selves in Christ. We are part of God's holy people and his royal priesthood. We, too, are transformed by the Holy Spirit, and enabled to live out our lives in fellowship with God, and each other, celebrating our sexual love in life-long committed relationships.

It is sometimes claimed that gays are recklessly pursuing their goal at the expense of the church and its unity. In fact, we respect diversity. In its submission to the Lambeth Commission,[3] the Lesbian and Gay Christian Movement engaged Canon Derek Belcher, a canon

---

3 http://www.aco.org/acns/acnsarchive/acns1800/acns1890.html.

lawyer, to argue the case that the ordination of homosexual people in sexual relationships remains part of the legitimate diversity present within the Anglican Communion. Our view was, and remains, that custom and practice in many provinces has for many years developed into an acceptance of homosexuals in same-sex relationships, even where there had been no clear decision to set aside discrimination, as in the United States. We believe such customary law is typically Anglican, and that decisions of Lambeth Conferences could not claim a higher authority, nor even the title of "quasi-law" (as this development was specifically denied to it at its conception), and has not been granted by its constituent provinces since.

The cool reception given to the Virginia Report by the Anglican Consultative Council, which tried to give more weight to the rather misnamed "Instruments of Unity" has been a key moment in the process of Anglican development. There was no will to see greater authority granted to these bodies, and a clear preference for the "local option". We know that developments have taken place within Anglicanism that have resulted in "impaired" communion (to some degree), even straining the bonds of affection and challenging the "normative" understanding of scripture, but that has happened without any church expressing a desire to "walk apart" and leave the Communion. The same could, and should, have happened with the ordination of homosexuals by ECUSA and the same-gender blessings by the Canadian Diocese of New Westminster. In fact, the earlier developments within Anglicanism offered a deeper *prima facie* challenge to unity, particularly in the area of the "normative" understanding of scripture.

We believe that the future for Anglicanism remains in Communion-development as its unique contribution to Christendom, rather than in trying to create a "united" church, which would inevitably be more authoritarian and hierarchical. If the Anglican Communion is to continue, it must be what it is: untidy, broad, diverse and not try and reinvent itself as something different, least of all should it become a pale shadow of the church it grew from. The current diversity within Anglicanism in such areas of common prayer, the ordination of women, and canon law, along with the changing discipline on marriage and divorce, have developed incrementally; acceptance of the Windsor recommendations about authority, and a universally agreed covenant, will mean an end to this process of development.

We want a solution where nobody feels un-churched. I accept that this may be a far more painful way, but the pain will be much more evenly spread than that involved in the proposals we are presently considering. The healing it can bring will not be temporary, and truth and unity will not be compromised. There are no temporary expedients or quick fixes, and no legal formula, that will protect us from future disagreements. Most lesbian and gay Anglicans, and our friends, such as the contributors to this volume, still hold that the process of changing hearts and minds across the Communion should continue as before. It is a pattern that has served the Communion well so far, allowing for the gradual reception of any development without the demand that such changes be adopted as universal practice. Where there is dissent within provinces adequate provision should be made for those who remain unconvinced.

But, some will ask: might that diversity one-day crumble when, and if, the Communion decides to adopt a universal anti-gay law? Well, that is a possibility, and if that actually happened, obviously gays would have to leave. If that kind of irrevocable step were taken, we would be left in a totally impossible position. But we are not there yet – and I honestly believe it won't happen. The fact is that there are hundreds of thousands, perhaps even millions of gays among the 60-odd million Anglicans in the world today. It is true that we haven't always been as vocal or as organized as we should, but we are not going to go away, unless given absolutely no alternative.

What Windsor and the Dromantine (Newry) communiqué appear to misunderstand is that no unity can now be achieved without us. There can be no credible or lasting resolution to the way the church deals with its homosexual membership unless they are at the heart of the process of healing. The present "crisis" has been described as a "battle for the heart and soul of the church" – but the problem with battles is that there are winners and losers, and the prevailing spirit of "winner takes all" is a recipe for disaster. The current disagreement has, perhaps needfully, been loud and raucous, bitter and hurtful, but that will pass. Homosexuals are not going away. We are here for the duration, and ultimately we will be listened to, and we will listen in our turn; no less in the future as in the past. There can be no real church without us, or in spite of us. We will work for unity, but we will not be *sacrificed* to it.

Despite everything, I am confident that some new, very Anglican, way will be found for us to sit and take counsel together. We have recommended from the beginning an international Anglican commission on sexuality, with an equal composition of lesbian and gay Anglicans and others. This would finally bring an end to all the displacement activities and the rhetoric, which inevitably characterize any debate or report formulated on a basis of excluding our experience. The current view expressed by the English house of bishops that the crisis has to be averted before we can sit down and talk is simply putting the cart before the horse. I refuse to believe that Anglicanism, which has survived so many "crises" and so much turmoil, cannot enable a way in which all of us can live Christianly together.

APPENDIX (1)

Lambeth Conference 1998: Resolution 1.10 Human Sexuality

This Conference:

1   commends to the Church the subsection report on human sexuality;

2   in view of the teaching of Scripture, upholds faithfulness in marriage between a man and a woman in lifelong union, and believes that abstinence is right for those who are not called to marriage;

3   recognises that there are among us persons who experience themselves as having a homosexual orientation. Many of these are members of the Church and are seeking the pastoral care, moral direction of the Church, and God's transforming power for the living of their lives and the ordering of relationships. We commit ourselves to listen to the experience of homosexual persons and we wish to assure them that they are loved by God and that all baptised, believing and faithful persons, regardless of sexual orientation, are full members of the Body of Christ;

4   while rejecting homosexual practice as incompatible with Scripture, calls on all our people to minister pastorally and sensitively to all irrespective of sexual orientation and to condemn irrational fear of homosexuals, violence within marriage and any trivialisation and commercialisation of sex;

5 cannot advise the legitimising or blessing of same sex unions nor ordaining those involved in same gender unions;

6 requests the Primates and the ACC to establish a means of monitoring the work done on the subject of human sexuality in the Communion and to share statements and resources among us;

7 notes the significance of the Kuala Lumpur Statement on Human Sexuality and the concerns expressed in resolutions IV.26, V.1, V.10, V.23 and V.35 on the authority of Scripture in matters of marriage and sexuality and asks the Primates and the ACC to include them in their monitoring process.

APPENDIX (2)

A Pastoral Statement to Lesbian and Gay Anglicans from Some Member Bishops of the Lambeth Conference.

Statement sponsored by the Rt Rev'd Ronald Haines, Bishop of Washington,

August 5, 1998.

Dear sisters and brothers,

The Lambeth Conference has spent nearly three weeks deliberating issues of human sexuality, among many other vital issues facing our world-wide Communion. We have met in a climate of enormous diversity and have attempted both to articulate our views and listen carefully to those of others.

Within the limitations of this Conference, it has not been possible to hear adequately your voices, and we apologise for any sense of rejection that has occurred because of this reality. This letter is a sign of our commitment to listen to you and reflect with you theologically and spiritually on your lives and ministries. It is our deep concern that you do not feel abandoned by your Church and that you know of our continued respect and support.

We pledge that we will continue to reflect, pray and work for your full inclusion in the life of the Church. It is obvious that Communion - wide we are in great disagreement over what inclusion would mean. We ourselves have varied views and admit, as the report of the Human Sexuality Sub-section of the Conference says, that there is much we do not yet understand. But we believe it is an imperative of the Gospel and our faith that we seek such understanding.

We call on the entire Communion to continue (and in many places, begin) prayerful, respectful conversation on the issue of homosexuality. We must not stop where this Conference has left off. You, our sisters and brothers in Christ, deserve a more thorough hearing than you received over the past three weeks. We will work to make that so.

Signatories to the Bishop's Pastoral Statement

By 30th October 1998, there were 182 signatories, including 8 Primates.

Signatories Indexes by country

Australia (12)
Brazil (1)
Canada (17)
Central Africa (2)
England (42)
Ireland (4)
Japan (1)
Mexico (1)
New Zealand (8)
Scotland (6)
South Africa (8)
United States (76)
Wales (5)

O

is a symbol of the world,
of oneness and unity. O Books
explores the many paths of wholeness
and spiritual understanding which
different traditions have developed down
the ages. It aims to bring this knowledge
in accessible form, to a general readership,
providing practical spirituality to today's seekers.
For the full list of over 200 titles covering:

- CHILDREN'S PRAYER, NOVELTY AND GIFT BOOKS
- CHILDREN'S CHRISTIAN AND SPIRITUALITY
- CHRISTMAS AND EASTER
- RELIGION/PHILOSOPHY
- SCHOOL TITLES
- ANGELS/CHANNELLING
- HEALING/MEDITATION
- SELF-HELP/RELATIONSHIPS
- ASTROLOGY/NUMEROLOGY
- SPIRITUAL ENQUIRY
- CHRISTIANITY, EVANGELICAL
AND LIBERAL/RADICAL
- CURRENT AFFAIRS
- HISTORY/BIOGRAPHY
- INSPIRATIONAL/DEVOTIONAL
- WORLD RELIGIONS/INTERFAITH
- BIOGRAPHY AND FICTION
- BIBLE AND REFERENCE
- SCIENCE/PSYCHOLOGY

Please visit our website,
www.O-books.net

SOME RECENT O BOOKS

The Windsor Report
A Critical Evaluation

The Anglican Church faces a crisis over questions of sexuality and authority, prompted by the consecration of Canon Gene Robinson as bishop of the Diocese of New Hampshire in 2003. The most serious split in its history seems to be imminent, with liberals on one side and conservatives on the other. The Windsor Report, produced in November 2004 by the Eames Commission that was established by the Archbishop of Canterbury to find a way forwards without schism, seems to offer the last hope of reconciliation.

For the conservatives, it's time to take stand on biblical authority and moral values. For the liberals, if the Church can't move forward with society and be more inclusive on questions of gender and sexuality, much as it has done in the past on questions like slavery and women's rights, then schism is preferable to unity. Both sides feel that further procrastination on what they see as essential is only more damaging in the long term. These cogently-argued articles by liberals closely involved in the discussion say that the kind of status quo offered by the Windsor report is no answer. There is too much at stake to continue compromising with the spirit of fundamentalism.

Jonathan Clatworthy is General Secretary of the Modern Churchpeople's Union. David Taylor is a graduate in theology from Oxford University who has worked for many years in publishing, now retired.

Church/Religion
1 905047 29 0
£7.99 $11.95

The Censored Messiah
Peter Cresswell

Peter Cresswell has a revolutionary new theory about the life of Jesus and the origins of Christianity. It is a thrilling story, based on modern scholarship, of how a Jewish man tried to change the direction of the religious leadership of his people. It describes a breathtaking piece of brinkmanship carried out against the Roman occupiers of Israel, a journey into the mouth of death and beyond which appeared to succeed.

Peter Cresswell is a freelance writer with degrees from Cambridge and York Universities in Social Anthropology.

1 903816 67 X
£9.99 $14.95

Reiki Mastery
For Second Degree Students and Masters
David Vennells

Reiki has many levels and forms, and has changed along the way from the pure, "original" practice of its Buddhist founder, Dr. Mikao Usui. Advanced Reiki, especially above First Degree, is about "facing the mirror," the inner mirror of our own mind. As we progress with our spiritual practice we can begin to clean away the layers of misconception that colour the way we view ourselves, others and the world around us. This is a compassionate, wise, handbook to making the most of the Life Force Energy that surrounds and informs us all.

David Vennells is a Buddhist teacher of Reiki and the author of *Reiki for Beginners, Bach Flower Remedies for Beginners, Reflexology for Beginners.*

1-903816-70-X
£9.99 $14.95

The Goddess, the Grail and the Lodge
Alan Butler

We're only just beginning to realise that Bronze Age people knew far more about astronomy and engineering than we have given them credit for, that the Goddess religion continued in various forms through Christianity in the worship of the Virgin Mary down to our own time, that small groups of families and brotherhoods of knights have been highly influential throughout European history. In the essentials of knowledge nothing is new, and the icon of this knowledge has been the Grail.

Reading like a thriller, *The Goddess, the Grail and the Lodge* explains why it was adopted and used, how it existed on different levels to different people, and shows what "Grail Knowledge" really was and is.

Alan Butler is a qualified engineer and an expert on Megalithic cultures and the Knights Templar.

1-903816-69-6
£12.99 $15.95

Good As New
A radical re-telling of the Christian Scriptures
John Henson

This radical new translation conveys the early Christian scriptures in the idiom of today. It is "inclusive," following the principles which Jesus adopted in relation to his culture. It is women, gay and sinner friendly. It follows principles of cultural and contextual translation, and returns to the selection of books that the early Church held in highest esteem. It drops Revelation and includes the Gospel of Thomas,

"a presentation of extraordinary power." Rowan Williams, Archbishop of Canterbury

"I can't rate this version of the Christian scriptures highly enough. It is amazingly fresh, imaginative, engaging and bold." Adrian Thatcher, Professor of Applied Theology, College of St Mark and St John, Plymouth

"I found this a literally shocking read. It made me think, it made me laugh, it made me cry, it made me angry and it made me joyful. It made me feel like an early Christian hearing these texts for the first time." Elizabeth Stuart, Professor of Christian Theology, King Alfred's College, Winchester

John Henson, a retired Baptist minister, has co-ordinated this translation over the last 12 years on behalf of *ONE for Christian Exploration,* a network of radical Christians and over twenty organisations in the UK

1-903816-74-2
£19.99 $29.95 hb

The Thoughtful Guide to the Bible
Roy Robinson

Most Christians are unaware of the revolution in how the Bible may be understood that has taken place over the last two hundred years. This book seeks to share the fruits of the Biblical revolution in an easily accessible manner. It seeks to inform you of its main features and to encourage you to do your own thinking and come to your own conclusions.

Roy Robinson is a United Reformed Church minister, now retired and living in England. A former missionary in Zaire this work arises from a lifetime of study and Bible teaching at the Oxted Christian Centre, which he founded.

1-903816-75-0
£14.99 $19.95

Torn Clouds
Judy Hall

Drawing on thirty years experience as a regression therapist and her own memories and experiences in Egypt, ancient and modern, *Torn Clouds* is a remarkable first novel by an internationally-acclaimed MBS author, one of Britain's leading experts on reincarnation. It features time-traveller Megan McKennar, whose past life memories thrust themselves into the present day as she traces a love affair that transcends time. Haunted by her dreams, she is driven by forces she cannot understand to take a trip to Egypt in a quest to understand the cause of her unhappy current life circumstances. Once there, swooning into a previous existence in Pharaonic Egypt, she lives again as Meck'an'ar, priestess of the Goddess Sekhmet, the fearful lion headed deity who was simultaneously the Goddess of Terror, Magic and Healing.

Caught up in the dark historical secrets of Egypt, Megan is forced to fight for her soul. She succeeds in breaking the curse that had been cast upon her in two incarnations.

Judy Hall is a modern seer who manages the difficult task of evoking the present world, plus the realm of Ancient Egypt, and making them seem real. There is an energy behind the prose, and a power in her imagery which hints that this is more than just a story of character and plot, but an outpouring from another age, a genuine glimpse into beyond-time Mysteries which affect us all today. Alan Richardson, author of *Inner Guide to Egypt.*

Judy Hall has been a karmic counsellor for thirty years. Her books have been translated into over fourteen languages.

1 903816 80 7
£9.99/$14.95